Avoiding Losses / Taking Risks

Avoiding Losses / Taking Risks
Prospect Theory and International conflict

Barbara Farnham, Editor

Ann Arbor

THE UNIVERSITY OF MICHIGAN PRESS

Copyright © 1994 by the University of Michigan
All rights reserved
Published in the United States of America by
The University of Michigan Press
Manufactured in the United States of America
⊚ Printed on acid-free paper

1997   1996   1995   1994   4 3 2 1

Library of Congress Cataloging-in-Publication Data

Avoiding losses/taking risks : prospect theory and international
  conflict / Barbara Farnham, editor.
      p.   cm.
"The articles in this book were originally published as a special
issue of the journal Political psychology, volume 13, number 2 (June
1992)."
   Includes bibliographical references and index.
   ISBN 0-472-08276-0
   1. International relations—Decision making. 2. Risk-taking
(Psychology)   I. Farnham, Barbara.
JX1311.A9   1994
327—dc20   94-30367
                                                        CIP

The articles in this book were originally published as a special issue of the journal,
POLITICAL PSYCHOLOGY, Volume 13, Number 2 (June 1992). Reprinted with
permission of Plenum Publishing Corporation, 233 Spring Street, New York, NY
10013.

Contents

Introduction
Barbara Farnham   1

An Introduction to Prospect Theory
Jack S. Levy   7

Political Implications of Loss Aversion
Robert Jervis   23

Roosevelt and the Munich Crisis: Insights from Prospect Theory
Barbara Farnham   41

Prospect Theory in International Relations: The Iranian Hostage Rescue Mission
Rose McDermott   73

Prospect Theory and Soviet Policy Towards Syria, 1966–1967
Audrey McInerney   101

Prospect Theory and International Relations: Theoretical Applications and Analytical Problems
Jack S. Levy   119

Prospect Theory and Political Analysis: A Psychological Perspective
Eldar Shafir   147

Conclusion
Barbara Farnham   159

Introduction

Barbara Farnham

Most traditional explanations of international relations assume that states act rationally in pursuing their interests.[1] How, then, do we account for instances of apparently suboptimal behavior? Some states cling to policies that are evidently failing and, as many believe the United States did in Vietnam, continue to invest resources in pursuit of goals that seem increasingly unattainable. Others, like Britain and Argentina in the Falkland Islands, are willing to take risks and spend blood and treasure on objectives that seem to outside observers far from worth the cost.

If states are indeed intent on maximizing expected utility, choices such as these are puzzling. Why would utility maximizers ever choose policies with less than the highest expected value? A number of analysts believe the answer to this is question is most likely to be provided by theories that focus on decision-making processes and/or leaders' personalities, rather than those that emphasize the impact of the international environment or domestic forces.[2]

---

[1] Theories that focus on the international environment, for example, emphasize the role of structural forces so obvious and compelling that no particular judgment is required to translate them into policy. All that is needed is a decision maker sufficiently rational to perceive the constraints and choose the appropriate course.

[2] As Robert Jervis (1980, p. 28) has observed, "When the situation is not so compelling as to produce uniform behavior in all people one must look to the differences among individuals for at least part of the explanation."

In recent years, political scientists have turned to the field of psychology for insight into behavior at the decision-making level of analysis. (On levels of analysis, see Jervis, 1976, ch. I; Singer, 1961, pp. 77–92; Waltz, 1979; Wolfers, 1962.) Psychological theories of judgment and choice explain departures from normative standards of rationality in terms of distortions arising from either cognitive limitations or strong emotion.

Cognitive models of decision making regard human beings as inherently limited in their ability to perform the operations required by analytical models (Stein, and Tanter, 1967, p. 7; Steinbruner, 1974, p. 8). Motivational models, on the other hand, see decision-making behavior as driven by emotion. Thus, they emphasize the influence on decision making of "desires and drives to minimize psychological discomfort" (Jervis, 1978, p. 328: On motivational models, see Janis and Mann, 1977; George, 1980, 1974; and Holsti and George, 1975).

As "an alternative account of choice under risk," prospect theory is generally considered part of the first tradition (Kahneman and Tversky, 1979, p. 263), although recently several analyses have suggested that emotion may also play a role in triggering at least some of the behavior it describes (see, for example, Farnham, 1994; Cusimano, 1993). The theory attempts to explain the decision-making processes people actually use and to show how these systematically produce outcomes that violate a number of the key assumptions of rational choice theory. Specifically, prospect theory predicts that, in making their decisions, people will often fail to maximize expected utility.

Thus, like other cognitive models of decision making, prospect theory is concerned with the intellectual limitations of the decision maker. It differs, however, in that it not only claims to explain decision-making processes but also links those processes directly to specific violations of rational norms. It predicts, that is, that people will respond to certain kinds of situations in ways that yield distinct and identifiable suboptimal outcomes.

This characteristic allows prospect theory to compete with the theory of rational choice on a different basis from most other psychological theories of decision. Rational choice theorists dismiss the quite robust findings of cognitive and social psychology that people often fail to use rigorous analytic processes by making the assumption that they behave "as if they were rational" (Friedman, 1957). Prospect theory, however, disputes the notion that process is irrelevant to the ultimate outcome of a decision by demonstrating a clear connection between the two. That is, it challenges the "as if" assumption by showing not merely that people frequently fail to act as if they were rational, but also that the ways in which they do act produce very different outcomes from those expected by rational choice theory.

Most striking in this regard are prospect theory's insight into the impact of loss aversion and problem representation on choice. In the first instance, according to prospect theory, losses have a greater impact than do gains—people mind incurring a loss considerably more than they are pleased by an equivalent gain, and this has significant consequences for their decision-making behavior. Second, prospect theory holds that the way the alternatives are presented can have great influence on the choices a person will make, even if it has no effect on the expected value of the alternatives. For example, people are willing to take risk to avoid an outcome framed as a loss that they refuse to take when the outcome is presented as a gain.

Many analysts believe that these insights have considerable potential for explaining behavior in international relations that is puzzling for the theory of rational choice, including the disposition to count sunk costs alluded to earlier. This volume is intended to explore the implications of prospect theory for the analysis of international relations in this and a number of other areas, an enterprise which is motivated both by the importance of the problems prospect theory promises to help us understand and by the possibility it offers of achieving a richer explanation of foreign policy choice.

Among the subjects discussed here that prospect theory may be able to illuminate are deterrence, the causes of war, bargaining behavior, crisis stability, the willingness to intervene in diplomatic disputes or in the affairs of other countries more generally, and the incentives for military action. Not only can prospect theory improve our understanding of these important matters, it may also be able to suggest strategies for dealing with them. For example, the insight that the framing of a problem has a significant impact on choice suggests that, in trying to influence the behavior of others, it would be a mistake to focus exclusively on directly affecting their cost-benefit calculations while overlooking the possibility of influencing those calculations indirectly by manipulating the way the choice is presented. An attempt at persuasion, for example, may well have a greater impact if it is framed in terms of avoiding a loss than it would if framed as making a gain.

Those interested in using prospect theory to develop a richer explanation of foreign policy decisions focus on a number of areas in which rational choice explanations seem to fall short. For one thing, considerable dissatisfaction has recently been expressed with the assumption that we need be concerned only with outcomes. Skeptical of the notion that process can be left out of account, some critics question "whether it is really possible to separate the task of making accurate predictions of choices from that of creating accurate explanations of choice processes" (McKeown, 1986, p. 51). Others point out that, in contrast to utility theory, prospect theory is able to offer some insight into the formation of preferences and to deal with values and changes in values.

In this volume, political scientists and psychologists join forces to explore these possibilities. Their method of inquiry is perhaps unusual in that they have not only tried to identify the questions prospect theory is best suited to address but have also examined empirical evidence that the theory can provide, in some instances, a more convincing explanation of foreign policy choices than its major competitors. Thus, their conclusions about prospect theory's future potential for enriching political analysis are grounded in an assessment of its success in explaining actual cases.

This way of proceeding has produced some interesting, and at times unexpected, results. As well as identifying areas of international relations where the insights of prospect theory may eventually prove fruitful and exposing the difficulties involved in using it to explain and predict political outcomes, this collection of articles suggests possible elaborations of the theory itself and indicates a direction for the continued collaboration of political scientists and psychologists in applying prospect theory.

Jack Levy's initial contribution introduces the theory, outlining its central propositions and comparing them to the predictions of rational choice theory. This effort is especially valuable because, although prospect theory poses a clear challenge to expected-utility theory, the two have seldom been analyzed systematically together. As Levy points out, however, empirical evidence alone cannot provide an adequate test of theory. Rather, theories must also be evaluated in the light of their competitors. Thus, his explicit comparisons of prospect theory and the theory of rational choice are particularly welcome.

Following Levy's general introduction, Robert Jervis discusses the implications of prospect theory for the analysis of conflict and bargaining in international politics. Focusing on loss aversion, Jervis notes that, while this phenonmenon may not always require a psychological explanation if political constraints are properly understood, there are still a number of cases, including those involving crucial war-peace decisions, that may be illuminated by insights derived from prospect theory.

The empirical studies by Barbara Farnham, Rose McDermott, and Audrey McInerney explore prospect theory's ability to explain three instances of behavior in political settings that are puzzling for the theory of rational choice. Analyzing President Franklin D. Roosevelt's decision making during the Munich crisis of 1938, Farnham shows that it exhibited a number of phenomena predicted by prospect theory, including framing effects, a reversal of preferences despite the absence of substantial change in the value of the options, and risk acceptance to avoid loss. She concludes that prospect theory provides a better account of Roosevelt's decision to intervene in the crisis than do competing explanations. She also argues that the Munich case strongly suggests that emotion may play a role in triggering changes in decision frames.

McDermott uses prospect theory to explain President Jimmy Carter's April 1980 decision to rescue the American hostages in Iran. Finding himself in the domain of loss as a consequence of the hostage taking, Carter authorized a rescue mission entailing considerable risk in order to regain status quo. McDermott contends that loss aversion predisposed the president to engage in risky behavior he would otherwise have shunned.

Finally, McInerney analyzes Soviet behavior toward its client Syria in 1966 and 1967. She argues that, having defined the status quo in the Middle East as resting, to some extent, on a socialist Syria aligned with the Soviet Union, Soviet leaders became risk acceptant in order to avoid losing such a regime—even to the point of pursuing policies that encouraged war in the Middle East.

Following these historical studies, Jack Levy and Eldar Shafir explore general issues relating to the application of prospect theory to international relations. Levy focuses on the potential of prospect theory to enhance the analysis of international politics, examining the conceptual and methodological problems associated with applying it in that context. He also attempts to develop some criteria for judging empirical applications of the theory which he uses to evaluate the three case studies.

As a psychologist who has had considerable experience with prospect theory, Eldar Shafir also identifies a number of problems and pitfalls in using it to analyze political events. In addition, however, he addresses the issue of how to assist future efforts to apply prospect theory to political behavior, suggesting a direction for further collaboration between political scientists and psychologists. Specifically, Shafir advocates a joint research program in which selected "variables are controlled and data collected in otherwise naturally occurring political settings." The objective of such a research program would be "to clarify how individual theories of choice apply to the analysis of political events," a goal which is shared by the contributors to this volume on prospect theory and international relations.

ACKNOWLEDGMENTS

I would like to thank James Davis, Lori Gronich, and Robert Jervis for their comments.

REFERENCES

Cusimano, M. (1993) Emotion and Frame. Paper presented at the American Political Science Association Annual Meeting, Washington, DC, September 2–5, 1993.

Farnham, B. (1994) Roosevelt and the Munich crisis: insights from prospect theory. This volume.

Friedman, M. (1957). The methodology of positive rationality. In M. Friedman (Ed.), *Essays in Positive Economics* (pp. 3–43). Chicago: University of Chicago Press.

George, A. (1974). Adaptation to stress in political decision making: the individual, small group, and organizational contexts. In G. Coelho, D. Hamburg, and J. Adams (Eds.), *Coping and Adaptation* (pp. 176–245). New York: Basic Books.

George, A. (1980). *Presidential Decisionmaking in Foreign Policy: The Effective Use of Information and Advice.* Boulder, CO: Westview Press.

Holsti, O. and George, A. (1975). Effects of stress on the performance of foreign policy-makers. In C. Cotter (Ed.), *Political science annual, 6* (pp. 255–319). Indianapolis: Bobbs-Merrill.

Janis, I. and Mann, L. (1977). *Decision-Making*. New York: Free Press.

Jervis, R. (1978). Foreign policy motivation: a general theory and a case study, by Richard Cottam. *Political Science Quarterly, 93*, 327-28.

Jervis, R. (1976). *Perception and Misperception in International Politics*. Princeton, NJ: Princeton University Press.

Jervis, R. (1980) Political decision-making: recent contributions. *Political Psychology, 2*, 86–101.

Kahneman, D. and Tversky, A. (1979). Prospect theory: an analysis of decision under risk. *Econometrica, 47*, 263–92.

McKeown, T. (1986). The limitations of "structural" theories of commercial policy. *International Organization, 40*, 43–64.

Singer, J. D. (1961). The level of analysis problem in international relations. *World Politics, 14*, 77–92.

Stein, J. and Tanter, R. (1967). *Rational Decisionmaking*. Columbus, OH: Ohio State University Press.

Steinbruner, J. (1974). *Cybernetic Theory of Decision*. Princeton, NJ: Princeton University Press.

Waltz, K. (1979). *Theory of International Politics*. Reading, MA: Addison-Wesley.

Wolfers, A. (1962). The actors in international politics. In Arnold Wolfers, *Discord and Collaboration* (pp. 3–24). Baltimore: Johns Hopkins University Press.

An Introduction to Prospect Theory

Jack S. Levy[1]

INTRODUCTION

Since its formulation by Kahneman and Tversky in 1979, prospect theory has emerged as a leading alternative to expected utility as a theory of decision under risk. Prospect theory posits that individuals evaluate outcomes with respect to deviations from a reference point rather than with respect to net asset levels, that their identification of this reference point is a critical variable, that they give more weight to losses than to comparable gains, and that they are generally risk-averse with respect to gains and risk-acceptant with respect to losses. The hypothesized pattern of loss aversion and the importance of framing have received tentative confirmation by a series of diverse and robust experimental tests that are now well-known in the literature on behavioral decision theory (Kahneman &

---

[1]Department of Political Science, Rutgers University, New Brunswick, New Jersey 08903-0270

Tversky, 1979; Tversky & Kahneman, 1986; Fishburn & Kochenberger, 1979; Schoemaker, 1980).

Over the last several years a handful of international relations scholars, most prominently Robert Jervis (1988, 1989, 1991), have begun to apply the concepts of framing, loss aversion, and varying risk propensities to foreign policy decision-making. These concepts have been used primarily in a supplemental role to modify other theoretical propositions in most applications of the theory (Jervis, 1988, pp. 696-698, 1989, pp. 94-95, 168-172; Lebow, 1987, p. 54; Levy, 1987, pp. 101-103; 1989a, p. 274; 1989b, pp. 126-127; Maoz, 1990; Huth, Gelpi, & Bennett, 1992). Recently, however, key components of prospect theory have been given a more central role in international relations theorizing (Stein, 1992; Jervis, 1992) and have been used as central organizing concepts to structure case studies of foreign policy decision-making (Farnham, 1992; McInerney, 1992; McDermott, 1992).

Although interest in prospect theory has been growing among international relations theorists, its details remain unfamiliar to the vast majority of scholars in the field. Consequently, this is a good time to review the essential elements of the theory and to evaluate the analytical problems that might affect its utility as a framework for research in international relations and foreign policy. Because prospect theory was developed in response to expected utility theory, I begin this introductory essay with a very brief review of expected utility, note some frequently observed empirical violations of that theory, and show how prospect theory integrates these observed patterns into an alternative theory of risky choice.

I will not deal here with debates in the social psychology, economics, and decision-theory literature regarding the empirical validity of prospect theory and experimental tests of the theory in the laboratory (Hershey & Shoemaker, 1980b; Machina, 1982; Slovic & Lichtenstein, 1983). Nor will I be concerned with the broader questions of whether observed violations of expected utility constitute "irrational' behavior or invalidate the theory, whether prospect theory is superior to expected utility theory, or whether normative and descriptive theories of decision are ultimately reconcilable (Tversky & Kahneman, 1986). I will analyze the potential contribution of prospect theory for international relations later in this issue (Levy, 1992).

EXPECTED-UTILITY THEORY—A BRIEF REVIEW

Expected utility is a theory of decision under conditions of risk, where each option leads to one of a set of possible outcomes and where the probability of each outcome is known. (Risk differs from uncertainty, where the probabilities of outcomes are not completely known, and from certainty, where the probabilities are known and equivalent to zero or one.) The expected-utility principle asserts that individuals attempt to maximize expected utility in their choices between risky options: they weight the utilities of individual outcomes by their probabilities and choose the option with the highest weighted sum (Luce & Raiffa, 1957, Ch. 2).

Since Bernoulli's (1954) proposal of the expected-utility principle in 1738, it has usually been assumed that the psychological value of money and most other goods does not increase proportionally with objective amount, but instead that there is diminishing marginal utility for money. This can be represented by a concave (downward curving) utility function. Individuals can also have increasing or constant marginal utility for a particular good, which can represented by a convex or linear utility function, respectively.

An actor's attitude toward risk is conventionally defined in terms of marginal utility or the shape of the utility function. An actor is risk-averse if the utility function is concave, risk-neutral if the utility function is linear, and risk-acceptant if the utility function is convex. Given a choice between two options, one involving a certain outcome of utility x and the other involving a lottery or gamble with the equivalent expected utility x, a risk-averse actor will prefer the certain outcome to the gamble, a risk-acceptant actor will prefer the gamble, and a risk-neutral actor will be indifferent between the two. Most people are risk averse with respect to monetary outcomes and prefer a certain payoff of $50 (or even $40) to a 50/50 chance of either nothing or $100.

Expected-utility theory has dominated the analysis of decision-making under risk, both as a normative model of rational choice and a descriptive model of how people actually behave. But not all of its predictions appear to be fully consistent with observed behavior.[2] These empirical anomalies in expected-util-

---

[2]For example, gambling and insurance behavior present a dilemma for expected-utility theory. The assumption of diminishing marginal utility for money implies that people should shy away from lotteries and other gambles to win large amounts of money at small probabilities, but this is inconsistent with the popularity of gambling. Expected-utility theory can account for gambling by assuming convex utility functions, but that would leave it at odds with a wide range of behavior for which individuals appear to be risk averse. This includes the proclivity to purchase insurance, which involves a certain small loss in order to avoid a small probability of a very large loss (Friedman & Savage, 1948). Expected-utility theory can easily explain gambling *or* insurance, but it cannot easily account for both gambling and insurance by a single individual. The dilemma can be eliminated if utility theory were to posit that individuals have different utility functions for different domains of behavior. But this would add significantly to the complexity of the explanation, involve a significant loss in parsimony, and possibly introduce a tautological element into a theory of behavior.

In fact, insurance behavior is rather complex. People commonly purchase insurance but often hesitate to insure against extremely improbable outcomes. They also tend to shun "probabilistic insurance" (Kahneman & Tversky, 1979, pp. 269–271), which should be attractive for individuals with diminishing marginal returns for money, and they deviate in other ways from predicted behavior regarding insurance (Slovic et al., 1977; Schoemaker, 1980, Ch. 5; Slovic, Fischoff, & Lichtenstein, 1988, pp. 156–158).

ity theory led Kahneman and Tversky (1979) to develop prospect theory as an alternative theory of decision under risk.

THE DESCRIPTIVE FOUNDATIONS OF PROSPECT THEORY

Kahneman and Tversky (1979) begin by presenting the results of a series of laboratory experiments involving hypothetical choices, and it would be useful to summarize some of the most important findings here. Most of their examples refer to risky choice regarding monetary outcomes, but many of their findings can be generalized to other forms of risky choice.

(1) People tend to think in terms of gains and losses rather than in terms of their net assets, and therefore encode choices in terms of deviations from a *reference point*. Kahneman and Tversky (1979, p. 273) argue that "the carriers of value or utility are changes of wealth, rather than final asset positions that include current wealth." They acknowledge that asset position matters in principle, but argue that "the preference order of prospects is not greatly altered by small or even moderate variations in asset position" (p. 277). The reference point is usually the status quo, but that need not necessarily be the case. One can also speak of deviations from an *aspiration level* or some other reference point which is not equivalent to the status quo. This possibility leads to some interesting questions regarding the framing of a choice problem, to which we will return.

(2) People treat gains differently than losses in two respects. First, individuals tend to be risk-averse with respect to gains and risk-acceptant with respect to losses. In a typical experiment (Kahneman & Tversky, 1979), 80% of respondents preferred a certain outcome of $3000 to an 80% chance of $4000 and 20% chance of nothing. If faced with the same two negative prospects, however, 92% of respondents preferred to gamble on an 80% chance of losing $4000 and 20% of losing nothing to a certain loss of $3000. In both cases respondents chose the option with the lower expected value and the combination of these two patterns is inconsistent with expected-utility theory. There is no conclusive evidence on exactly *how* risk-averse or risk-acceptant people are (or how much they are willing to sacrifice in expected value in order to avoid a certain loss or secure a certain gain), but figures in the 20%–30% range are not uncommon in laboratory experiments.

These experiments suggest that individual utility functions are concave in the domain of gains and convex in the domain of losses, a pattern which Kahneman and Tversky (1979, p. 268) refer to as a *reflection effect* around the reference point. This means, among other things, that the sensitivity to changes in assets decreases as one moves further from the reference point in both directions, which would not be true of a utility function which was either strictly concave or strictly convex. This pattern has been found repeatedly for a variety of individuals and situations (Fishburn & Kochenberger, 1979), but it may break down for very small probabilities or for catastrophic losses, which we will consider later.

(3) Gains are also treated differently than losses in that "losses loom larger than gains." As Jimmy Conners exclaimed, "I hate to lose more than I like to win." This phenomenon of *loss aversion* implies that people prefer the status quo (or another reference point) over a 50/50 chance for positive and negative alternatives with the same absolute value. It also implies that people value what they have more than "comparable" things they do not have. The very process of acquiring an object enhances the value of that object, even for items as trivial as candy bars or coffee mugs. This over-evaluation of current possessions has been called the *endowment effect* (Thaler, 1980, pp. 43–47).

Loss aversion and the endowment effect imply that selling prices should be higher than buying prices: the minimal compensation people demand to give up a good is often several times larger than the maximum amount they are willing to pay for a commensurate entitlement. The endowment effect and evaluation disparities have been repeatedly demonstrated in the experimental literature (Knetsch & Sinden, 1984; Knetsch, 1989; Kahneman, Knetsch, & Thaler, 1990).[3] They largely account for the tendency for people to overweight out-of-pocket costs (losses) relative to opportunity costs (foregone gains), and there is evidence that they affect peoples' judgments of fairness and justice (Kahneman, Knetsch, & Thaler, 1991, pp. 203–204). The endowment effect and evaluation discrepancies are also reflected in legal doctrine, which recognizes an asymmetry between acts of commission and omission, and which distinguishes between "loss by way of expenditure and failure to make a gain." People are more likely to be entitled to compensation for actual losses than for denied opportunities to secure gains (Kahneman, Knetsch, & Thaler, 1990, p. 1246, 1991, pp. 202–204).

The endowment effect also has important implications for utility theory. It challenges the assumptions that preferences are invariant under different representations of equivalent choice problems (because framing affects preferences), that indifference curves are reversible and nonintersecting, and that preferences are independent of endowments (one's preference between A and B may depend on whether A is currently part of one's endowment) (Knetsch, 1989;

---

[3] The gap between compensation demanded and willingness to pay may be up to 3 or 4 to 1 (Kahneman, Knetsch, & Thaler, 1990, p. 1336; Hartman, Doane, & Woo, 1991, p. 142). Some studies have proposed and tested alternative explanations for these "evaluation disparities" between buyers and sellers. Knez, Smith, and Williams (1985) suggest that the observed gap is a manifestation of routine application of normally sensible bargaining habits to laboratory experiments (for sellers to inflate and buyers to deflate prices for strategic reasons), and Coursey, Hovis, and Schulze (1987) report that these discrepancies diminish with learning in repeated trials. But Kahneman, Knetsch, and Thaler (1990) and Knetsch and Sinden (1987) control for these possible effects and find that these evaluation disparities do not disappear under a wide range of conditions.

Slovic & Lichtenstein, 1983; Tversky, Slovic, & Kahneman, 1990; Kahneman et al., 1990).

The endowment effect exists even if the endowment is a windfall and therefore somewhat artificial, though the effect may be slightly weaker under such conditions. For this reason, we might expect laboratory studies to underestimate the true magnitude of endowment effects (Knetsch, 1989, p. 1282). Moreover, the longer one possesses a good, and particularly the greater the effort and resources expended to acquire it, the greater its perceived value, as cognitive dissonance theory would suggest (Jervis, 1989, p. 169). The symbolic value of political and economic assets in international relations should further strengthen the endowment effect.

It should be noted, however, that the endowment effect and loss aversion do not appear to apply to normal commercial transactions. Money expended on an item is not treated as a loss, and goods purchased for eventual sale or barter—as opposed to use—generally do not generate an endowment effect (Kahneman et al., 1991, p. 200). In addition, the experimental evidence, though tentative, suggests that endowment effects are stronger and more consistent if one is given physical possession of a good, as opposed to a property right to receive the good at some point in the future or a chance (as opposed to certainty) to receive such a good (Kahneman et al., 1990, p. 1342).

(4) Because of the encoding of outcomes in terms of a reference point and the differential treatment of gains and losses, the identification of the reference point, or *framing* of a choice problem, becomes critical. One striking demonstration of the significance of the framing effect is illustrated by the following medical example (Tversky & Kahneman, 1981, p. 453). Subjects were given a hypothetical choice between alternative programs to combat the outbreak of a disease which was expected to kill 600 people. The identical statistics (asserted to be a consensus of scientific opinion) regarding the expected consequences of the epidemic and the two treatment programs were presented to one group in terms of the number of people who would be saved (the "survival frame"), and to another group in terms of the number of people who would die from the disease (the mortality frame). Specifically, in program A, 200 people would be saved (or 400 would die), and in program B there was a one-third chance that 600 people would be saved (none would die) and two-thirds probability that none would be saved (600 would die). A strong majority (72%) favored the cautious alternative A in the survival frame, but a comparable majority (78%) favored the risky alternative in the mortality frame.[4]

---

[4]There is a potential levels-of analysis problem or ecological fallacy which needs to be explored in problems of this kind. Experimental tests on risk propensities in the domains of losses and in the domain of gains are conducted on two distinct sets of subjects so that aggregate results do not necessarily imply a reflectivity effect in *individuals*. Experiments which adopt an individual-level

In effect, the survival frame involves a downward shift in the reference point, which is equivalent to adding a positive constant to all outcomes. This downward *translation effect* (Abelson & Levi, 1985, p. 248) influences outcomes by increasing the tendency toward risk aversion. Thus whether a respondent frames the issue in terms of gains or losses has a significant impact on preferences in spite of the mathematical equivalence of the two choice problems. The importance of framing has been demonstrated by a number of other experimental studies (McNeil, et al., 1982; Levin et al., 1985; Tversky & Kahneman, 1986; Fleishman, 1988). The preference of gas stations and other businesses for offering customers a cash discount rather than requiring a credit card surcharge, in order to frame the issue as a gain rather than a loss for the consumer, reflects an anticipation of framing effects.

Although in many simple choice problems the framing of the problem is largely predetermined by the situation (or the experimental design), in other situations it is more subjective and sensitive to how the individual responds to a situation and encodes a decision. This is particularly likely where the situation involves a sequence of successive choices and where there is ambiguity regarding the status quo. Is the reference point for each choice problem framed cumulatively with respect to one's asset position at the beginning of the series of choices, or with respect to one's asset position at each individual choice? A gambler who sustains a series of losses will be more inclined to be risk acceptant if he or she adopts the cumulative frame of the asset position at the beginning of the evening and attempts to recover losses, whereas one who uses current asset levels would be more risk averse. Someone on a winning streak, however, will be more risk averse if he or she frames the choice in terms of initial assets rather than total assets at the time of each new bet.

This example illustrates the importance of how individuals *accommodate* to gains or losses. Accommodation to losses induces a tendency toward risk aversion (relative to nonaccommodation), whereas accommodation to gains induces risk-seeking behavior to keep those gains (Abelson & Levi, 1985, p. 249). This leads to the question of how quickly individuals or states adjust or *renormalize* (Jervis, 1992) to a new status quo, and under what conditions or types of situations. The literature speaks of an instant endowment effect (Kahneman et al., 1990, p. 1342) and implies that actors accommodate to gains more quickly than to losses. This has significant consequences for strategic interaction in dynamic situations. If A has just made a gain at the expense of B, B's attempt to recover his losses (from the old status quo) will be perceived as a potential loss by A (from the new status quo), so that both parties will be in a domain of losses

---

(as opposed to aggregate) focus (Hershey & Schoemaker, 1980b) show weaker tendencies toward reflectivity.

and be more risk-seeking. We will return to applications of this hypothesis to bargaining situations in international relations.

(5) A number of studies have shown that individuals overweight outcomes which are certain relative to outcomes which are merely probable—the *certainty effect* (Allais, 1979; Kahneman & Tversky, 1979). They also overweight small probabilities and underweight moderate and high probabilities, and the latter effect is more pronounced than the former. Extremely likely but uncertain outcomes are often treated as if they were certain, which Kahneman and Tversky (1986, p. S268) call the *pseudocertainty effect*. Consequently, changes in probabilities near 0 or 1 have a greater impact on preferences than comparable changes in the middle of the probability range, which leads to the *ratio-difference principle* or *subproportionality:* the impact of any fixed positive difference between two amounts increases with their ratio (Quattrone & Tversky, 1988, p. 728; Tversky & Kahneman, 1986, p. S263).

The differential evaluation of the complete elimination as opposed to the reduction of risk is illustrated by the fact that people are willing to pay far more to reduce the risk of a catastrophic loss from .10 to 0 than from .20 to .10, even though the change in expected utility is the same. More graphically, people in a hypothetical game of Russian roulette are willing to pay far more to reduce the number of bullets in a revolver from 1 to 0 than from 4 to 3 (Quattrone and Tversky, 1988, p. 730). These forms of behavior are contrary to the expectation rule (that the utilities of risky outcomes are weighted linearly by their probabilities) and ratio-scale properties of expected-utility theory.

The effects of the overweighting of small probabilities may be reinforced by the availability heuristic (Tversky & Kahneman, 1982), in which dramatic events which come readily to mind (television images of disaster, for example) are perceived to be more likely than they actually are. Note, however, that the *overestimation* or exaggeration of probabilities, which may arise from the availability heuristic or from other cognitive or motivational biases (Jervis, 1976; Janis & Mann, 1977), is analytically distinct from the *overweighting* of low probabilities. Overestimation refers to the subjective assessment of probabilities, and may be influenced by the vividness of an event category or by other cognitive or motivational biases. Overweighting is a property of the weighting function, which operates on subjective probabilities assessments independently of the processes by which they are generated, as demonstrated by laboratory experiments in which probabilities are given (Kahneman & Tversky, 1979, p. 281).

(6) There is also evidence that in order to simplify the choice between alternatives, individuals often disregard components that are common to each alternative option, and focus on components which are different (Tversky, 1972). This *isolation effect* (or *cancellation*) can lead to different preferences because there may be more than one way to decompose prospects into shared and dis-

tinctive elements, as Kahneman and Tversky (1979, p. 271) demonstrate in experiments involving two-stage choice problems.[5]

The aforementioned patterns of behavior with respect to judgment and decision violate several of the basic assumptions of expected-utility theory in nontransparent choice situations (as opposed to more transparent choice situations in which the similarities between problems is more obvious), including transitivity, dominance, invariance, and cancellation (or the independence of irrelevant alternatives).[6] In an attempt to incorporate these behavioral patterns, scholars have formulated a number of alternative models of risky choice (for a brief review and evaluation see Tversky & Kahneman, 1986, pp. S271–S273; Abelson & Levi, 1985, pp. 250–254). Prospect theory is the most comprehensive and best known of these.

PROSPECT THEORY: A SUMMARY

Prospect theory attempts to incorporate the observed violations of expected utility into an alternative theory of risky choice. It distinguishes two phases in the choice process: (1) The *editing phase* involves a preliminary analysis of the choice problem. It includes the identification of the options available to the actor, the possible outcomes or consequences of each, and the values and probabilities associated with each of these outcomes. It also includes the organization and reformulation of perceived options so as to "simplify subsequent evaluation and

---

[5]Consider the following two-stage problem from Kahneman and Tversky (1979, pp. 271–272). In the first stage there is a .75 probability of ending the game with zero payoff and .25 probability of moving to the second stage. In this second stage, there is choice between a certain payoff of $3,000 and an .80 probability of $4,000. The choice between these two prospects must be made before the outcome of the first stage is known. In this "sequential" frame, 78% of 141 subjects chose the second prospect. Note that this choice problem is equivalent to a one-time choice between a .20 probability of a payoff of 4,000 and a .25 probability of 3,000. In this "standard" frame, 65% of 95 respondents selected the first prospect. Kahneman and Tversky (1979) hypothesize that subjects ignored the first stage of the game in the sequential game because it was common to both prospects. This results in a fourfold increase in the probabilities to be evaluated, the introduction of a certain prospect, a corresponding change in probability weightings, and a preference reversal and violation of the invariance axiom (see fn. 6).

[6]*Transitivity* requires that if A is preferred to B and B to C, then A is preferred to C. *Dominance* means that if one option is better than another in one state of the world and at least as good in all other states, the dominant option should be chosen. *Cancellation*—which is equivalent to the substitution axiom (von Neumann and Morgenstern, 1944), the extended surething principle (Savage, 1954), and the independence of irrelevant alternatives—refers to the elimination of any state of the world that yields the same outcome regardless of one's choice. *Invariance*, or "extensionality" (Arrow, 1982), requires that different representations of the same (i.e., mathematically equivalent) choice problem should yield the same preferences (Tversky & Kahneman, 1986, pp. S253–S254). On the axiomatic foundations of utility theory, see Luce and Raiffa (1957, Ch. 2). For a discussion of behavioral violations of these axioms, see Kahneman and Tversky (1979), Arrow (1982), Tversky and Kahneman (1986, pp. S252–S254), and Tversky, Slovic, and Kahneman (1990).

choice" (Tversky & Kahneman, 1981, p. 453; Kahneman & Tversky, 1979, p. 274). (2) In the *evaluation* phase, the edited prospects are evaluated and the preferred prospect is selected. Kahneman and Tversky have developed a formal model to explain the evaluation of prospects, but the theory of editing or framing is less well-developed. Both the editing and evaluation phases are essential to prospect theory, although the former has received less attention.

Editing involves several mental operations which simplify the choice problem by transforming the representation of outcomes and probabilities. *Coding* involves the identification of a reference point and the *framing* of outcomes as deviations (losses or gains) from that reference point, and this can affect orientation toward risk. *Simplification* involves rounding off probabilities or outcomes, including discarding extremely unlikely outcomes by rounding their probability to zero, and can distort expected utility calculations. *Detection of dominance* entails the search for and elimination of dominated alternatives. There is also a *combination* of probabilities associated with identical outcomes and a *segregation* of a riskless component of a prospect from a risky component which is then evaluated with respect to its deviation from the assured minimum. There is often the *cancellation* of components common to all prospects or the elimination of irrelevant alternatives, which can lead to preference reversals and violations of invariance. These editing operations are discussed in more detail by Kahneman and Tversky (1979, pp. 284–285).

Editing is an integral component of the choice process and is essential if prospect theory is to be able to explain violations of invariance, preference reversal, intransitivities, and other anomalies of preference described above (Abelson & Levi, 1985, p. 250). In complex choice situations, however, exactly how choice problems are edited is difficult to predict because the process is influenced by the "norms, habits, and expectancies of the decision maker" as well as the features inherent in a choice problem (Tversky & Kahneman, 1986, p. S257). Moreover, the outcome of the editing process may be a function of the sequence of editing operations. Whether simplification takes place before or after combination and/or segregation, for example, may make a difference in the final editing of choices and introduces an additional element of unpredictability in decision-making.

For these reasons, Kahneman and Tversky (1979, p. 275) restrict themselves to choice problems "where it is reasonable to assume either that the original formulation of the prospects leaves no room for further editing, or that the edited prospects can be specified without ambiguity." That is, Kahneman and Tversky focus on the evaluation of prospects rather than the editing of choices, and the behavior they observe is determined primarily by the evaluation phase of decision-making. Needless to say, editing plays a much greater role in choice situations in international relations and requires far more theoretical and empirical attention.

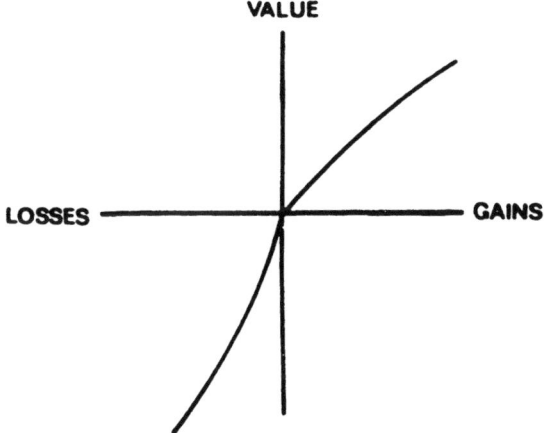

Fig. 1. A hypothetical value function.

Once the individual edits the available options, she then evaluates the edited prospects and selects the one with the highest value, as determined by the product of a value of an outcome and a decision weight. The weighted value of a prospect V is given by

$$V = \Sigma w\ (p_i) * v(x_i),$$

where p is the perceived probability of outcome x, $w(p)$ is the probability-weighting function, and $v(x)$ is the value function.

The *value function* has three main characteristics, which reflect the behavioral patterns summarized above: (1) It is defined on deviations from a reference point, rather than on net asset position (thus if the reference point shifts, the value function shifts accordingly); (2) it is generally concave for gains and convex for losses, reflecting risk aversion in the domain of gains and risk seeking in the domain of losses; (3) it is steeper for losses than for gains (perhaps by a ratio of 2:1, according to the experimental evidence [Tversky & Kahneman, 1981]). This captures the phenomenon of loss aversion and implies that the marginal utility of gains decreases faster than the marginal disutility of losses. A typical S-shaped value function is presented in figure 1.

The *probability-weighting function* measures the impact of the probability of an event on the desirability of a prospect. It is not a linear function of probability, however, and decision weights are not themselves probabilities. Technically, decision weights could be influenced by factors other than probability, including "ambiguity," or uncertainty about the level of uncertainty or risk (Kahneman & Tversky, 1979, p. 280; Ellsberg, 1961; Einhorn & Hogarth, 1985).

A typical probability-weighting function, induced from experimental evi-

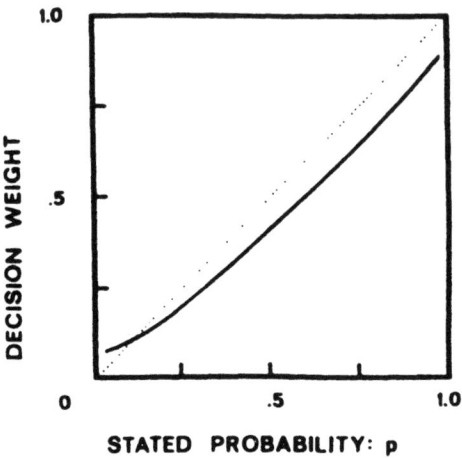

Fig. 2. A hypothetical weighting function.

dence, is given in figure 2. It has several characteristics. First, the weighting function is not well-behaved near its endpoints. This reflects the unpredictability of behavior under conditions of extremely small or extremely large probabilities. In other words, the variance in the probability weighting function is not constant and is quite large in the region near 0 or 1. Kahneman and Tversky (1979, pp. 282–283) acknowledge this unpredictability, and argue that "because people are limited in their ability to comprehend and evaluate extreme probabilities, highly unlikely events are either ignored or overweighted, and the difference between high probability and certainty is either neglected or exaggerated."

The fact that the weighting function is not well-behaved near its endpoints, and that by definition $w(0) = 0$ and $w(1) = 1$, leads to a second important characteristic: there is a sharp (though somewhat indeterminant) increase in the weighting function in these regions. Thus changes in probabilities near 0 or 1 have disproportionately large effects on the evaluation of prospects.

A third characteristic of the weighting function is that its slope is less than 1 across its entire range, except for the small region near its endpoints. Because the slope is a measure of the sensitivity of decision weights— and therefore of preferences—to changes in probabilities, this means that preferences are generally less sensitive to variations in probability than the expectation principle would suggest (with the important exception of the region near 0 and 1). One implication is that the sum of decision weights associated with complementary events is generally less than the weight given to a certain event, which reflects the certainty effect described above (Kahneman & Tversky, 1979, p. 282).

Fourth, other than the indeterminacy of behavior for extremely small probabilities, small probabilities are overweighted while larger probabilities are underweighted. Although there is no conclusive evidence as to the specific point at which overweighting shifts to underweighting, or whether this point varies significantly across individuals or conditions, it appears from typical experiments that this point falls in the .10–.15 range (Hershey and Shoemaker [1980] use .12). Thus it is clear that probabilities are underweighted over most of their range. This leads to a fifth characteristic of the weighting function: for all $0 < p < 1$, $w(p) + w(1 - p) < 1$. In other words, decision weights do not sum to 1 for choices between two options. Kahneman and Tversky (1979, p. 281) refer to this as *subcertainty,* and this property of the weighting function is somewhat controversial (Abelson & Levi, 1985, pp. 250–251).[7]

It is important to note that attitudes toward risk are not determined by the S-shaped value function alone, as is commonly assumed in most applications of prospect theory to international relations. Rather, risk propensities are determined jointly by the value function and probability weighting function. In the domain of gains where perceived probabilities are above the transition point from overweighting to underweighting (where the weighting function crosses the 45-degree diagonal, at approximately $p = .10 - .15$), the underweighting of probabilities works together with the concavity of the value function to undervalue the gamble relative to the certain outcome, and thus to encourage risk aversion. In the domain of losses, the underweighting of probabilities (above the probability transition point) reduces the weights given to risky negative prospects, makes them less unattractive, and thus encourages risk-seeking. In these probability ranges, the effects of the value function and the probability weighting function are thus mutually reinforcing.

This is not the case where probabilities are small, below the transition point from overweighting to underweighting (but above the very small region in which the value function is not well-behaved). Here the overweighting of probabilities works to increase the value of positive gambles and to increase the negative value of negative gambles, and thus to encourage risk-seeking in the domain of gains and risk aversion in the domain of losses, tendencies which are contrary to the effects of the value function. Which of these counteracting tendencies will dominate depends on the precise shapes of these functions over this range of small probabilities.

It is easy to show that the overweighting of probabilities is a necessary but not sufficient condition for risk-seeking in the domain of gains and for risk

---

[7]Subcertainty leads to an interesting paradox. Consider a choice between (1) $100 with certainty and (2) a fair coin flip which yields $100 for heads and $100 for tails. Subcertainty and the underweighting of the probabilities in the second option would lead to a preference for the first option, even though the two are mathematically equivalent. The paradox can be removed if editing by combination or cancellation is allowed. This demonstrates why editing is a necessary component of prospect theory (Abelson and Levi, 1985, p. 250).

aversion in the domain of losses. Given the shape of the weighting function and the transition point, this means that for prospect theory the "reversal" of risk propensities can occur only in the range of small probabilities. Whether it will occur in this range depends, however, on the relative shapes of the value and probability weighting functions. The indeterminacy of risk orientation is compounded in the range of extremely small probabilities, where the value function is still concave for gains and convex for losses but where the probability weighting function is indeterminant.

As Kahneman and Tversky (1979, pp. 285–286) note, the conditions for risk acceptance in the domain of gains and risk aversion in the domain of losses (i.e., small probabilities) are precisely those under which lottery tickets and insurance policies are sold. Thus the overweighting (and perhaps the exaggeration) of small probabilities is one possible explanation for the appeal of long-shot gambling, and it also might reinforce the tendency for risk averse individuals to insure against rare but catastrophic losses (Payne et al., 1981; Tversky & Kahneman, 1986, p. S258).[8]

Thus prospect theory challenges some basic assumptions and propositions of expected-utility theory and provides an important alternative theoretical framework for the analysis of social and political behavior. The theoretical and empirical studies in this issue are among the first comprehensive efforts to apply prospect theory to international relations and foreign policy.

ACKNOWLEDGMENTS

I would like to thank Patrick James, Cliff Morgan, Ed Rhodes, and Janice Stein for their helpful comments on earlier drafts of this paper.

REFERENCES

Abelson, R. P., & Levi, A. (1985). Decision making and decision theory. In G. Lindzey & E. Aronson (Eds.), *The handbook of social psychology*, 3rd. ed., vol. 1 (pp. 231–309). New York: Random House.

---

[8]We know, however, that while some people are highly risk-averse with respect to rare catastrophes and overinsure against them, other people basically ignore such potential catastrophes altogether. The unpredictability of behavior involving rare disasters is illustrated by the vast range of responses to the risks of airline disasters, earthquakes, or AIDS. Studies of insurance behavior often find a tendency to insure against losses in the medium range of probabilities but not against rare catastrophes (Slovic et al., 1977; Kunreuther et al., 1978), although these findings have been challenged by others (Hershey & Shoemaker, 1980a). Moreover, there is some evidence that decisions regarding the purchase of insurance are quite sensitive to relatively minor changes in the formulation (or framing) of the problem (Slovic et al., 1977).

Allais, M. (1953). Le comportement de l'homme rationnel devant le risque: Critique des postulats et axiomes de l'ecole Americaine. *Econometrica, 21,* 503–546.
Arrow, K. J. (1982). Risk perception in psychology and economics. *Economic Inquiry, 20,* 1–9.
Bernoulli, D. (1954). Exposition of a new theory on the measurement of risk. *Econometrica, 22,* 23–36.
Coursey, D. L., Hovis, J. L., & Schulze, W. D. (1987). The disparity between willingness to accept and willingness to pay measures of value. *Quarterly Journal of Economics, 102,* 697–690.
Einhorn, H. J., & Hogarth, R. M. (1985). Ambiguity and uncertainty in probabilistic inference. *Psychological Review, 92,* 433–461.
Ellsberg, D. (1961). Risk, ambiguity, and the Savage axioms. *Quarterly Journal of Economics, 75,* 643–669.
Farnham, B. (1992). Roosevelt and the Munich crisis: Insights from prospect theory. *Political Psychology, 13,* 205–235.
Fishburn, P. C., & Kochenberger, G. A. (1979). Two-piece Von Neumann-Morgenstern utility functions. *Decision Sciences, 10,* 503–518.
Fleishman, J. A. (1988). The effects of decision framing and others' behavior on cooperation in a social dilemma. *Journal of Conflict Resolution, 32,* 162–180.
Friedman, M. & Savage, L. J. (1948). The utility analysis of choices involving risk. *Journal of Political Economy, 56,* 279–304.
Hartman, R. S., Doane, M. J., & Woo, C. (1991). Consumer rationality and the status quo. *Quarterly Journal of Economics, 106,* 141–162.
Hershey, J. C., & Shoemaker, P. J. H. (1980a). Risk taking and problem context in the domain of losses: an expected utility analysis. *Journal of Risk and Insurance, 47,* 111–132.
Hershey, J. C., & Shoemaker, P. J. H. (1980b). Prospect theory's reflection hypothesis: a critical examination. *Organizational Behavior and Human Performance, 25,* 395–418.
Huth, P., Gelpi, C., & Bennett, D. S. (1992). International conflict among the great powers: Testing the interactive effect of system uncertainty and risk propensity. *Journal of Conflict Resolution, 36.*
Janis, I. L., & Mann, L. (1977). *Decision making.* New York: Free Press.
Jervis, R. (1988). War and misperception. *Journal of Interdisciplinary History, 18,* 675–700.
Jervis, R. (1989). *The meaning of the nuclear revolution.* Ithaca, NY: Cornell University Press.
Jervis, R. (1991). Domino beliefs and strategic behavior. In R. Jervis & J. Snyder (Eds.), *Dominoes and bandwagons: Strategic beliefs and great power competition in the Eurasian rimland* (pp. 20–50). New York: Oxford University Press.
Jervis, R. (1992). Political implications of loss aversion. *Political Psychology, 13,* 187–204.
Kahneman, Daniel, Knetsch, J. L., & Thaler, R. H. (1990). Experimental tests of the endowment effect and the Coase theorem. *Journal of Political Economy, 98,* 1325–1348.
Kahneman, D., Knetsch, J. L. & Thaler, R. H. (1991). The endowment effect, loss aversion, and status quo bias. *Journal of Economic Perspectives, 5,* 193–206.
Kahneman, Daniel, & Tversky, A. (1979). Prospect theory: An analysis of decision under risk. *Econometrica, 47,* 263–291.
Knetsch, J. L. (1989). The endowment effect and evidence of nonreversible indifference curves. *American Economic Review, 79,* 1277–1284.
Knetsch, J. L., & Sinden, J. A. (1984). Willingness to pay and compensation demanded: experimental evidence of an unexpected disparity in measures of value. *Quarterly Journal of Economics, 99,* 507–521.
Knetsch, J. L., & Sinden, J. A. (1987). The persistence of evaluation disparities. *Quarterly Journal of Economics, 102,* 691–695.
Kunreuther, H., Ginsberg, R., Miller, L., Sagi, P., Slovic, P., Borkan, B. & Katz, N. (1978). *Disaster insurance protection.* New York: Wiley.
Lebow, R. N. (1987). *Nuclear crisis management.* Ithaca, NY: Cornell University Press.
Levin, I. P., Johnson, R. D., Russo, C. P., & Deldin, p. (1985). Framing effects in judgment tasks with varying amounts of information. *Organizational behavior and human decision processes, 36,* 362–377.
Levy, J. S. (1987). Declining power and the preventive motivation for war. *World politics, 40,* 82–107.

Levy, J. S. (1989a). The diversionary theory of war: a critique. In M. I. Midlarsky (Ed.)., *Handbook of war studies* (pp. 259-288). Boston: Unwin Hyman.

Levy, J. S. (1989b). Quantitative studies of deterrence success and failure. In P. C. Stern, R. Axelrod, R. Jervis, & R. Radner (Eds.). *Perspectives on deterrence* (pp. 98-133). New York: Oxford University Press.

Levy, J. S. (1992). Prospect theory and international relations: theoretical applications and analytical problems. *Political Psychology, 13,* 283-310.

Luce, R. D. & H. Raiffa. (1957). *Games and decisions.* New York: Wiley.

McDermott, R. (1992). The failed rescue mission in Iran: an application of prospect theory. *Political Psychology, 13,* 237-263.

McInerney, A. (1992). Prospect theory and Soviet policy towards Syria, 1966-1967. *Political Psychology, 13,* 265-282.

McNeil, B. J., Pauker, S. G. Sox, H. C., Jr., & Tversky, A. (1982). On the elicitation of preferences for alternative therapies. *New England Journal of Medicine, 306,* 1259-1262.

Machina, M. J. (1982). Expected utility analysis without the independence axiom. *Econometrica, 2,* 277-332.

Maoz, Z. (1990). Framing the national interest: the manipulation of foreign policy decisions in group settings. *World Politics, 43,* 77-110.

Payne, J. W., Laughhunn, D. J., & Crum, R. (1981). Aspiration level effects in risky choice behavior. *Management Science, 27,* 953-959.

Peterson, S. A., & R. Lawson. (1989). Risky business: prospect theory and politics. *Political Psychology, 10,* 325-339.

Quattrone, G. A., & Tversky, A. (1988). Contrasting rational and psychological analyses of political choice. *American Political Science Review, 82,* 719-736.

Schoemaker, P. J. H. (1980). *Experiments on decisions under risk: the expected utility hypothesis.* Boston: Martinus Nijhoff.

Slovic, P., Fischhoff, B., & Lichtenstein, S. (1988). Response mode, framing, and information-processing effects in risk assessment. In D. E. Bell, H. Raiffa, & A. Tversky (Eds.), *Decision making: descriptive, normative, and prescriptive interactions* (pp. 152-166). New York: Cambridge University Press.

Slovic, P., Fischhoff, B., Lichtenstein, S., Corrigan, B., & Combs, B. (1977). Preference for insuring against probable small losses: insurance implications. *Journal of Risk and Insurance, 44,* 237-258.

Slovic, P., & Lichtenstein, S. (1983). Preference reversals: a broader perspective. *American Economic Review, 73,* 596-605.

Stein, J. G. (1992). International cooperation and loss avoidance: framing the problem. In J. G. Stein & L. Pauly (Eds.), *Choosing to cooperate: How states avoid loss.* Baltimore: Johns Hopkins University Press.

Thaler, R. (1980). Toward a positive theory of consumer choice. *Journal of Economic Behavior and Organization, 1,* 39-60.

Tversky, A. (1972). Elimination by aspects: a theory of choice. *Psychological Review, 76,* 31-48.

Tversky, A., & Kahneman, D. (1981). The framing of decisions and the psychology of choice. *Science, 211,* 453-458.

Tversky, A., & Kahneman, D. (1986). Rational choice and the framing of decisions. *Journal of Business, 59* (no. 4, pt. 2), S251-S278.

Tversky, A., Slovic, P., & Kahneman, D. (1990). The causes of preference reversal. *American Economic Review, 80,* 204-217.

Political Implications of Loss Aversion

Robert Jervis[1]

INTRODUCTION

Is prospect theory valid? If it is, what are the implications for political decision-making, international politics, and social life in general? I do not have full answers, but this sketch may prove a useful stimulant to further thinking (also see Quattrone & Tversky, 1988; Kanwisher, 1989; Peterson & Lawson, 1989).

In summary, the theory argues that people tend to be risk-averse for gains (this was generally known before) but simultaneously to be risk-acceptant for losses (this was the surprise). People are loss-averse in the sense that losses loom larger than the corresponding gains. Losing ten dollars, for example, annoys us more than gaining ten dollars gratifies us. What is peculiar about this is that, contrary to most versions of expected utility theory, the reference point—usually the status quo—is crucial (Tversky & Kahneman, 1986). More than the hope of gains, the specter of losses activates, energizes, and drives actors, producing great (and often misguided) efforts that risk—and frequently lead to—greater losses. Furthermore, the choice between alternatives will be influenced by the

---

[1]Department of Political Science and Institute of War and Peace Studies, Columbia University, New York, New York 10027.

way in which the question is posed. People will choose the risky alternative when the choice is framed in terms of avoiding losses when, in the exact same case, they would take the less risky course of action if the frame of reference is the possibility of improving the situation. Although a setback might be quite minor when compared to the person's total value holdings, he will see it in terms of where he was shortly before and so may take the gamble of an even greater loss in order to gain a chance of reestablishing his position.

The evidence as to the theory's validity is far from conclusive. The bulk of it comes from the answers people give to questionnaires asking them to choose between alternatives of different risks and payoffs. The results could be a hothouse artifact of the laboratory (Wittman, 1991; Smith, 1991, pp. 890–892), as I suspect is in part the case for the supposed tendency of people to pay insufficient attention to base rate information (Jervis, 1986). Perhaps the main reason for thinking that the effect is real is that the tendency for people to be risk-acceptant for losses resonates with personal experience. I doubt if I am alone in having been willing to tolerate an unusually high risk of significant losses in return for the chance of paying no penalty at all or in having been willing to invest significant additional resources in a venture in the hope—I cannot say the expectation—of recouping a recent loss. It is not an accident that people are warned against throwing good money after bad—they often do. Similarly, economists tell us that it is not rational to be influenced by "sunk costs"—having put a lot into a venture is not a good reason to continue with it. But the fact that this is a valid prescription does not mean the behavior is not common—indeed if it were not, there would be no need for economists to stress the point.

If loss aversion occurs in political life, the explanation may not be entirely psychological. Both domestic and international politics could explain the pattern. A leader who accepts even a limited defeat is likely to be punished at the polls. Gambling by accepting a chance of a greater loss in return for a chance of no loss (or even a victory) might be irrational from the standpoint of the national interest, but rational from the standpoint of the power-seeking politician. The difference between smaller and larger national losses may not translate into a similar difference in the loss of political power; a small loss might be sufficient to lose the politician the next election and a larger loss might even rally support to him. Similarly, Dennis Ross argues that during the Cold War Soviet leaders would run high risks to avoid losses because retreating would significantly damage the ruling domestic coalition (Ross, 1984).

Losses may not scale in their international impact either. That is, it is possible that in terms of reputation and credibility a small loss would cost the country not much less than a significantly larger one. (This effect would not hold for more concrete kinds of losses, such as territory and economic strength.) Indeed, decision-makers (Jervis, 1991)—or at least American decision-makers (Morgan, 1985)—seem to believe that small losses will multiply via the domino effect. Gains are not expected to have such consequences. So a rational statesman would not be willing to run high risks in order to secure a moderate gain but would accept much higher risks to avoid a short-run loss of the same magnitude because it would lead to greater losses over a longer period of time.

To say that the explanation for this odd behavior is political rather than psychological is actually misleading, however. While we may not need prospect theory to explain statesmen's choices if we can show that they are based on an analysis of how others will reward or punish them, the theory may tell us how others are reaching their judgments. Thus if it is true that the political costs that leaders incur from losses are not proportional to the magnitude of the loss, the reason may be that domestic opinion operates according to prospect theory in finding even small losses so painful that it prefers high risks to accepting them and will punish any leader who permits them to occur. Prospect theory may also help account for the belief in domino effects because it indicates that people will focus more on losses than on gains. Thus in the late 1970s the United States was deeply concerned that the loss of influence in Ethiopia would have widespread repercussions but paid little attention to the simultaneous gain of influence in Somalia. Similarly, earlier in the Cold War the United States was preoccupied with what it saw as losses that might lead to further dominoes falling but paid little attention to the reversal of Soviet fortunes in Egypt, the Central African Republic, Ghana, or even China. These events constituted major gains for American power and interests that dwarfed many of the defeats that loomed so large in American eyes. But the very fact that this was not understood was crucial to American behavior and can be explained at least in part by the psychological processes discussed here.

GENERAL EFFECTS OF LOSS AVERSION

There seem to be many instances where people and organizations are risk-acceptant for losses. One nice example is that betting is said to be particularly heavy on the last horse race. People who have lost money throughout the afternoon place heavy bets on the final race; they are willing to risk more money in order to gain a chance of recouping their earlier losses. Again, the problem is more complicated than those in the standard pencil-and-paper tests. A husband or wife who returns home having lost a part of his or her paycheck may suffer a price that is relatively insensitive to the amount of the loss. Even without a spouse, the cost to the person's ego may be significant and again much more sensitive to the *fact* of a gain or loss than to the *magnitude* of the gain or loss. But this fact, far from undermining prospect theory, may constitute one of the reasons why it operates.

Perhaps the best generic example of the willingness to take great risks to avoid any loss is cover-ups. If a person has committed a nontrivial transgression, she may devote significant resources to trying to cover it up even though doing so exposes her to much greater penalties if the activities are later discovered. Knowledge of the Watergate break-in would not have cost Nixon his presidency; even sponsorship of it might not have. It was the cover-up that destroyed him. Of course, the objective odds are not known and so a standard expected-utility model can be built to account for Nixon's behavior, although it is far from clear that such a model would be consistent with the rest of his life. Furthermore, there could be large numbers of cases in which people admit to their transgressions, but since these do not give rise to major political scandals, we tend to overlook them. But although firm evidence is lacking, I suspect that cover-ups are more frequent than they would be if people acted on unbiased estimates of costs and probabilities instead of being driven by the need to get off without paying any penalty at all.

More generally, prospect theory leads us to expect people to persevere in losing ventures much longer than standard rationality would lead one to expect. Vietnam is an obvious case, but as usual the situation is not entirely clear. First, as I noted earlier, a person believing in the domino theory would pay high costs to avoid a limited defeat. Second, instances of long, losing wars are a sample of cases biased in the same way that cover-ups are. Instances in which actors cut their losses are less dramatic and so may be lost sight of. Third, continuing along a difficult or costly path sometimes pays off in the long run. Loss aversion may then contribute to useful perseverance. Albert Hirschman (1976) speaks of the "hiding hand." That is, sometimes we embark on a program without much sense of the many obstacles. Were we aware of them at the start, we would never begin. But if we see the obstacles only after we have put in a great deal of time and effort, we will be reluctant to write off our investment and so will continue, and perhaps succeed. The refusal to accept a loss then can be functional, even though the difference in the stance toward losses than toward gains still needs to be explained. These arguments cannot be definitively refuted, but neither do they deny that prospect theory can explain cases like Vietnam: American leaders were continually willing to escalate even though they knew that the prospects of eventual victory were far from certain and that their actions would greatly increase the domestic and international costs they would pay in the event of failure. Sunk costs, furthermore, loomed large in the secret deliberations.

In other wars as well, statesmen lose all sense of proportion about the magnitude of losses when some loss appears certain. Thus Iklé points out that in February 1918 the Germans objected to the Austrian suggestion that they shift their war objectives and agree that "their two countries were obliged to fight for the pre-war possessions of Germany. But Ludendorff granted this concession only after vehement opposition: 'If Germany makes peace without profit, then Germany has lost the war.' What curious inability to distinguish between loss of some territories and loss of the nation!" (Iklé, p. 82). Cutting losses after the expenditure of blood and treasure is perhaps the most difficult act a statesman can take; the lure of the gamble that persevering will recoup the losses is often too great to resist. Furthermore, and what is crucial to the claim that this behavior cannot be explained by a normal expected-utility approach, the same people who gamble in this way are cautious when faced with choices that involve gains: they will take much greater risks to try to return to where they were than they will to make major improvements in the status quo.

The Ford administrations' reaction to the possibility of a swine flu epidemic illustrates some of the dynamics of the choice between a sure but small loss and the chance of a much larger one, although it also brings out several ambiguities. The government launched a program to inoculate everyone in the belief that there was a significant danger that without inoculation massive deaths would occur. The political leaders knew, although they did not focus on it, that mass inoculation was both costly and would certainly kill a few people because of side effects. Whether or not the medical officials did a good job of presenting the issues to political leaders (Neustadt & Fineberg, 1978; Silverstein, 1981), the logic of the argument for mass inoculations was fairly straightforward. As Silverstein (p. 135) put it:

> It mattered a little that the experts could not tell whether the chance of pandemic influenza was 30 percent, or 3 percent, or even less than 1 percent. What the assistant secretary for Health, the secretary of HEW, the president, and Congress heard was that there was *some* chance of pandemic flu and this was enough. No responsible politician at any level wished to put himself in the position of opposing the program, thus running the risk that pandemic illness and death might prove him a villain.

This story does not fit entirely well with prospect theory. Assuming decision-makers realized that inoculations would cause at least a few deaths and that the outbreak of swine flu was less than certain, they chose a small but sure loss in order to eliminate the possibility of a larger catastrophe. Three factors help unravel this. First, the deaths from inoculation were probably seen as an insurance payment, a normal cost of doing business. As Tversky and Kahneman (1986) have shown (but I think not fully explained), people are much more willing to accept an outcome if it can be portrayed not as a loss but as an expected payment for the activity. Thus people buy insurance, which means preferring a small but sure loss to the slight chance of a much greater one. Second, politics was a driving force (not to imply that there is anything wrong with this). Leaders knew that if there was an epidemic that could have been greatly reduced by a program of vaccinations that they had rejected, their political losses would be enormous. Indeed, even if the epidemic did not materialize, a decision not to inoculate might harm them if the public believed this stance was imprudent. Here, as in the foreign policy case mentioned at the outset, we may have to shift our attention from the decision-makers to the beliefs and values of those who can reward and punish them. Third, once deaths from inoculations were real rather than an abstract expectation—and occurred in greater numbers than predicted—the program was immediately called off. Sure losses had a greater impact when they involved particular human beings than when they were projections. (Fortunately for the U.S., but unfortunately for tests of the theory, it simultaneously became clear that little or no swine flu was going to materialize.)

EFFECTS ON BARGAINING, DETERRENCE, AND CAUSES OF WAR

The proposition that actors react very differently to the prospect of losses than to the chance of making gains has important implications for international bargaining and conflict. If loss aversion is widespread, states defending the status quo should have a big bargaining advantage. That is, a state will be willing to pay a higher price and run higher risks if it is facing losses than if it is seeking to make gains. A related proposition which is consistent with the literature (Schelling, 1966; Jervis, 1989) is that coercion can more easily maintain the status quo than alter it—deterrence is usually easier than what Schelling calls "compellence." These arguments, however, assume that it is clear to the actors which of them is the defender and which is the challenger. Sometimes this is true, but often it is not. This yields a third implication: Conflicts and wars are more likely when each side believes it is defending the status quo.

Since the reason why the perceived status quo will be vehemently defended is that states will run high risks rather than suffer even a small but certain loss, the proposition can be broadened to argue that conflicts and wars are most likely when each side believes it will suffer significant losses if it does not fight. Perceptual biases are likely to enter in here. When states overestimate others' hostility, as they frequently do, they will expect losses unless they take strong if not aggressive action. Both sides can readily come to believe this. Not only will each accept high risks in order to avoid a bad outcome, but each is likely to think that the other side is merely striving for gains and so is likely to be willing to back down. Furthermore, Lebow, Stein, and others have shown (Lebow, 1981; Lebow & Stein, 1987; Jervis, Lebow, & Stein, 1985), states that are desperate—that face severe losses—feel strong motivated biases to believe that the policy that offers a way out can in fact succeed. These states are then likely to convince themselves that they can successfully coerce others when a disinterested perspective would reveal that this is implausible. As Lebow and Stein (1987) note, deterrence theory is designed primarily to explain how to deal with countries that are seeking gains. In these circumstances, deterrence may be effective. But if the other is driven by the fear of losses, threats and coercion are likely to backfire, producing a spiral of greater hostility. (For deterrence versus the spiral model, see Jervis, 1976, Ch. 3).

A fourth implication is that during the Cold War a superpower's threat to intervene in a local conflict was greater the more its local client was suffering. This was exemplified twice in the 1973 war, first increasing the credibility of the American intervention, then increasing the credibility of a Soviet move when the tide of battle shifted against Egypt. Superpowers are less prone to intervene, and their threats to do so are less credible, when such actions would bring gains to the client. Again, the danger is that both sides will fear losses (and will not understand either the other's perspective or the chances of success), thereby generating not only conflicts but undesired and unforeseen ones. But to the extent that perceptions are shared, loss aversion should stabilize local conflicts by making it unlikely that either side can "win big." Assuming the local clients realize this, they will have to moderate their demands and actions.

More generally, by giving a bargaining advantage to the side that fears or suffers losses, loss aversion supports stability. This affects day-to-day diplomacy as well as crisis bargaining. For example, loss aversion and the resulting caution probably is part of the explanation for why neither the U.S. or the Soviet Union was anxious to gamble on a reunited Germany. The result might have been to greatly improve either side's position, but it would mean foregoing the sure and current advantage of controlling part of that country. To call the results stability, however, is to miss the other half of the story—because actors place a higher valuation on what they have than on what they might gain, they will refuse to accept bargains that a third party would judge to make them better off. The general level of trading within and among countries will then be lower than most theories would lead one to expect. Economists have come to argue that these activities are less than previously expected because scholars had neglected the role of "transaction costs"—the costs of acquiring information, drawing contracts, and guarding against cheating (Coase, 1937; Williamson, 1985). But loss aversion may be equally important.

WAR-PEACE DECISIONS

Prospect theory produces inferences about both the short- and the long-run causes of wars. If it is correct, we would expect that wars and other conflicts would be more strongly and more commonly motivated by the desire to avoid perceived losses than by the hope of making gains. States should be more often pushed into war by the fear that the alternative to fighting is a serious deterioration in their position than pulled in by the belief that war can improve a situation that is already satisfactory. As I will note below, sometimes the status quo itself is unsatisfactory. But more often, even if it leaves a great deal to be desired, the status quo is at least tolerable in the sense that the state is willing to live with it rather than running a significant risk of suffering the greater losses than a war might bring. Fear is usually a more potent motivator than the desire for expansion. A statesman will run a significant risk of destruction of his own power and his regime and devastation of his country if he thinks the alternative is a certain and significant deterioration in his power and security. But he would not be willing to run similar risks if he believed that the status quo could be maintained by diplomacy even though war, if successful, could bring great gains. Wars are then less frequently caused by aggression than by spirals of fear and insecurity (Jervis, 1976, Ch. 3).

Thus it now appears that Saddam Hussein's attack on Kuwait cannot be described entirely as an attempt to increase his power and influence. Rather, he seems to have believed that if he did not attack, his position would get steadily worse. Not only would there be little hope for economic recovery in the absence of a Kuwaiti willingness to forgive Iraqi debt and stop driving oil prices down by producing more than their OPEC quota, but he seems to have seen an American-led conspiracy to trim his power (Viorst, 1991, pp. 67–68). The famous historian A. J. P. Taylor exaggerates as usual when he claims that "every war between Great Powers [between 1848 and 1918] started as a preventive war, not a war of conquest" (Taylor, 1954, p. 166), but the preventive motive indeed is frequent (Levy, 1987).

Loss aversion similarly implies that the restraints in a limited war are more likely to be broken by a side that fears that failing to do so will result in significant losses than by the side that believes that expansion can bring it significant gains. By contrast, approaches that give no special place to the status-quo point would lead us to think that states should escalate when doing so is expected to yield more utility than maintaining the restraint. Since there is no reason why states should adopt a different stance toward avoiding losses than toward making gains, they should be as likely to increase the level of violence in order to break stalemate and secure a decisive victory as to ward off a defeat. In fact, I doubt if this is actually true. The United States threatened escalation at the final stages of the Korean War (Foot, 1990), but it is far from clear what it would have done if the Chinese had not agreed to a truce. The Chinese, in turn, intervened not in the summer of 1950, when such action might have pushed the United States off the peninsula, but in the fall when the alternative was to accept a hostile regime on its borders (that is, when it was certain that the status quo would deteriorate badly if she did not fight). The risks China was willing to run to regain Quemoy and Matsu and threaten Formosa—objectives of presumably great value—were much less.

Although it is often said, especially of aggressors, that the appetite grows with the eating, this does not seem to be as true as it would be were gains and losses to be treated symmetrically. Although states sometimes do overreach themselves (as the United States did in crossing the 38th parallel in Korea), it is relatively unusual for the side with the upper hand to increase the level of violence or continue to fight to gain additional objectives, even if doing so seems militarily feasible. Thus the Chinese did not push deeper into Indian territory in 1962 when their initial attack met with great success and, contrary to Kissinger's argument, India probably would not have turned on West Pakistan in 1971 even if the U.S. had not tried to deter such a move. Only in the last of his wars did Bismarck yield to the temptation to make extra gains, and even in this situation he took Alsace and Lorraine only because he was convinced that even if he did not the French would be immutably hostile. Although it was Hitler who taught the world that ambitions and risk-taking increased with success, this picture actually is not accurate: Hitler's outlook and stance remained remarkably unchanged throughout his monstrous career.

This does not mean that unprovoked aggression never occurs. Hitler, to take only the most obvious example, was driven by the desire to drastically alter the status quo, not by the fear that he was encircled by hostile powers that would destroy Germany unless he took arms against them. The case of postwar Soviet foreign policy is ambiguous in this regard, and it would not be surprising if both motives were at work. Indeed, it should be stressed that prospect theory does not deny that actors may want to change the status quo or that the combination of the strength of the motivation to do so and the perceived possibilities of success can lead to expansion and war. Actors will take some risks to improve their situations even if they are risk-averse for gains. But, the theory argues, actors should be much more willing to run risks when they believe that failing to do so will result in certain losses. Wars will then frequently be triggered by fear of loss; fighting in order to act on an opportunity will be relatively rare.

Great methodological problems plague the attempt to develop fully convincing comparisons (see below), but it appears that when states take very high risks it is usually the case that they believe they will have to accept certain losses if they do not do so. Furthermore, this recklessness surprises other countries—both those who are attacked and neutrals—because they expect the state to be more cautious, which it usually is because the more normal context is one of facing gains rather than losses. Thus Japan attacked Great Britain and the United States in December 1941 not because her leaders had much confidence they could win, but because they saw—quite correctly—that the alternative to fighting was to surrender much of their position in Southeast Asia and China. This loss would have been a major one. But a military withdrawal would still have permitted her a great deal of influence in the area and would have left the Japanese islands, industry, armed forces, and cities intact. Others thought the choice for war was odd because it was—and in retrospect still is—hard to empathize with the pressures people feel when faced with losses.

This case is far from unique in its general outlines. Although the German motivation in 1914 was mixed, one important component was the belief that the diplomatic and military situation was deteriorating and that German security would be much lower in a few years if Germany did not fight. Her leaders knew that victory was far from certain; I find it hard to believe that they would have run this risk is they thought that the status quo could have been maintained by peaceful means and that the only reason to fight was to gain even more territory, power, and prestige. The other participants in World War I also were much more strongly driven by fears than by hopes. All were worried that their power and security were being undermined by the course of events. While they had expansionist ambitions, these were not sufficient to lead them to stake the future of their countries on a war that they all entered with great trepidation. Similarly, although Israel's 1967 war resulted in its gaining territory, the motivation, as in 1956 and in the war of attrition of 1969–70, was the belief that unless these risky actions were taken, the status quo would deteriorate badly.

The other side of this coin is harder to see because it consists of nonevents: states are slow to take advantage of opportunities to expand at some risk (Lebow, 1984), especially when compared with their behavior when they feel their position is under attack. We tend to take peace and even the lack of demands for change as natural. But they are not: given the postulates of power politics and expected utility, we should see states pushing to alter the status quo in their favor as often as they exert themselves to maintain it. We should see more Hitlers, at least in smaller versions of power and ruthlessness. These are not absent: Bismarck fought in order to expand, or really create, his state; the dramatic weakening of a country or empire often draws others to attack; aggression of course occurs. But are these events as frequent as they would be if opportunity were as strong a motivation as the fear of loss?

In some cases, the reference point is not the status quo but something better. The gap between this desired state of affairs and the current one can lead to high risk-taking. (Of course, the danger here is that this argument will become tautological unless we can specify a priori what this reference point will be and when it will be used. We also need to rule out the possibility that the same forces which determine the reference point also directly lead to the risky behavior. Some work has been done to establish what the likely reference points will be, but more work needs to be done.) At times, the reference point will be an earlier status quo, before the actor suffered serious losses. Thus for at least a period after a country has lost significant territory or influence, the previous situation is likely to be the standard and the continuation of the current situation will be experienced as a loss. This was clearly the case for Egypt after the 1967 war. She could not accept Israeli occupation of Sinai as normal and the 1973 war was triggered by the belief—probably correct—that although war was risky, there was no chance that peaceful diplomacy could succeed (Stein, 1985).

The fact that both sides can have different reference points and so can simultaneously be impelled by loss aversion can render dangerous the strategy of the fait accompli. George and Smoke note that deterrence can alter the status quo before the defender has time to react (George and Smoke, 1974, pp. 536–40). But unless the latter quickly adjusts to the new situation, it may be willing to run unusually high risks to regain its previous position. The other side, expecting the first to be rational, will be surprised by its continued resistance. Because each side will see itself as defending the status quo, it will therefore have strong incentives to stand firm and—believing the adversary sees the situation as the state does—will expect the other side to retreat. Each will be driven by a strong resistance to accept what it sees as an unfavorable change.

The belief in inevitable progress can produce a different, and steadily changing, reference point. If and when the Soviet leaders believed the communist ideology, they expected a steady increase in the power of communism and the number of countries that were freed from the grip of capitalism. The status quo was not only politically but psychologically arbitrary and so stagnation for them would have the same psychological impact as losses for others. This might explain what Western observers saw as the unusual propensity of the Soviet Union to take risks to increase its influence and aid leftist regimes.

Crisis Stability

Prospect theory also addresses the short-run causes of war in the nuclear era. Almost all analysts agree on the importance of "crisis stability." The existence of nuclear weapons means that states are deterred more by the fear of retaliation than by the expectation that they might suffer military defeat. But if one or both sides believe that a first strike can destroy the other's strategic forces, a strike might occur. By contrast, the configuration is stable if each side believes that striking first produces little advantage or even, in the extreme case, reduces the state's capability more than it does that of the adversary. In this case, it is very hard to start an all-out war and expectations of the war's starting will not produce a self-fulfilling prophecy, as they do under crisis instability.

Psychological processes contribute strongly to the presence or absence of crisis stability (Jervis, 1989, Ch. 5). Prospect theory in particular can explain some of the forces that might be at work (for further discussion, see Jervis, 1989, pp. 168–73). Because people are willing to take unusual risks to recoup recent losses, even if these setbacks are quite minor when compared with their total value holdings, a decision-maker might risk costly escalation or even world war if such a move held out the possibility of reversing a defeat. In cases in which a standard expected-utility model would predict the actor to cut his losses, he might up the ante. This would not lead directly to nuclear war, but it could create a situation that was extremely dangerous and one in which the momentum of military moves might lead to the use of nuclear weapons.

The danger would be especially great if both sides were to feel that they were losing, something that could easily happen because antagonists often have different perspectives and use different baselines. The Middle East crisis of 1973 may be an example of such a situation, with the Americans feeling that they could not allow Israel to lose and the Russians feeling that at least a limited Arab victory was necessary to regain their influence.

A second consequence of loss aversion for crisis stability is that if the decision-maker thinks that a small war—and therefore enormous loss—is certain if he does not strike and that attacking provides even a chance of escaping unscathed even if it risks a much larger war, he may decide to strike even if the standard probability-utility calculus calls for restraint. Similar dynamics could operate on a smaller scale in less severe crises, such as those set off by a hostile coup in an important Third World country or the limited use of force by the adversary in a disputed area. With his attention riveted on the deterioration which will occur unless he acts strongly to reverse the situation, the decision-maker might take actions which entail an irrationally high chance of major escalation.

The powerful aversion to losses could lead the decision-maker to attack in the situations described in the previous paragraphs, but it could lead him to hold back if he thought that even though striking first could be advantageous, it would lead to certain retaliation while he might be able to keep the peace if he did not fire. As long as there is any hope of avoiding total war, decision-makers are likely to recoil from the thought of starting it. Even General Curtis LeMay's successor as head of SAC, General Thomas Power, argued against preemption "so long as there is the slightest hope that we can prevent a Soviet attack through diplomatic means of a strong posture of deterrence" (Power & Arnhym, 1964, pp. 80–81). Similarly, Neville Chamberlain argued for continued appeasement on the grounds that "we were in no position to justify waging a war today in order to prevent a war hereafter" (quoted in Mommsen, 1983, p. x).

The response can be influenced by how the decision is framed. If the decision-maker takes as his baseline not the existing situation, but the casualties that would be suffered in a war, his choice between the same alternatives might be different. He would then judge the policies according to lives that might be saved, not lost, with the result that he would choose a course of action that he believed would certainly save some lives rather than another that might save more, but might not save any. The obvious danger is that a first strike, which would significantly reduce the other side's strategic forces and one's own casualties, would be preferred to restraint which could not provide the certainty of saving any lives. The result would not only be unfortunate for public policy, but is hard to square with rational choice theories if the person would respond differently if she focused on the possibility of avoiding war, not reducing casualties. Furthermore, as noted earlier, there is also some evidence indicating that people are more willing to accept disadvantages which are seen as costs (as in insurance premiums) rather than losses. The evidence is not strong and the theorizing is a bit ad hoc, but if the phenomenon is real it could lead decision-makers to take higher risks when these are seen as the cost of conducting foreign policy than when risks are conceptualized as a sacrifice in the status quo. It is hard to believe that a first strike could ever be seen in the former terms, but a strategy that increases the chance of war could be.

Of course, in laboratory experiments it is the professor who gives one group one frame and another group another. In real situations, we need to explore why people come to frame the situation in one way rather than another (Farnham, 1992). Alternatively, we should try to see whether actors manipulate frames—so that an actor who knows what decision he wants others to make should frame the question in a way that is more likely to elicit this answer. For example, in the 1930s appeasers should have stressed the fact that their policy provided a chance of avoiding war; anti-appeasers should have stressed that Germany would grow stronger—and British casualties greater—the longer the war was postponed and that appeasement was certain to sacrifice other British values, such as power, prestige, and morality. Thus as the Munich crisis reached its peak, the pro-appeasement British ambassador to Czechoslovakia stressed to the Czechs that they should not be lured into believing that standing firm might succeed in avoiding all losses— "refusal or evasion [of the Anglo-French plan] at this last moment meant the destruction of their beautiful country, while acceptance meant retention of most of what mattered to Czechs and Slovaks" (quoted in Taylor, 1979, p. 788).

RENORMALIZATION

Prospect theory argues for the importance of the status quo because it is usually from this that gains or losses are computed. But there is a problem with the argument that people will take high risks if doing so holds out some chance of reversing recent losses. Once one has suffered a loss, why is not the new—if less desired—position considered the status quo, rendering the person risk-averse for moves that could improve it (including those that might bring about a return to the old status quo)? This raises the question of what can be called "renormalization"—that is, the length of time it takes for actors to adjust to a new status quo. When you have suffered a loss that you cannot immediately recoup, when does this get incorporated into your new sense of the status quo? By mid-October 1962, did the Russians consider the strategic balance with missiles in Cuba as the benchmark from which gains and losses would be measured? If the blockade and associated bargaining had not succeeded in removing the missiles, how long would it have taken for the U.S. to treat the new situation as the status quo? A personal anecdote illustrates some of these questions. On a recent vacation, I tried to body-surf an undisciplined wave and ended up crashing into the sand. For a minute or two I was paralyzed, and the thought that the paralysis would be permanent obviously crossed my mind. But the paralysis passed quickly, to be replaced by nasty pain and a very unpleasant stiff neck. If the paralysis had lasted much longer, I would have treated the pain and suffering that accompanied movement as a major gain over the other outcome. But because my paralysis was so short-lived, and I did not have time to assimilate it, I compared my current situation to that which existed before the injury and so was annoyed and grumpy.

In international politics—and in social life in general—I suspect that we renormalize for gains much more quickly than we do for losses. We rapidly, if not effortlessly, adjust to good fortune and any improvement in our lives. Indeed, we get accustomed to it so readily that the immediate burst of pleasure produced by the change soon dissipates. Neither individuals nor nations are so accepting of losses, however. We remain unhappy, unreconciled, and often bitter for a prolonged period. But what determines the exact length of this period is not known. It is clear, however, that it is the slow renormalization for losses that drives the risk-acceptance and indeed creates situations in which both sides are impelled by loss aversion. Thus in the Cuban missile crisis the status quo for the United States was the situation in which there were no Soviet missiles or bombers on the island; for the Soviet Union the status quo may have been the world as it was before the blockade. Of course Khrushchev chose to withdraw (although Kennedy in turn made significant concessions). Perhaps he would have been less accommodating if the installation had been completed and the new status quo formalized by an official announcement.

A related problem is that when a state has made a pledge—even a secret one—to change the situation, it may consider that pledged future as the new reference point. This may help explain aspects of the Cuban missile crisis and the Fashoda crisis of 1898. The Soviets had started to put missiles in Cuba before the U.S. made its formal warnings in September 1962; the French moved toward Fashoda before the British had issued formal prohibitions. In a fully rational world, it would not matter that the defender made its commitment—which surely should have been credible—only after the challenger had decided (but not announced) that it would move. But psychologically, the challengers' decisions perhaps led them to feel that backing away would be a loss rather than a foregoing of a gain.

IMPLICATIONS FOR SOCIAL EFFICIENCY AND STABILITY

Experiments have revealed an "endowment effect" related to loss aversion—being given an object increases one's valuation of it (Knetsch et al.,

1987). Students who were given a mug would only part with it for a price much higher than they had earlier (before they received it) said it was worth. While in laboratory situations these striking effects decrease social efficiency by inhibiting trades, the implications for the real world may be quite different. As people endow their possessions, lives, and perhaps self-images with greater value, their level of satisfaction increases. Social stability is enhanced as an added force of inertia operates. You like what you have—be it your job, apartment, or spouse—and so are unwilling to trade it for an object that would seem to an outsider to be of greater value. Trades that are rational from an expected-utility standpoint will be rejected, presumably producing considerable inefficiency. But greater efficiency might come at too high a price. Imagine a world in which everyone was willing to change what he or she was doing in the hope of making greater gains. Efficient in some sense surely; but what would be the societal costs of constant and rapid change? What would be lost in the sense of the stability, regularity, and solidity of social life? Furthermore, envy and jealousy would be increased if people did not place a higher valuation on what they have than on other's possessions. The fact—if it is a fact—that people are less anxious to change than they otherwise would be raises the general level of contentment within societies and helps make them work; the knowledge that others will fight very hard to keep what they have increases predictability and decreases overt social conflict.

Internationally, the effects probably are less benign. While valuing what it has contributes to the state's sense of well-being and so counteracts the desperation that leads to many wars, negotiations are inhibited as each side feels that the cost of making a concession is greater than the gain received from the concession by the other side. For example, each side might be more pained by giving up 1,000 missiles in an arms control agreement than it would be gratified and made secure by having the adversary's force reduced by the same amount. Or two countries might be better off by most measures if they would exchange some bits of territory, but the bargain would be made impossible by the high subjective evaluations each side placed on what it had.

Other difficulties are caused by the "certainty effect"—the tendency for actors to over-weight outcomes whose likelihood is 1 or 0. Thus while an expected utility model might lead one to expect that a state would be willing to make an agreement that would significantly increase the chance of peace at the cost of having to fight a war at some disadvantage if armed conflict did break but, loss aversion would inhibit this bargain. Statesmen would ask, "If we sign this agreement, will we certainly be worse off if war should come?" and, when the answer is yes, they would conclude that this is too high a price to pay for even a large decrease in the chance of war.

A second consequence is that actors are likely to be willing to pay more to reduce uncertainty to close to zero than they are to reduce uncertainty the same amount in the middle range. That is, a policy that reduces the chance of war from 35% to 25% would be valued much less than one that would reduce it from 11%

to 1%, let alone from 10% to zero. Agreements and measures of the latter type are rare; states may not be willing to pay as much as they should for the significant increases in the chance of desired outcomes that leave a good deal of uncertainty remaining. Logically, arrangements that provide complete certainty should be especially valuable only if they yield disproportionate benefits, such as permitting the state to disband its army. But the attraction of certainty is not sensitive to such considerations and cannot be explained by them.

METHODOLOGICAL DIFFICULTIES

Getting good evidence for any of these effects will not be easy. The endowment effect is difficult to verify because states and people in society are not given things the way people in experiments are given mugs and candy bars at random. Furthermore, it would be difficult to specify that the added valuation comes immediately rather than as a result of the ties that are built up between the country and the territory or other value that has been gained. But it might be possible to find cases in which countries conquered or otherwise gained territory almost accidentally—areas they had not been seeking as primary goals—and then see how much they were willing to pay to keep them.

It is at least as difficult to gather firm evidence on the main inferences from prospect theory. Crucial is the argument that people will run much higher risks to avoid losses than to make gains. The experimenter gives the subjects the payoffs and probabilities; in real life people construct their subjective estimates of both of these elements. Similarly, the experimenter can frame the same question differently and see how people respond; in social and political life actors do their own framing. Thus while we can find cases in which different actors employ different frames (McDermott, 1992), correlations between differences in framing and differences in choice and preferences may be spurious—the same factors that lead an actor to frame the situation in a particular way may drive her choice. Even if we find that actors' preferences change as the way they frame the choice changes, third variables may still be at work.

Showing that people are loss-averse obviously means demonstrating much more than that they do not like losses. Rather, what is crucial is demonstrating that differences in risk-taking propensity vary according to the direction of the expected changes from the status quo. The difficulties are formidable. First, we can rarely specify with great precision the risks that an actor perceives in various courses of action. Thirty years after the Cuban missile crisis we still argue about how risky Khrushchev believed his move would be. Furthermore, showing that people are more risk-acceptant for losses than for gains requires comparisons that are quite difficult because they call for a measure of the subjective utility of various outcomes. Most decisions lack an objective yardstick of lives or dollars;

we cannot readily find comparisons as convincing as those which arise when people are faced with the possibility of a loss or a gain of a given amount of money or a certain number of lives. Thus even if we can show that a statesman took risks when the alternative would have been to accept a smaller but certain loss, we need also to show that in other situations he preferred continuing the status quo to accepting a similar gamble that might have resulted in an improvement equal in magnitude to the loss he found unacceptable. Without precise—or at least decent—measures of the magnitude of the gains and losses (which are of course subjective), greater risk-taking in the latter cases can be attributed to differences in the utilities in the cases. Of course, confirmation of expected-utility theory is plagued by similar difficulties of measurement, but without a set of very good comparisons there will always be a great deal of room for dispute. Nevertheless, it is clear both that prospect theory yields important and counterintuitive propositions and that many cases—cited here and in the other articles in this issue—indicate that statesmen are indeed more risk-acceptant for losses than for gains. The psychological world does not appear to be symmetrical, and the implications for human and national behavior are many and important.

REFERENCES

Coase, R. (1937). The nature of the firm. *Economica N.S., 4*, 386–405.
Farnham, B. (1992). Roosevelt and the Munich crisis: Insights from prospect theory. *Political Psychology, 13*, 205–235.
Foot, R. (1985). *The wrong war: American policy and the dimensions of the Korean conflict, 1950–1953.* Ithaca, NY: Cornell University Press.
Foot, R. (1990). *A substitute for victory: The politics of peacemaking at the Korean armistice talks.* Ithaca, NY: Cornell University Press.
George, A. and Smoke, R. (1974). *Deterrence in American foreign policy.* New York: Columbia University Press.
Hirschman, A. (1976). *Development projects observed.* Washington, D.C.: Brookings Institution.
Iklé, F. (1971). *Every war must end.* New York: Columbia University Press.
Jervis, R. (1976). *Perception and misperception in international politics.* Princeton, NJ: Princeton University Press.
Jervis, R. (1986). Representativeness in foreign policy judgements. *Political Psychology, 7*, 483–505.
Jervis, R. (1989). *The meaning of the nuclear revolution.* Ithaca, NY: Cornell University Press.
Jervis, R. (1991). Domino beliefs and strategic behavior. In R. Jervis & J. Snyder (Eds.), *Dominoes and bandwagons: Strategic beliefs and great power competition in the eurasian rimland* (pp. 20–50). New York: Oxford.
Jervis, R., Lebow, R. N., & Stein, J. G. (1985). *Psychology and deterrence.* Baltimore, MD: Johns Hopkins University Press.
Kanwisher, N. (1989). Cognitive heuristics and American security policy. *Journal of Conflict Resolution, 33*, 652–675.
Knetsch J., Thaler, R., & Kahneman, D. (1987). Experimental tests of the endowment effect and the Coase theorem. Unpublished manuscript.
Lebow, R. N. (1981). *Between peace and war.* Baltimore, MD: Johns Hopkins University Press.
Lebow, R. N. (1984). Windows of opportunity: Do states jump through them? *International Security, 9*, 147–186.

Lebow, R. N. & Stein, J. G. (1987). Beyond deterrence. *Journal of Social Issues, 43,* 5–72.
Levy, J. (1987). Declining power and the preventive motivation for war. *World Politics, 40,* 82–107.
McDermott, R. (1992). The failed rescue mission in Iran: An application of prospect theory. *Political Psychology, 13,* 237–263.
Mommsen, W. (1983). Foreword. In W. Mommsen & L. Kettenacker, (Eds.), *The fascist challenge and the policy of appeasement* (pp. ix–xii). Boston: Allen & Unwin.
Morgan, P. (1985). Saving face for the sake of deterrence. In R. Jervis, et al. (Eds.), *Psychology and deterrence* (pp. 125–152). Baltimore: MD: Johns Hopkins University Press.
Neustadt, R. & Fineberg, H. (1978). *The swine flu affair.* Washington, DC: Government Printing Office.
Peterson, S., & Lawson, R. (1989). Risky business: Prospect theory and politics. *Political Psychology, 10,* 325–340.
Power, T., & Arnhym, A. (1964). *Design for survival.* New York: Coward-McCann.
Quattrone, G., & Tversky, A. (1988). Contrasting rational and psychological analyses of political choice. *American Political Science Review, 82,* 719–736.
Ross, D. (1984). Risk aversion in Soviet decisionmaking. In J. Valenta & W. Potter (Eds.), *Soviet decisionmaking for national security* (pp. 237–251). Boston: Allen & Unwin.
Schelling, T. (1966). *Arms and influence.* New Haven, CT: Yale University Press.
Silverstein, A. (1981). *Pure politics and impure science.* Baltimore, MD: Johns Hopkins University Press.
Smith, V. (1991). Rational choice: the contrast between economics and psychology. *Journal of Political Economy, 99,* 877–897.
Stein, J. G. (1985). Calculation, miscalculation and conventional deterrence: the view from Cairo. In R. Jervis, et al. (Eds.), *Psychology and Deterrence* (pp. 34–59). Baltimore, MD: Johns Hopkins University Press.
Taylor, A. J. T. (1954). *The struggle for mastery in europe.* New York: Oxford.
Taylor, T. (1979). *Munich: the price of peace.* Garden City, NY: Doubleday.
Tversky, A., & Kahneman, D. (1986). Rational choice and the framing of decisions. *Journal of Business, 59,* S251–S278.
Viorst, M. (1991). Report from Baghdad. *New Yorker,* June 24, 1991.
Wittman, D. (1991). Contrasting economic and psychological analyses of political choice: an economist's perspective on why cognitive psychology does not explain democratic politics. In K. Monroe, (Ed.), *The economic approach to politics* (pp. 405–432). New York: Harper Collins.
Williamson, O. (1985). *The economic institutions of capitalism.* New York: Free Press.

Roosevelt and the Munich Crisis: Insights from Prospect Theory

Barbara Farnham[1]

INTRODUCTION

Recently, there have been a number of attempts to use prospect theory to explain political decision-making behavior (e.g., Quattrone & Tversky, 1984 and 1988). Because such efforts challenge the claim of theories of rational choice to provide a more convincing account of similar phenomena (e.g., Bueno de Mesquita, 1981), an attempt to examine these competing models in the light of an historical case should have considerable theoretical interest.

President Franklin D. Roosevelt's decision-making behavior during the Munich crisis in September 1938 provides a suitable vehicle for such an explora-

[1]Institute of War and Peace Studies, Columbia University, New York, 10027.

tion because it appears to exhibit a number of phenomena associated with prospect theory, such as a change in the framing of the choice problem and corresponding preference reversal, risk acceptance to avoid loss, and the operation of certainty effects. During the course of the crisis, Roosevelt moved from a firm conviction that American intervention was inappropriate to the belief that it was not only desirable, but necessary. At the same time, he became willing to accept at least two risks he had previously desired to avoid: that such intervention might be ineffective or, worse, have an adverse effect on the crisis, and that it might have unfortunate domestic political repercussions.

What is most striking about Roosevelt's reversal of preferences is that it seems to have been a consequence of a change in the way he represented the crisis to himself, or framed it, rather than a response to new information about its implications for the United States.[2] Initially, Roosevelt believed that the European crisis, even should it end in war, did not represent an immediate threat to the United States. In mid-crisis, however, he apparently became convinced that it did pose such a threat, despite the fact that, from an American point of view, the objective situation was unaltered. Roosevelt had in fact come to regard an outcome of war as in some sense a loss for the United States and thus felt impelled to take action to avoid it.

This behavior is puzzling from a rational choice perspective because a preference reversal based on a different representation of the same decision problem clearly violates the expectations of utility theory (Tversky & Kahneman, 1986, p. S523). Prospect theory, on the other hand, by providing "an alternative account of choice under risk" which holds that people are frequently less analytical in making their decisions than expected-utility theory would predict (Kahneman & Tversky, 1979, p. 263), offers the possibility of explaining such behavior.

In addition to illuminating an important episode in American foreign policy, however, the application of prospect theory to the Munich case offers at least three theoretical benefits. For one thing, while several of the predictions of prospect theory have received experimental support, there has been relatively little work demonstrating their applicability to political decision-making. Direct evidence of the ability of prospect theory to explain behavior in an actual political decision-making situation, therefore, could increase confidence in its ecological validity and extend its range (For experimental evidence in general, in addition to the work of Tversky and Kahneman cited below, see Davis & Bobko, 1986, pp. 125–126; Bazerman, 1983, p. 214; Levin et al., 1985, p. 372; and Shapira, 1981, pp. 334, 344–348, 250. For attempts to use prospect theory to illuminate

---

[2]According to Tversky and Kahneman a decision frame includes the decision-maker's conception of "the acts or options among which [he or she] must choose, the possible outcomes or consequences of these acts, and the contingencies or conditional probabilities associated with a particular choice." Taken together, these elements serve to define the decision problem (Tversky & Kahneman, 1981, p. 453).

political judgment, see Quattrone & Tversky, 1988 and 1984. On the need to relate psychological theories to decision-making behavior in political settings, see Tetlock, 1985; and Farnham, 1990).

A second benefit of using prospect theory to explain the Munich case is that in suggesting a possible cause of changes in decision frames, it may contribute to an elaboration of the theory itself. Tversky and Kahneman have said relatively little on this subject. Stating only that "the frame that a decision-maker adopts is controlled partly by the formulation of the problem and partly by the norms, habits, and personal characteristics of the decision-maker," they have addressed neither the issue of how a decision problem is formulated in the first place nor the question of what factors might cause that formulation to change spontaneously (Tversky & Kahneman, 1981, p. 453). The Munich case, however, suggests the intriguing possibility that at least some frame changes may be triggered by affect. Apparently, that is, President Roosevelt reframed the European crisis as a matter of direct concern to the United States only after the idea of impending war had become emotionally compeling to him.

Finally, because the Munich crisis ultimately produced considerable stress for Roosevelt, it offers an opportunity to look more closely at Janis and Mann's (1977) decisional conflict model of decision-making. Since the crisis manifested many of the conditions under which that model is expected to apply, its failure to do so raises a question about the model's usefulness for explaining decision-making behavior in political settings.

In the discussion which follows, after first describing Roosevelt's behavior during the Munich crisis, an attempt will be made to compare explanations for it derived from both prospect theory and the theory of rational choice. The implications of this analysis for prospect theory, as well as for decision-making in general, will then be explored.

THE COURSE OF THE MUNICH CRISIS

The Munich crisis began in mid-September 1938 as Great Britain and France sought to cope with German pressure on Czechoslovakia while avoiding war and preserving at least the appearance of honoring their commitments to the latter. The crisis was resolved, however temporarily, with the signing of the Munich agreement on September 30.

The proximate cause of the crisis was the escalation of German Chancellor Adolf Hitler's claims on Czechoslovakia from autonomy for the Sudeten Germans, to which the Czechs had already agreed, to outright cession of the Sudetenland to Germany. Rather than give in to such pressure, Czechoslovakia turned to France and Britain for help. As a consequence of this appeal, Neville Chamberlain, the British prime minister, offered to conduct direct negotiations with Hitler (brief descriptions of the Munich crisis may be found in Taylor, 1979, pp. 7–11; Offner, 1969, pp. 259–68; Divine, 1965, pp. 51–55, and 1969, pp. 20–21).

On September 15, Chamberlain met Hitler at Berchtesgaden and heard his demand for the cession of the Sudeten provinces. The British prime minister then undertook to persuade the French, and pressure the Czechs, into agreeing to this ultimatum. Having succeeded in both aims, he met again with Hitler at Godesberg on September 22 only to discover that the Fuehrer was now also requiring the cession of territory in which Germans were a minority and insisting that all transfers be carried out by October 1. In reaction to this development, "British and French public opinion stiffened, and by September 25 it seemed likely that Chamberlain and Edouard Daladier, the French Premier, would fight rather than surrender completely to Hitler" (Divine, 1969, p. 20).

At this point President Roosevelt chose to intervene, first with an appeal to the states involved not to break off negotiations, and then with a message to Hitler alone proposing that the talks be expanded into a conference which would include all interested parties. After a further intervention by Mussolini, Hitler issued invitations to Great Britain, France, and Italy to meet at Munich on September 29 and 30 (Taylor, 1979, pp. 9–10).

The outcome of this conference, as Divine has noted, "marked the climax of appeasement. In return for Hitler's promise not to seek an additional foot of territory in Europe, Britain and France agreed that Germany should occupy the Sudeten area in four stages. . . . The Czechs agreed to the terms on the morning of September 30, and thus became the sacrificial victims of the worldwide demand for peace at any price." At this point, the democracies having found a way to give Hitler what he wanted without putting him to the trouble of fighting for it, the crisis ended (Divine, 1965, p. 54; see also Hull, 1948, pp. 595–596).

ROOSEVELT'S RESPONSE TO THE MUNICH CRISIS

From the perspective of Roosevelt's decision-making behavior, the Munich crisis can be divided into two stages, with the Godesberg meeting serving as the line of demarcation. The first stage, which was characterized by his marked disinclination to intervene in the crisis, extended from September 13 to September 22, coming to a climax with his conversation with British Ambassador Sir Ronald Lindsay on September 19. The second stage began on September 23, when the initial reports of the Godesberg ultimatum reached the president, and ended with the signing of the Munich Agreement on September 30. From an American perspective, the high point of this stage was Roosevelt's dramatic change of policy about intervention in the crisis culminating in his two appeals on September 25 and 27.

Stage I: September 13–September 22, 1938

During the first phase of the crisis, Roosevelt's assessment of the likelihood of general war fluctuated with the reports he received from Europe. His determination not to intervene, however, remained unaltered.

At the outset, both the president's analysis of the situation and his policy preferences mirrored those of the pre-crisis period. In assessing the worsening climate in Central Europe in the summer of 1938, Roosevelt had exhibited concern about the possibility of war as well as uncertainty about the intentions of the major players owing to contradictory reports from abroad, the conflicting views of members of his administration, and his own suspicions about both the resolve of the British and French and their motives in attempting to involve the United States.[3]

The mixture of uncertainty and concern which underlay the president's diagnosis of the Czech situation in the weeks before the crisis was reflected in his determination not to involve the United States. While sympathetic to the democracies, and frustrated by his inability to discover some positive way to support them, Roosevelt refused to join openly in their attempts to deal with the German threat, notwithstanding the determined efforts of members of his administration, like Ambassador Bullitt, to persuade him to do so.[4]

The onset of the crisis itself brought no dramatic changes in Roosevelt's policy preferences. While his assessment of the likelihood of war during the first stage of the crisis varied according to the news from Europe, his determination to avoid intervening did not.

Initially, Roosevelt believed that there would be no general war because the French and British would not resist Hitler. On September 16 or 17, for example, he advised Secretary of the Interior Harold Ickes that

---

[3]For a sample of reports from abroad during this period, see "Bullitt to FDR, May 20, 1938," Schewe, 1979, #1180; "Kennedy to Hull, August 31, 1938," United States Department of State, *Foreign Relations of the United States,* (hereafter *FRUS*) 1938, vol. I, pp. 565–566; "William C. Bullitt, Ambassador to France, to Roosevelt, August 31, 1938," Schewe, 1979, #1260; "Roosevelt to Cordell Hull, Secretary of State, August 31, 1938," *Ibid.*, #1259; "William Phillips, Ambassador to Italy, to Roosevelt, September 1, 1938," *Ibid.*, #1263; "Bullitt to Hull, September 12, 1938," *FRUS,* 1938, vol. I, p. 589; and "Kennedy to Hull September 9 and 10, 1938," *Ibid.*, pp. 584–585. The views of various members of the Administration at this time may be found in "Memo from Adolf Berle to the President, September 1, 1938;" Kaufmann, 1963, pp. 662–664; Blum, 1965, pp. 452, 457; Ickes, 1954, pp. 381–382. For Roosevelt's and Morgenthau's suspicions that the British were trying to manipulate the United States, see "Morgenthau Diary," September 1, 1938, vol. 138, pp. 33–55.

[4]See, for example, Bullitt's letter of May 20, 1938 (Bullitt, 1972, pp. 261–262). For evidence of Roosevelt's reluctance to support the democracies openly, see "Press conference, Hyde Park, September 9, 1938, 5:30 P.M.," Schewe, 1979, #1273; Taylor, 1979, pp. 525–526; Blum, 1965, p. 518; Langer and Gleason, 1952, pp. 32–33; and Haight, 1960, pp. 345–348. A detailed discussion of Roosevelt's attitudes and policy preferences during this period may be found in Farnham, 1991, pp. 385–398.

> Chamberlain is for peace at any price. . . . Czechoslovakia apparently has resisted pressure from England and France to agree to a plebiscite. Lacking a plebiscite, Hitler will move in. . . . Because it will not have submitted to the demands of France and England, Czechoslovakia will be left by these supposed allies to paddle its own canoe. This will mean a swift and brutal war . . . [which] will leave Czechoslovakia dismembered and prostrate. . . . [Then] . . . England and France . . . will "wash the blood from their Judas Iscariot hands. (Ickes, 1954, p. 468)

Given the pusillanimity of the states most concerned, Roosevelt concluded that there was no meanful action he could take. On September 13, for example, he agreed with Hull that it would be best to do nothing at all. Instead, the president confined himself to offering a few minimal gestures of support for the democracies, such as sending the light cruiser Nashville to England in readiness to transport British gold reserves to New York ("Morgenthau Diary," vol. 141, pp. 69, 115. Hull communicated this decision to the French Ambassador on September 14 [Alsop and Kintner, 1940, pp. 7–8; Memorandum of a conversation between Hull and the French Ambassador, *FRUS*, 1938, vol. I, pp. 598–599]. As Assistant Secretary of State Moffat reported in his diary, this decision was reaffirmed on September 16 [Hooker, 1956, pp. 202–203, 205].)

Between September 17 and 19, the president assimilated the bad news from Berchtesgaden and adjusted his expectations about the likelihood of war. On the morning of the 19th, for example, predicting that Czech resistance to Hitler's demands would now force the democracies to fight, Roosevelt repeated to Secretary Morgenthau a recipe for winning a general war in Europe he had outlined to Secretary Ickes on September 17 and expressed the belief that, despite German preponderance in military aviation, the democracies would prevail in an air war (Ickes, 1954, pp. 469–470. Representative of the kind of news about the Berchtesgaden meeting Roosevelt received is Ambassador Kennedy's September 17 account of Chamberlain's statement that Hitler "was perfectly willing to take on a world war" over the principle of self-determination for the Sudeten Germans [Kennedy to Hull, September 17, 1938, *FRUS*, 1938, vol. I, pp. 607–608]. Other reports emphasizing the seriousness of the situation may be found in Kennedy to Hull, September 17, 1938, *FRUS*, 1938, vol. I, pp. 609–12; Wilson to Hull, September 18, 1938, *Ibid.*, pp. 612–614; and Carr to Hull, September 18, 1938, *Ibid.*, pp. 614–615. The nearly unanimous conclusion of these communications was that war was virtually certain to occur unless the democracies acceded to Hitler's demands.).

Convinced that a defensive war based on a blockade offered Britain and France their best chance of vanquishing the Germans, Roosevelt discussed with Morgenthau how best to get this idea across to them. Because of his reservations about the ability of Ambassadors Kennedy and Bullitt to convey his meaning effectively, the president decided to do the job himself, making an appointment with the British ambassador for that evening (Morgenthau Diary, 1938, vol. 141, p. 115. Also in Blum, 1965, pp. 519–520).

According to Ambassador Lindsay's account of this meeting, Roosevelt declared that while he would like to be of some immediate assistance, "having no illusions as the effect of his previous public statements," he was reluctant to make any pronouncements about the present situation:

> Today he would not dare to express approval of the recommendations put to the Czechoslovak Government. He would [also] be afraid to express disapproval of German aggression lest it might encourage Czechoslovakia to vain resistance. He thus felt unable to do anything and thought at his press conference tomorrow (he has postponed the last two) he would confine himself to refusing to make any comment at all.[5]

What the president really wanted to discuss with the ambassador was the proper strategy for conducting the war he believed the Western powers would soon be forced to fight. Declaring that Great Britain and France "would be beaten if they tried to wage war on classical lines of attack," Roosevelt recommended that they should conduct the war "purely by blockade and in a defensive manner." He also indicated that, within the limits of his domestic constraints, he would give the democracies as much help in such a war as he could.

Clearly then, while the news from Berchtesgaden did lead President Roosevelt to take some sort of action, what is most striking is the type of the action he chose. Roosevelt's heightened expectation of war led him neither to try to avert it, nor to alter his policy of nonintervention in the crisis itself. Instead, he responded to the deteriorating situation in Europe by attempting to bolster the courage of the democracies in the present and guide their strategy in any future struggle. (That this was Roosevelt's purpose in speaking to Lindsay is also Dallek's view [1979, pp. 164–165].)

After the president's meeting with the British ambassador, there followed several days of waiting. Ultimately, the Czechs, having received no support for their position, "accepted flatly and unconditionally the British-French proposal," acceding to virtually all of Hitler's demands. Since Roosevelt's expectation of war had been based on the belief that the Czechs would fight, this development reduced his estimate of its likelihood. The forthcoming meeting of Prime Minister Chamberlain and Hitler at Godesberg would now merely be a matter of arranging the details (Bullitt to Hull, September 21, 1938, *FRUS*, 1938, vol. I, pp. 630–631. According to Dallek, the president was surprised at

---

[5] "Sir R. Lindsay (Washington) to Viscount Halifax, (Received September 20, 1:40 a.m.)," (Butler and Woodward, 1951, pp. 627–629. On the meeting between Roosevelt and Lindsay, see also Taylor, 1979, pp. 846–848; Lash, 1976, pp. 25–28; Offner, 1969, p. 261; Cole, 1983, p. 300). Other evidence of Roosevelt's disinclination to intervene directly in the crisis even after Berchtesgaden is found in a memorandum of his conversation with a French trade unionist on September 18 or 19 in which he "pointed out that he did not feel the situation warranted any initiative from him. Such an initiative, if not accepted, might make the situation even worse than it was" ("Memorandum by J. Pierrepont Moffat, Chief, Division of European Affairs, Department of State, September 20, 1938," Schewe, 1979, #1289a. Also in *FRUS*, 1938, vol. I, pp. 625–626, and Hooker, 1956, pp. 206–207).

the Czech decision but felt that there was now "agreement in principle" between the German and Czech governments [Dallek, 1979, p. 165].).

However dramatic the president's conversation with Ambassador Lindsay may appear, therefore, it did not in fact constitute a departure from the policies he had been following all along. Even after Berchtesgaden had greatly increased his assessment of the probability of war, Roosevelt remained reluctant to intervene openly in the crisis.

Stage II: September 23–September 29, 1938

For President Roosevelt, as for other Americans, the Munich crisis began in earnest on September 23. Primarily as a consequence of the talks between Hitler and Chamberlain at Godesberg on September 22 and 23, expectations of war increased dramatically in Washington and elsewhere (Dallek, 1979, p. 165. For a detailed account of the Godesberg meeting itself, see Taylor, 1979, pp. 806–819).

Ickes has described Roosevelt's initial reaction to the news from Godesberg in his account of a cabinet meeting on the afternoon of September 23 at which the European situation was "canvassed very fully" (Ickes, 1954, pp. 473–474). Opening the meeting with a worst-case analysis of the possible consequences of the latest developments, Secretary Hull declared that there were "undoubtedly" defensive alliances between Italy, Germany, and Japan, and Japan would support Germany and Italy in their bid to dominate Europe while itself trying to gain complete control over Asia. Consequently, in Ickes' words,

> . . . France may soon find itself to be a helpless country lying between an enlarged and strengthened Germany and Italy. England might even be reduced to the status of a third- or fourth-rate power with many of her colonies gone. If this should happen, there might follow attempts on the part of Germany, Italy, and Japan to penetrate South America. This would mean that the United States would have to go to the defense of South America, in which event we would be called upon to defend both the Atlantic and the Pacific seaboards from powerful enemies. (Ickes, 1954, p. 473–474)

Roosevelt, on the other hand, in line with his previously expressed views, was considerably less pessimistic about the democracies' chances, repeating that they should fight a strictly defensive war, and declaring that the British and French would control both the Atlantic Ocean and the Mediterranean and would thus be able to bottle up the Germans and the Italians. For the first time, however, he did express some concern about German preponderance in the air, labeling it "the worst thing about the situation." The meeting closed with the president reading from an analysis of the situation from Ambassador Bullitt just handed to him, which predicted "that Germany might be crossing the [Czech] frontier this morning and that Poland might go across even before morning"

(Ickes, 1954, p. 473–474; "Memorandum to Roosevelt, September 23, 1938," Schewe, #1294).

Clearly, then, the news of Hitler's unreasonable demands at Godesberg produced an immediate upward revision in Roosevelt's estimate of the likelihood of war in Europe. It did not, however, lead to a change in policy. Although war now seemed imminent, the president still had no thought of intervening to prevent it. According to Ickes' account, as late as the afternoon of September 23, there was "no doubt of the President's desire to avoid any embroilment in European quarrels."[6] That he had decided to intervene in the crisis by at least the afternoon of September 25 is thus a puzzle which must be solved.

The First Intervention

Throughout the day on September 24, bad news poured into the White House. Despite the six-day respite Hitler had generously granted the Czechs, the situation remained menacing.[7] As Ickes reported in his diary, much of Europe was gearing up for war (Ickes, 1954, p. 473. See also Czechoslovak Legation to the Department of State, September 24, 1938, *FRUS,* vol. I, pp. 645–646; Haight, 1960, p. 352).

Moreover, the diplomatic traffic, in emphasizing Hitler's total unreasonableness, left no doubt that responsibility for war would rest solely with him. For example, Kennedy cabled that the British

> have just received Hitler's answers and they are . . . preposterous. Hitler not only wants what everybody was willing to give him but it looks as if he wants a great deal more. . . . Cadogan feels that . . . they have taken every possible opportunity to demonstrate they believed there was some sanity in Hitler and to save the world from the horrible results of war. . . . Hitler's answers prove there is no sanity left in the man. (Kennedy to Hull, Sep-

---

[6]In fact, the message from Bullitt, which Roosevelt read to the Cabinet, had suggested that he should now act directly with respect to the crisis and referred obliquely to the Ambassador's previous idea of calling an international conference. Roosevelt, however, apparently made no mention of this proposal to his Cabinet. That immediate action was not at the forefront of his thinking on September 23 is also shown by his negative reply to Nicholas Murray Butler's suggestion that he make an appeal to the parties ("Memorandum to Roosevelt, September 23, 1938," "Roosevelt to Nicholas Murray Butler, President, Columbia University, September 23, 1938," Schewe, 1979, #1294, 1295; Ickes, 1954, pp. 473–474.).

[7]On September 24 Ickes reported that, while "the situation still looks threatening," it was "not as critical as the message read by the President yesterday indicated," because "Hitler has given six days for acceptance of his terms by Czechoslovakia." (Ickes, 1954, p. 473). Roosevelt himself had this news by the afternoon of September 23, though not at the time of the Cabinet meeting where he was nevertheless still clearly disinclined to intervene. Moreover, since the clock continued to run and all the news from Europe was bad, it is doubtful that Hitler's gesture greatly reduced the pressure ("Memorandum by Henry M. Kannee, Assistant to Marvin H. Mc Intyre, September 23, 1938," and "Memorandum to Roosevelt, September 23, 1938," Schewe, 1979, #1293, #1294. Note that Schewe reverses the order of these two memoranda. However, it is clear that #1294 was received in time to be read to the Cabinet which met at 2 p.m., whereas #1293 bears the time 4.50 P.).

tember 24, 1938, *FRUS*, 1938, vol. I, pp. 642–643, received 10 a.m. In a similar vein, see Carr to Hull, September 24, 1938, *Ibid.*, pp. 643–644, received 4:40 p.m.)

Meanwhile, Ambassador Bullitt, certain that the American people would desire "some effort by our Government . . . even though the effort may prove to be a failure," renewed his plea that Roosevelt appeal to the parties to confer at The Hague. Bullitt also thought that the United States should send a representative to such a conference and issue a "strong warning against armies crossing frontiers" (Bullitt to Hull, September 24, 1928, *FRUS*, 1938, vol. I, pp. 641–642. See also Hull, 1948, p. 590).

Despite such entreaties, Roosevelt took no action of any kind on September 24. Apparently, however, he was not unmoved and was beginning to think that some kind of intervention might be desirable. In fact, by the morning of the 25th, the impulse to act had affected even the State Department (Berle, 1973, p. 186; Hooker, 1956, pp. 211–212; Hull, 1948, pp. 590–591; Alsop and Kintner, 1940, p. 9).

By September 25 war clearly seemed imminent, as throughout the day Roosevelt continued to receive reports about both the draconian terms Hitler sought to impose and their complete unacceptability to any of the other parties, which made war a virtual certainty. There was, for example, a "flood" of telegrams from Ambassador Bullitt detailing Hitler's demands and emphasizing their extraordinary harshness. According to Bullitt, the German note to Chamberlain was "totally unacceptable. The terms asked by Hitler are virtually those imposed on a defeated German Army for evacuation of northern France" (Haight, 1960, p. 352; Bullitt to Hull, September 25, 1938, *FRUS*, 1938, vol. I, pp. 648–649, received 11:35 a.m. See also Bullitt to Hull, September 25, 1938, *Ibid.*, pp. 646–648, received 9:15 a.m.; and Bullitt to Hull, September 25, 1938, *Ibid.*, pp. 650–652, received 12:25 p.m.).[8]

While these alarming reports poured in, the planning for an American response initiated in the State Department continued. Berle and Moffat had volunteered to produce the draft of a presidential statement and, after considering and ruling out Bullitt's conference plan, settled on a message which would be, as Berle desired, "not merely an appeal but a definite suggestion that we would use our good offices in a draft leading to the revision of the Versailles Treaty." Hull, while disapproving of the idea of treaty revision as "too dangerous," took the draft

---

[8]Bullitt's reports were supplemented by a cable from Ambassador Carr transmitting the Czech president's plea to prevent "the assassination of the state" by urging the British and the French not to desert Czechoslovakia. Moreover, the American ambassador to Germany, Horace Wilson, telegraphed later in the day to convey the opinion of the British Ambassador to Germany that unless the British and French managed to pressure the Czechs into accepting the German troops, there would almost certainly be war (Carr to Hull, September 25, 1938, *Ibid.*, pp. 649–650, received at 10:20 a.m.; and Wilson to Hull, September 25, 1938, *Ibid.*, pp. 654–56, received 7 p.m.. See also, Hull, 1948, pp. 590–591).

statement to the president at six o'clock (Berle, 1973, p. 186, Hooker, 1956, pp. 211–212; Offner, 1969, pp. 262–263 [Offner's account is based on the original Moffat diary]; Haight, 1960, p. 353, Alsop and Kintner, 1940, p. 9).

Clearly, by this point Roosevelt wanted to act to affect the crisis. His desire to influence the manner in which a general war in Europe would be fought had been totally supplanted by a determination to prevent it. Henceforth he was completely focused on the imminence of war and the need to end the crisis before it could occur (Hull informed Moffat on the night of the 25th that Roosevelt had gotten such bad telephone reports from both Bullitt and Kennedy that he could no longer keep silent [Hooker, 1956, pp. 212–213; Hull, 1948, pp. 591–592]. On Roosevelt's anxiety to stop the war by this time, see also Morgenthau Diary, vol. 142, p. 342).

Thus, the drafting of the appeal went forward. Bullitt had suggested that it should include an offer by the president to arbitrate. Hull disliked this idea. (In fact he opposed sending any appeal whatever.) Along with Normal Davis, he was also against the somewhat less extreme step of a tender of good offices (according to Hull, he kept urging the president to go slow, while Welles egged him on [Hull, 1948, pp. 591–592. Hooker, 1956, pp. 212–213; Berle, 1973, pp. 186–187]).

In the end, Roosevelt acceded to these objections, and any hint of mediation was removed from the appeal. According to Moffat, this was done both because of his fear of "untoward domestic effects," and because he believed the notion of good offices to be implicit in the appeal in any case (Berle, 1973, p. 187; Hull, 1948, p. 592; Hooker, 1956, pp. 212–213; Offner, 1969, p. 263).

The president finished revising the final draft by midnight, and it was sent to Hitler, Chamberlain, Daladier, and Czechoslovakian President Edvard Benes at 1 a.m. on September 26. In the message, Roosevelt declared that the "fabric of peace . . . is in immediate danger," and stressed that, while the United States eschewed "political entanglements," it could not escape the consequences of a general war. He, therefore, reminded the parties of their obligation to settle their differences peacefully, and called on them not to break off negotiations (Alsop and Kintner, 1940, p. 10; Offner, 1969, p. 263; Roosevelt to Hitler, September 26, 1938, *FRUS,* 1938, vol. I, pp. 657–658. The responses to Roosevelt's appeal may be found in *Ibid.,* pp. 661–673).

Exactly what did Roosevelt hope to accomplish with this message? Hull, who had serious reservations about the efficacy of such an appeal, has stated that Roosevelt was motivated by the feeling that nothing could be worse than inaction: "The President . . . believed with Bullitt that something should be done, even if it were not successful. He said to me: 'It can't do any harm. It's safe to urge peace until the last moment.' "

Welles, on the other hand, told the French ambassador that the message reflected Roosevelt's attempt to balance his desire to affect the course of the crisis with his concern about possible domestic repercussions. In Haight's words, Welles gave Ambassador St. Quentin to understand that "in his first message Roosevelt aimed at bringing the weight of the United States to bear upon the European crisis and at the same time to avoid stirring American isolationist feelings" (Hull, 1948, p. 591; Haight, 1960, p. 356, n. 129). That the president was disposed to be cautious about arousing domestic opinion can also be seen by his refusal to allow Chamberlain's proposed radio address to be broadcast directly to the United States (memorandum of a phone conversation between Welles and Kennedy, September 26, 1938, 1:30 p.m., *FRUS,* 1938, vol. I, pp. 660–661. See also, Hull, 1948, p. 593).

In any case, the day following the president's appeal was marked by considerable anxiety. According to Hull, they "waited almost breathlessly" for the replies, especially Hitler's.

Unfortunately, no word from the Fuehrer was immediately forthcoming. However, Roosevelt received ample evidence of the democracies' continued resolve, as well as numerous expressions of their gratitude for his message and assurances about its positive influence which he found particularly gratifying (Hull, 1948, p. 592. Memorandum of a phone conversation between Welles and Kennedy, September 26, 1938, 1:30 p.m., *Ibid.,* pp. 660–661. For accounts of Allied determination, see Kennedy to Hull, September 26, 1938, *FRUS,* 1938, vol. I, p. 659; Bullitt to Hull, September 26, 1938, *Ibid.,* p. 668. For expressions of appreciation see Kennedy to Hull, September 26, 1938, *Ibid.,* p. 659, received 8:30 a.m.; Bullitt to Hull, September 26, 1938, *Ibid.,* pp. 659–660, received 2 p.m.).

Hitler's answer to the president's message, when it finally arrived, was not nearly so pleasing. In a speech heard in the United States on the afternoon of September 26, the Fuehrer was far from conciliatory, declaring at one point "that if the Czechs did not give the Sudeten Germans immediate freedom, 'we will go and fetch this freedom for ourselves.' " As Ickes described it, Hitler "ranted and raved for over an hour. At times he seemed to be almost incoherent. He shrieked his defiance to the whole world, bragging of the prowess of Germany. . . . War seemed to be inevitable, with every tick of the clock bringing it closer" (Offner, 1969, pp. 263–264; Ickes, 1954, p. 477). For an account of Hitler's intransigence during this period see Taylor, 1979, pp. 870–875).

Moreover, Hitler's formal reply to Roosevelt's message offered no more solace than his speech. Disclaiming all responsibility should further developments lead to war, he recited at length German grievances against the Czechs and ended with the ominous declaration that "the possibilities of arriving at a just settlement by agreement, are . . . exhausted with the proposals of the German memorandum. It does not rest with the German Government, but with the Czechoslovakian Government alone, to decide, whether it wants peace or war." As the president reported to his cabinet on the following day, the tone of Hitler's reply was "truculant and unyielding" (Hitler to Roosevelt, September 26, 1938, *FRUS,* 1938, vol.

I, pp. 669–672, received 9:14 p.m.. This message was not received in written form in the White House until September 27. However, Assistant Secretary of State George Messersmith phoned the substance of it to Roosevelt on the evening of the 26th ["Adolf Hitler, Chancellor of Germany, to Roosevelt, September 27, 1938," Schewe, 1979, #1302, Berle, 1973, p. 187. Ickes, 1954, p. 478]).

The Second Intervention

On the morning of the 27th, a group of State Department officials met to consider an appropriate response to the latest developments. Berle and Welles were deputized to draft a second message to Hitler, which they did, opting for the path of "boldness" by including in it a call for a conference at The Hague. Just before lunch, Hull and Welles took this draft statement to the President (Berle, 1973, p. 187).

By this time, still more evidence of Hitler's refusal to cooperate had arrived. For example, both Kennedy and Bullitt cabled that the Fuehrer's reception of Chamberlain's latest notes had been "completely and definitely unsatisfactory." In Bullitt's words, Hitler's reply "was the most violent outburst possible; . . . nothing could have been more unhelpful." By way of contrast, moreover, this demonstration of Hitler's intransigence was accompanied by a number of reports of continued expressions of gratitude for the president's message from Great Britain and France (Kennedy to Hull, September 27, 1938, *FRUS*, 1938, vol. I, p. 673, received 7:05 a.m.; Bullitt to Hull, September 27, 1938, *Ibid.*, pp. 673–674, received 9:15 a.m., and pp. 674–675, received 11:10 a.m.. A cable from Ambassador Carr also underlined the unreasonableness of Hitler's demands from the point of view of Czech military security Carr to Hull, September 27, 1938, *Ibid.*, p. 679, received 1:20 p.m.).

The news of Hitler's obduracy and aggressive posturing had two implications for Roosevelt's diagnosis of the crisis. First of all, it underlined the Fuehrer's sole responsibility for the continued slide toward war. Secondly, it increased expectations that war would actually occur unless something happened to prevent it.[9] Apparently the confluence of these two perceptions shaped Roosevelt's decision, at some point during the course of the morning of September 27, to take further action.

---

[9]Supporting the first point is Welles's statement to Bullitt that any action by the president would be directed solely at Hitler (Memorandum of telephone call between Welles and Bullitt, September 27, 1938, 2:40 p.m., *FRUS*, 1938, vol. I, pp. 675–676). The second point is corroborated by Welles's later statement that on September 27 " 'Information of unquestioned authenticity' had come through that at 2:00 p.m. on the next day, September 28, Hitler would march his armies into Czechoslovakia unless the Godesberg terms were met" (Haight, 1960, p. 355). This account was confirmed by Roosevelt himself when he told Arthur Murray on October 14, 1938, that he had received news on the 27th that Hitler would take action the next day (Murray, 1946, p. 95).

At the president's lunchtime meeting with Welles and Hull, two proposals discussed earlier in the State Department (a request to other governments to support the American appeal to continue negotiations and a personal appeal to Mussolini) were approved without reservation. However, the third proposal that Roosevelt should call for a conference did not fare quite as well because Hull, "depressed" by the possible dangers which might arise from so bold a step, opposed it. In this he was apparently supported by Roosevelt.

Ultimately, Welles was instructed to ask Bullitt and Kennedy to get Daladier's and Chamberlain's views on the desirability of such a plan. If they approved, the message addressed to Hitler might then suggest a conference at a neutral European capital, although the promise of American participation would be omitted (Berle, 1973, p. 187; Alsop and Kintner, 1940, p. 10).

While Welles made these calls and worked with Berle on redrafting the message from the president to Hitler, Roosevelt met with his cabinet in a special session. He had arranged for them to listen to Chamberlain's speech at 2:00 p.m., and, as he told Arthur Murray two weeks later, it was a moving experience:

> When it was finished I looked round the table and there were tears in the eyes of at least four Members of the Cabinet, and I felt that way myself. I had listened to Hitler on the Monday, and so had most of my Cabinet. The contrast between the two just bit into us—the shouting and violence of Hitler, and the roars, through their teeth, of his audience of 'Krieg, krieg,' and then, the quiet, beautiful statement of Chamberlain's. (Murray, 1946, p. 95. According to Murray, these are Roosevelt's own words as noted at the time by Murray himself. Ickes [1954, p. 477] also gives an account of this emotional episode, and Berle noticed later that day that the president had been "much impressed" with Chamberlain's speech [1973, p. 189].)

For the rest of the meeting, "the European situation was the almost exclusive subject of discussion." Informing the cabinet of Hitler's unsatisfactory reply to his first message, Roosevelt raised the possibility of sending a second. He then led a discussion of this idea which, despite the emotion generated by Chamberlain's speech, amounted to a fairly dispassionate appraisal of the various alternatives. The president also reiterated his belief that in the event of war the democracies would be the victors, theorizing that "the French would speedily mop up the Italian colonies in northern Africa and would promptly liquidate Franco in Spain. . . . Italy itself could shortly be driven to the wall and . . . then England, France, Russia, Czechoslovakia, Romania, Yugoslavia, Turkey, and other anti-German countries could concentrate against Germany" (Ickes, *Diary*, vol. II, p. 481). Clearly then, at this point in the crisis Roosevelt was still confident that the democracies could be victorious in a war with Germany.

Sometime during the course of the afternoon on which this cabinet meeting was held, Roosevelt decided that a second message should go to Hitler as soon as possible. As he told Murray,

> I had intended to send a message to Hitler on the Wednesday morning. But on the top of Chamberlain's radio speech came news from our people in Berlin that Hitler was to take

action at two o'clock on Wednesday afternoon. So I got down at once about five o'clock to the draft of my message, and Hull came across again from the State Department. By about nine o'clock we had hammered out the message, and Hitler had it with his breakfast. (Murray, 1946, p. 95. Apparently, Roosevelt had decided not to wait to hear the views of Chamberlain and Daladier. In fact, by the time Kennedy called at 5:45 p.m. to relay Chamberlain's opinion, Welles was able to state his belief that the President "will send his message tonight without fail." [Memorandum of a Telephone Conversation between Kennedy and Welles, September 27, 1938, *FRUS*, 1938, vol. I, pp. 679–680])

Following his conversation with Kennedy, Welles took Roosevelt the new draft of the message to Hitler which the whole State Department group had already approved. After dinner, the president met with Welles, Hull, and Berle to work on this draft. There followed a two-hour session which has been graphically depicted by Alsop and Kintner: "The President worked at his littered desk, smoking incessantly and shooting questions at the other three. They sat nervously near him, Berle fidgeting, Hull swearing softly under his breath, and Welles for once almost out of countenance."

A moment of considerable tension occurred when "a report came in that the Germans might march in the night, forcing a war to no purpose. For a moment the President showed real anger." However, as the report was not confirmed, the drafting continued. By 9 p.m. the draft was well enough in hand to allow the secretary of state to go home to bed, and at 9:30 it was signed by the president (Alsop and Kintner, 1940, pp. 10–11. See also Berle, 1973, p. 188, and Murray, 1946, p. 95).

Roosevelt's second message to Hitler was sent at 10:18 p.m. Recalling his earlier emphasis on the peaceful settlement of disputes and the complete lack of justification for any threat of force which might result in general warfare, the president pointed out to the German chancellor that these considerations were even more relevant now that agreement in principle had been reached between Germany and Czechoslovakia. He therefore urged continuation of the negotiations, raising the possibility of widening them to include "all the nations directly interested in the present controversy." While reiterating that the United States had "no political involvements in Europe," Roosevelt nevertheless closed by stating that "the conscience and the impelling desire of the people of my country demand that the voice of their government be raised again and yet again to avert and to avoid war" (Roosevelt to Hitler, September 27, 1938, *FRUS*, 1938, vol. I, pp. 684–685. Farnham [1991, pp. 431–435] analyzes several opposing views of Roosevelt's intentions in sending the second appeal to Hitler and concludes that it was a genuine attempt to prevent war by pressuring Hitler into peaceful settlement of the dispute along the lines which had already been agreed upon.).

The period of anxious waiting for Hitler's reply following the dispatch of this message ended on the morning of the 28th. As Berle dramatically recorded in his diary, Hitler had invited Britain, France, and Italy to discuss the Czech crisis ("The 'break'! Thank God."). Roosevelt was also relieved by the news and at 1 p.m. sent his famous two-word message to Prime Minister Chamberlain: "Good Man." (Berle, 1973, p. 188; Hull to Kennedy, September 28, 1938, *FRUS*, 1938, vol. I, p. 688. While the meaning of Roosevelt's message has been debated, most agree with Langer and Gleason that it signaled relief at the continuance of negotiations rather than approval of the policy of appeasement per se. One who disputes this interpretation is Offner. Haight, on the other hand, believes that, at this point, Roosevelt "assumed that Chamberlain still stood with Daladier as an opponent to capitulation. . . . He expected Chamberlain to negotiate at Munich on the basis of 'reason and equity' " [Langer and Gleason, 1952, p. 34; Offner, 1969, p. 269; Haight, 1960, p. 356, n. 132. See also, Haight, 1970, p. 22.]).

Thus, although the terms of the Munich settlement were not made known until September 30, emotionally the crisis ended on September 28 with the announcement of the agreement to meet. In comparison with that achievement the settlement itself seemed almost beside the point. What little concern remained about matters of substance was rapidly engulfed by the universal rejoicing over a procedural victory: Hitler had agreed to a peaceful meeting rather than war as the means of accomplishing his goals. Ironically, in the atmosphere of widespread relief that war had been averted, few seemed to notice that the issue over which it had almost been fought (the conditions under which the Czechs would give up the Sudetenland) had been all but forgotten.

EXPLAINING ROOSEVELT'S BEHAVIOR

During the first stage of the Munich crisis, Roosevelt's attention was focused primarily on the general political and military problems of Europe as they related to American concerns and he seemed only minimally concerned with the crisis per se, contemplating even an outcome of war with some detachment. Moreover, although he was beginning to develop some notion of the crisis' possible consequences for the United States, he still had no sense that he ought to be directly involved in its resolution, viewing overt intervention as a course which involved considerable risk. Nor did Roosevelt alter his policy in this respect even after the news from Berchtesgaden had caused him to believe that war was virtually inevitable.

After Godesberg Roosevelt's attitude changed, but not at once. Initially, although reports of that meeting on September 23 led him to believe that war was imminent, he still had no thought of intervening. Sometime during September 24, and almost certainly by the morning of the 25th, however, his thinking underwent a dramatic change, and he decided to act directly. As Morgenthau reported to his aides early on the morning of the 26th, the president had suddenly become "very anxious to get in and stop this war in Europe" (Morgenthau Diary, September 26, 1938, vol. 142, p. 342).

Within less than two days, therefore, Roosevelt's attention had shifted away from the general long-run implications of the European situation for the United States and toward the crisis itself. This shift in focus, moreover, was accompanied by a change in policy from nonintervention to active intervention, its attendant risks notwithstanding. Before Godesberg, the most Roosevelt would do was to advise the democracies about how to fight the prospective war; thereafter, such considerations were overwhelmed by his desire to prevent it. For Roosevelt, *that* had become the central problem and one which he believed required direct action on his part. Such a dramatic shift in preferences obviously requires explanation.

The Rational Choice Explanation

One interpretation of the president's preference reversal might be that it was simply a rational response to new information which altered the subjective expected utility of intervention. However, while one or more changes in the environment—in the value of the outcome of war, for example, or its probability, or the risks of intervention—could conceivably have triggered such a shift, there were in fact no changes in any of these factors sufficient to justify Roosevelt's reversal of preferences.

If, for example, Roosevelt's post-Godesberg belief that an outcome of war would now be a loss had been based on new information about the costs of war to the United States, it would have been rational for him to decide to intervene to prevent war, even if doing so involved some risk. However, the crisis did not provide any new information about the value of the war. No matter how certain or imminent general war in Europe had become after Godesberg, it was in reality no more of a threat to the United States than it had been when it was merely probable. No one imagined for a moment that the United States would be *directly* threatened by war, certainly not Roosevelt who firmly believed that Britain and France would win. Yet despite his unaltered belief that the democracies would emerge victorious, the president behaved as though the prospect of war had become a direct threat to the United States. What is embarrassing to the theory of rational choice is that after Godesberg Roosevelt redefined what was essentially the same objective situation as a loss (The reports Roosevelt received emphasizing the dreadful consequences of war for European civilization might possibly be viewed as new information which changed his valuation of the outcome of war. Such arguments were not new to Roosevelt, however, and he had ignored them when they were made earlier [see, for example, Bullitt's letter of May 20, Bullitt, 1972, pp. 261–262].).

Not only was there no change in the perceived value of war which could have explained Roosevelt's policy shift, there was also no such alteration in his perception of the risks involved in intervening. Risk assessment can entail calculations both about the probability of the success of an option and about its utility in terms of costs or benefits (McDermott, 1991, p. 10), and Roosevelt evaluated intervention as a risky option on both grounds. That is, he believed that intervening in the crisis might very well be ineffective and, indeed, even make matters worse (see the president's remarks to Ambassador Lindsay and the French trade unionist on September 19), and that intervention could have unfortunate domestic repercussions as well.

With respect to the latter, not only did he manifest a concern with domestic opinion during his conversation with Ambassador Lindsay, but also prior to the crisis, he acceded to Hull's fears that taking even some quite modest economic steps to deter Germany would be "doing too much" and could "get the American people up on their toes over the European situation" ("Morgenthau Diary," August 31, 1938, vol. 137, pp. 229–230). Moreover, Roosevelt's caution about what Ambassador Bullitt would be allowed to say in a September 4 speech at Pointe de Graves, while not as exaggerated as Hull's wariness, also showed his concern about the impact of his actions in Europe on domestic opinion. Indeed, Hull told Bullitt that the president agreed with him that they both "had gone as far as our people would well understand" (Haight, 1960, p. 345. See also Roosevelt's hostile reaction to French Foreign Minister Bonnet's attempts in early September to get him to intervene, and his public disavowal of any such intention ["Press conference, Hyde Park, September 9, 1938, 5:30 P.M.," Schewe, 1979, #1273; Taylor, 1979, pp. 525–526; Blum, 1965, p. 518; Langer and Gleason, 1952, pp. 32–33; and Haight, 1960, pp. 345–348]).

Both before the crisis and during its first stage, then, Roosevelt clearly believed that intervening involved significant domestic risks, probably because such intervention would have meant taking a public stand. Indeed, Roosevelt was frequently prepared to engage in a good deal of behind the scenes diplomatic activity which seemed risky enough to others (such as his talk with Lindsay), but he was exceedingly cautious about what he did in public. As Hull pointed out, public involvement during the Munich crisis might have stirred up isolationist sentiment in the country, raising fears that the president was embarking on an activist course that would take the United States into war. (Evidence of Roosevelt's habitual caution about taking public positions may be found in the discussion of his decision-making before and during the Nine Power Conference in Brussels in the fall of 1937, in Farnham, 1991, pp. 314–321, and Appendix. An analysis of Roosevelt's attitudes toward American isolationism and domestic opinion before the crisis is in Farnham, Ch. 3).

At the outset, then, Roosevelt considered intervention to be risky because it might fail, entail domestic repercussions, or both. Moreover, there is ample support for the idea that he continued to believe so even after he had made the decision to intervene.

With respect to the risk of failure, nothing had occurred at Godesberg which entitled Roosevelt to infer that he could now act more effectively than he might have done earlier. On the one hand, while new evidence that Britain and France were at last willing to resist Hitler might have made American action more palatable to Roosevelt because he no longer needed to feel that the democracies were trying to get the United States to do their dirty work for them, Hitler's response to their firmness provided little reason to hope that United States intervention could now succeed in preventing war. On the other hand, although Roosevelt now thought that Czech agreement to the substance of Hitler's demands had removed any rational basis for waging war, since Godesberg he had had nothing but evidence that the Fuehrer was unreasonable in the extreme. Thus, there was less justification than ever for believing that his appeal could be effective.

Nor had anything changed on the American side of the equation to allow the president to think that he had the means to act more effectively. Certainly, he had no more ammunition than he had possessed before the Godesberg meeting. Nothing that transpired there in any way altered the fact that the United States would not, under any circumstances, actually intervene militarily in the Czech crisis, or even threaten to do so.

Moreover, despite his decision to intervene, Roosevelt himself seems to have believed that it was still a risky choice in terms of effectiveness. The amount of effort he put into learning whether his second intervention had been successful, as well as the considerable anxiety this issue seemed to cause him, indicates his awareness that the move could well have failed (Farnham, 1991, pp. 435–436). Clearly, the president seems to have been seeking reassurance that the risk he had taken had succeeded. (This calls into question Secretary Hull's assertion that Roosevelt decided to make his first intervention not because he thought it would be successful but because he wanted to do *something* and sending a message would at least do no harm. Of course, once war appeared virtually certain, there is a sense in which nothing the president did could make things worse. However, the evidence suggests that Roosevelt, while continuing to fear that he risked failure, hoped for more.)

Not only did Roosevelt still worry about the risk of failure, however, he also remained concerned about the domestic risks involved in intervening. That he was worried on this score is demonstrated by his acquiescence to Hull's and Davies's reservations during the drafting of his first appeal and supported by the testimony of Moffat and Welles cited earlier. Moreover, during the planning for his second intervention, Roosevelt displayed sensitivity to the possible risks of intervening by supporting Hull's wish to omit any mention of American participation in a proposed conference (in retaining the conference idea, however, he also showed willingness to accept some risk).

Finally, not only were there no changes in the risk of intervening sufficient to justify Roosevelt's reversal of preferences, there were also no such changes on the probability side of the equation. While it is possible to imagine that the president's decision to intervene was merely an appropriate reaction to an admittedly accurate diagnosis of the increased likelihood of war, this interpretation is not supported by an examination of the pattern of his responses during the crisis. Rather, the evidence shows that neither of his two shifts toward a heightened expectation of war was accompanied by a change in policy from inaction to intervention.

After Berchtesgaden, when Roosevelt first came to expect war, he seemed quite relaxed about the prospect and reacted, not by trying to prevent it, but by attempting to influence the manner in which it would be fought. Moreover, even the post-Godesberg diagnosis that war was imminent did not immediately move him to act. As late as the afternoon of September 23, he still believed that the democracies could win if they followed his strategic advice, and he manifested neither a sense of immediate threat to American security nor any sign of feeling a need to intervene in the crisis.

Thus, although Roosevelt had clearly assimilated the information that war was imminent, he apparently did not believe that this news indicated the kind of change in the environment which would have warranted an alteration in his policy of nonintervention.[10] An explanation for his behavior must, therefore, be sought elsewhere. One possibility is that, in accordance with the predictions of prospect theory, Roosevelt's reversal of preferences about intervening in the crisis resulted from a change in his framing of the decision problem.

The Prospect Theory Explanation

According to Tversky and Kahneman, the way a decision is framed in part determines how people see the consequences of choice. It is entirely possible for an individual to frame the same decision problem in different ways, and prefer-

---

[10]The slight increase in the probability of war between the afternoon of the 23rd and the morning of the 25th is insufficient to account for the dramatic reversal in Roosevelt's policy preferences which occurred that day. That small change in probability had a much greater impact on the president's decision-making than rational choice theory would predict. (I am indebted to Eldar Shafir for pointing this out.) Moreover, neither Roosevelt's perception of an increased likelihood of war nor its imminence afforded adequate justification either for the feeling that the United States had become directly threatened or the belief that American action might now be effective in ending the crisis.

ences between options have been shown to reverse with changes in frame, despite the fact that rational choice theory requires that such preferences should not do so. In other words, the way a problem is perceived can have a significant impact on the treatment of values and probabilities (Tversky and Kahneman, 1981, pp. 453, 457; Kahneman and Tversky, 1982, p. 166).

Furthermore, according to prospect theory, people evaluate prospective outcomes against a neutral reference point, usually the status quo. Outcomes that lie above the reference point are viewed as gains, while those falling below it are seen as losses. The importance of this concept for decision-making theory is that framing an outcome as a loss rather than a gain changes the way people respond to it, even to the point of causing them to reverse their order of preference among equivalent options. In particular, they are likely to be risk-averse when it is a matter of achieving a gain, but risk-acceptant when striving to avert a loss. As Quattrone and Tversky express it, prospect theory implies that "shifts in the reference point induced by the framing of the problem will have predictable effects on people's risk preferences" (Tversky and Kahneman, 1981, p. 454, 1986, p. S258; Quattrone and Tversky, 1988, p. 721).

Roosevelt's behavior during the Munich crisis accords with the expectations of prospect theory in a number of respects. Most importantly, in the aftermath of the meeting at Godesberg, there was at least one major change in his framing of the problem of whether or not to intervene in the Czech crisis which could have led to his preference shift: after Godesberg, Roosevelt suddenly came to view the impending war in Europe as a loss for the United States.

Not that he had previously seen a European war as a gain but, as has been demonstrated repeatedly, neither did the prospect greatly disturb him. By September 25, however, he unquestionably regarded war as a potential catastrophe.[11] Nevertheless, as has just been seen, and this is crucial for the argument, there is not the slightest evidence that Roosevelt actually believed, even then, that such a war would threaten America (except possibly in the sense that all wars are to some extent dangerous). Rather, he had come to view a European war as a loss without having changed his mind about its actual consequences.

Moreover, Roosevelt's increased willingness to intervene in the crisis as a consequence of perceiving war as a loss seems to have been reinforced by another change in his decision frame produced by what Tversky and Kahneman have called the *certainty effect*. This phenomenon manifests itself as a tendency to over-weight outcomes which are considered certain relative to those which are merely probable (Kahneman & Tversky, 1979, p. 265; Tversky & Kahneman,

---

[11]In terms of prospect theory, Roosevelt's reference point was a European political situation which did not threaten the United States and he believed that even war, while not a desirable outcome, did not constitute such a threat, i.e., it lay above his reference point. After Godesberg, however, having reframed the outcome of war in Europe as a catastrophe, Roosevelt's reference point shifted upward, and he now viewed war as a departure from the status quo in the domain of loss.

1986, pp. S263-S270; Fischoff, 1983, p. 144). Since, after Godesberg, Roosevelt viewed war as a virtual certainty, the certainty effect made the outcome of war seem considerably worse than it had when it was merely probable. His growing conviction that war was inevitable, that is, exacerbated his perception of it as a loss.

Moreover, the certainty effect may have combined with the so-called *pseudo-certainty effect* to reinforce Roosevelt's sense that war would be a disaster. That is, people tend to treat extremely likely but uncertain outcomes as though they were certain. Thus, as the probability of war rose after Godesberg, Roosevelt may first have converted it into a certainty in line with the pseudo-certainty effect and then overweighted it because of the certainty effect (Tversky & Kahneman, 1986, p. S268).

The impact of Roosevelt's frame change, reinforced by the certainty effect, was to transform what had been merely a potential problem for American foreign policy into a serious loss which was certain to occur. Furthermore, because this reframing caused Roosevelt to view the crisis from a different point of reference, it could also have been responsible for the reversal of preferences which led him to favor intervention in the crisis over inaction, despite the fact that the threat to the United States had not actually increased. As Jervis points out, "losses which are quite certain will be avoided even if they are relatively slight" (Jervis, 1989, p. 6).

As has been noted, framing effects on decision-making behavior occur when the same alternatives are evaluated in relationship to different points of reference. One way in which this may operate is that "the framing of an action sometimes affects the actual experience of its outcomes" (Tversky & Kahneman, 1981, p. 458). Accordingly, framing the decision problem posed by the European crisis so that the outcome of war seemed like the United States' loss, rather than merely that of others, could have changed the way in which Roosevelt experienced the consequences of nonintervention, which in turn altered his evaluation of the alternatives for dealing with the crisis. Thus the president came to prefer acting to halt the crisis before it ended in war to the passive stance he had adopted when he regarded war as the loss of others. In a way, now that he viewed the impending war as in some sense a loss for the United States, Roosevelt was no longer evaluating the alternatives as merely an observer, but as a sort of participant.[12] By reframing the war as a loss for the United States, he had also reframed the crisis as an American crisis.

[12]This interpretation is supported by the fact that, from this point forward, Roosevelt's behavior exhibited all the characteristics which, according to Raymond Cohen (1979, pp. 4, 24), identify a decision-maker who has perceived a threat. The consequent change in the president's behavior also accords with Hermann's (1972, p. 208) finding during a crisis simulation of differences in perception and behavior between participants and observers.

Moreover, as prospect theory predicts, in deciding to act to avert the war which he now viewed as a loss, Roosevelt became risk-acceptant. That is, he showed a willingness to incur the two risks he had previously avoided: the chance that his intervention might be ineffective, or even have an adverse impact on the crisis, and the danger that such action might provoke "untoward domestic effects."

Finally, a prospect theory explanation of Roosevelt's behavior is supported by his apparently complete lack of awareness that he was framing the crisis differently. At no time did the president link his decision to intervene in the crisis to a change in his feelings about the significance of war; he seems not to have noticed that they had changed, let alone to recall that, only days before, he had not thought a European war such a calamity that he wished to intervene to prevent it. This lack of recognition accords with Tversky and Kahneman's observation that "decision-makers are not normally aware of the potential effects of different decision frames on their preferences." (Roosevelt's behavior is also in line with their perception that, unless a conscious effort is made, a decision-maker may not be able to anticipate how he or she will feel about a future experience [Tversky & Kahneman, 1981, p. 457–458. See also, Kahneman & Tversky, 1984, pp. 349–350].)

Accounting for the Frame Change: The Role of Affect

If Roosevelt did not initially consider war in Europe to be a serious threat to the United States, why did he come to view it as such after Godesberg? What caused him to change his reference point so that he now counted that outcome a loss?

Unfortunately, prospect theory itself does not offer many clues about what causes decision frames to change. Nor do the various laboratory experiments on framing shed much light on this question. The experimenter alone manipulates the frame, providing subjects with both its initial and its altered version, the differences between the two being purely cognitive.

The Munich case, however, suggests that in the real world something more than cognition may at times be involved. It would appear, that is, that the frame change Roosevelt underwent in the midst of the crisis was triggered by the strong emotions he experienced in the aftermath of the Godesberg meeting. In other words, he seems to have reframed the crisis as a matter of direct concern to the United States only after the idea of impending war had become emotionally compelling to him.

This hypothesis is supported by several considerations. First of all, from a purely cognitive perspective, Roosevelt's reframing of the problem posed by the crisis is puzzling. As has already been shown, the cognition that war was virtually certain to occur was not by itself sufficient to provoke either a perception of threat or the desire to intervene.

Second, the period in which the frame change occurred was unquestionably a time of great emotion as Americans observed Europe's headlong rush toward war. Writing on September 30, Ickes testified to the common experience:

> The war scare in Europe has occupied all minds during the last few days practically to the exclusion of everything else. With troops rushing to their respective borders in France, Germany, Czechoslovakia, Hungary, and Poland; with France preparing to evacuate Paris and boxing up the treasures of the Louvre and the priceless glass of Chartres Cathedral for transport to areas where they might be safe from German shells and bombs; with England concentrating its fleet at strategic points in the Baltic and the Mediterranean, with Mussolini rattling his sabre; it seemed that war was only a matter of hours. (Ickes, 1954, vol. II, pp. 476–477)[13]

Finally, and perhaps most significantly, in the brief period between the initial reports from Godesberg and his decision to intervene, Roosevelt received numerous affect-laden communications, many of them from Bullitt and Kennedy who, emotionally at least, had already adopted the perspective of the parties to the crisis.

Before Godesberg Roosevelt, unlike his two ambassadors, had tended not to dwell on the disastrous immediate consequences of a general European war. Rather, as his remarks to Ambassador Lindsay suggest, he was thinking in a general way about the eventual implications for the United States should an unappeasable and aggressive Hitler prove successful in Europe. This difference in focus may account for the fact that, in contrast to the emotional response of Bullitt and Kennedy, Roosevelt's attitude toward the anticipated conflict was curiously detached. Initially, the idea of impending war seems to have lacked emotional reality for him.

This sense of detachment, as well as his continued refusal to intervene despite the imminence of war (both of which Roosevelt exhibited as late as the afternoon of September 23), contrasts quite dramatically with the anxiety about stopping the impending war that Morgenthau described to his staff early on the 26th (and which Roosevelt must, therefore, have shown at least by the 25th). Thus, the president's shift in preferences was not the culmination of a gradual process of reevaluation. Rather, it was an immediate response to a sudden change

---

[13] An indication of the strength of the emotional impact of the Munich crisis in the United States is that it seems to have been a major contributor to the panic generated by Orson Welles's contemporary radio drama about an invasion from Mars. As Heywood Broun noted at the time, "I doubt if anything of the sort would have happened four or five months ago. The course of world history has affected national psychology. Jitters have come home to roost. We have just gone through a laboratory demonstration of the fact that the peace of Munich hangs over our heads, like a thundercloud" (Klass, 1988, p. 1. See also, Cantril, 1940, pp. 159–161).

in mood most probably induced by the emotionally charged communications he was receiving from Europe.

In fact, from 23rd to the 25th of September, Roosevelt was bombarded with increasingly dramatic messages which, among other things, predicted a war which would spell the end of European civilization, underlined Hitler's brutality and intransigence, graphically described Chamberlain's growing pessimism, conveyed the heart-rending pleas of the Czechs for help, and, from Ambassador Bullitt in particular, urged in the strongest possible terms American action to avoid the tragedy. Not only must these messages have had a considerable emotional impact of their own, but also their effect was probably magnified by the highly stressful atmosphere produced by the continuing crisis.

It appears that these communications served primarily to focus Roosevelt's attention on the dreadful consequences of the impending conflict, making it emotionally real to him. Thus, by September 25, the President not only *believed* that war was bound to occur unless steps were taken to prevent it, he had also begun to *feel* that it would be so terrible that he himself had to stop it.

Strong emotion, then, was apparently behind Roosevelt's transformation from a detached observer of someone else's crisis to a sort of participant. In the language of prospect theory: as the president became increasingly affected by the emotional impact of the news from Europe, he began to experience the prospect of war as a loss. This in turn led him to understand the choice of whether or not to intervene in a fundamentally different way, and, as a consequence, to want to prevent the war rather than merely to advise others on how to fight it.

This process continued as on the 25th itself, already desiring to act, Roosevelt underwent another day of great emotional tension which finally culminated in his decision to intervene. Even after he made that choice, however, the psychological pressure continued to build. September 26 began as a day of anxious waiting for Hitler's response to the president's message and ended with disappointment at his violent speech and unyielding reply. That Roosevelt's feelings had by this time become very much engaged indeed is shown both by his own account of his emotional reaction to Chamberlain's speech during the September 27 cabinet meeting and by reports of the tension which characterized the drafting session for his second appeal, particularly his display of anger at the news that Hitler might be preparing to march immediately. Clearly, outrage at Hitler's behavior and great sympathy for the democracies had joined Roosevelt's already considerable anxiety about the consequences of war.

It may also be that Roosevelt's awareness of the imminence of war added to his emotional distress in several ways. For one thing, the imminence of a threatening event may generate greater emotion and stress than certainty alone. During the Munich crisis, the war which had seemed certain after Berchtesgaden, after Godesberg appeared imminent as well. While that was not in itself sufficient to cause Roosevelt to reverse preferences about intervening, it may well have

Table I. Roosevelt's Beliefs and Preferences during the Munich Crisis

Time	Reference Point	Frame of Choice Problem	Attitude to Risk	Preference
Pre-crisis War not expected	No threat to U.S. from Europe	Crisis (including outcome of war) = within status quo	Averse	Do not intervene
9/16 Berchtesgaden War expected Allies → win	"	"	"	"
9/23 Godesberg War = certain War = imminent Allies → win	"	"	"	"
FRAME CHANGE				
9/24–25 Affect-laden reports War = certain War = imminent Allies → win	"	War = loss	Acceptant	Intervene #1
9/27 Hitler rebuff War = certain War = imminent Allies → win	"	"	"	Intervene #2

exacerbated the effect of the emotions which did. That is, imminence increased the salience of war by making clear that the war which seemed certain to occur would do so now rather than later. Not only might this awareness have heightened the painful emotions that Roosevelt was already feeling, it could also have intensified his stress by adding the pressure of time (Janis and Mann, 1977, pp. 54, 59; I am indebted to Alexander George for pointing out that imminence may have a different impact on a decision-maker's assessment of threat than does certainty).

In any event, there is considerable empirical evidence pointing to the experience of strong emotion as the crucial element in Roosevelt's post-Godesberg change of frame and subsequent reversal of preferences. Moreover, the idea that such emotion can mediate cognitive change has received ample theoretical support in the literature dealing with the relationship between cognition and affect. As Hoffman has pointed out, "cognitive psychologists often view affect as providing the motivating force for initiating cognitive processes" (Hoffman, 1986, p. 260; for Hoffman's view of the ways in which affect may influence information processing, see pp. 245–246).

Any account of what Roosevelt experienced after Godesberg, however, is incomplete without an awareness that the reverse process can occur as well. That is, a change of frame can affect the emotions felt by the decision-maker. In fact, Tversky and Kahneman themselves usually speak of changes in emotional response as the *outcome* of frame changes, rather than their cause (Tversky & Kahneman, 1981, p. 458; Kahneman & Tversky, 1984, pp. 341–350).

Clearly, this process could also have occurred in the Munich case. That is, framing the crisis as in some sense Roosevelt's own could have intensified the emotional involvement which caused the frame to change to begin with. This, in turn, could have had the effect of reinforcing the new frame in which an outcome of war was seen as a loss (It is a commonly held view that a decision-maker's personal experience of a crisis generates considerable emotion and stress. Morgan, for example, defines a national security crisis "as a severe threat to important values which, for the decision maker, means an increase in emotional intensity. . . ." Morgan, 1977, p. 168; see also, Holsti, 1972 and 1971; Holsti and George, 1975).

Again, the literature on the relationship between cognition and affect affords solid backing for the idea that changes in cognition can result in changes in affect. Indeed, as Hoffman observes, "the dominant approach to affect" has long been one "in which feelings are the consequences of cognitive appraisal" (Hoffman, 1986, p. 24).

Moreover, evidence that the causal connection between affect and cognition runs in *both* directions has recently led a number of scholars to conclude that, as appears to have been the case during the Munich crisis, these processes are mutually reinforcing. Thus, with respect to "the dynamic interplay between cognitive and affective/motivational processes as they unfold in natural situations," Sorrentino and Higgins argue that,

> motivation and cognition are, in fact, inseparable. . . . [I]t is not simply that cognition leads to motivation and motivation leads to cognition. Rather, each is a property or facet of the other. They are *synergistic* in that they operate together to produce combined effects. (Sorrentino and Higgins, 1986, pp. 12, 8. The relationship between cognition and affect is, of course, the subject of a long-standing controversy, about which there is as yet no consensus. For opposing views on this issue, see Zajonc, 1980; and Lazarus, 1982.)

Thus, the news from Godesberg may have touched off a rather complex interaction between affect and cognition, the effect of which was to transform Roosevelt from a somewhat detached observer of the crisis into a kind of participant. He had come to feel that war would be a loss, not only for Europe but for the United States as well, and, in this sense, the crisis had moved, at least in emotional terms, from being someone else's crisis to being in some sense his own. As a consequence of this change in frame, the president reversed his preferences and chose to intervene directly in the crisis.

A final question about the role of affect in Roosevelt's decision-making behavior during the Munich crisis concerns its implications for Janis and Mann's decisional conflict model of decision-making. Clearly, Roosevelt was subject to a number of the variables they cite as leading to biased information processing, such as significant negative emotion and time pressure, and he apparently also experienced considerable stress. Moreover, these factors had an important impact on his cognitive processes, causing him to redefine the choice problem and change his preferences.

What may be embarrassing for the decisional-conflict model, however, is that not only does it not predict this particular kind of response to stress, but also Roosevelt did not otherwise react to stress in the ways that it does predict. Contrary to the expectations of the model, there is not the slightest indication that the need to make a painful decision was itself the source of Roosevelt's negative emotion and stress. Nor did he show the least disposition toward defensive avoidance (Janis, 1959; Janis & Mann, 1977, pp. 57–58, 73–74). Moreover, there is no evidence that the stress experienced by the president resulted in the kind of biased information processing and cognitive rigidity predicted by the decisional-conflict model. Apart from helping to trigger the change of frame, stress does not appear to have impaired Roosevelt's ability to process information in a fairly rational manner (for a discussion of this point, see Farnham, 1991, pp. 459–466).

Janis and Mann, of course, might explain this anomaly by asserting that, while Roosevelt's stress was sufficient to result in "vigilant information processing," it was not great enough to cause impaired processing (Janis & Mann, 1977, pp. 50–52). Nevertheless, the president's behavior in this period at least raises a question about how much stress is enough. If a decision-maker can experience a degree of stress sufficient to trigger an unacknowledged frame change which then motivates him to act in a way he had previously thought unwise and yet leaves the general quality of his information processing unaffected, just how much stress is actually required to activate the pattern Janis and Mann predict? (This question is all the more compelling because it cannot be answered by pointing to individual differences in tolerance for stress. However high Roosevelt's tolerance for stress may have been, he was clearly subject to it on this occasion. For other criticisms of the usefulness of this model in explaining crisis behavior, see Morgan, 1977, pp. 177–179; and Levi & Tetlock, 1980)

CONCLUSION

This study has sought to evaluate the competing claims of prospect theory and rational choice theory to explain political decision-making in the light of an actual historical case. In applying the predictions of both theories to Franklin D. Roosevelt's decision-making during the Munich crisis, the study makes it clear that prospect theory provides a more satisfactory explanation of his behavior at that time than does the theory of rational choice.

In particular, the evidence uncovered by a detailed analysis of Roosevelt's decision-making behavior shows that his reversal of preferences about the desirability of American intervention in the crisis was not the result of a reassessment of the expected utility of intervening on the basis of new information. Rather, in the midst of the crisis, despite the fact that the objective situation had not changed materially from an American point of view, Roosevelt suddenly reframed the outcome of war as a loss and became anxious to prevent it, even to the point of incurring risks he had previously judged unacceptable. Such behavior cannot be accommodated within the framework of the theory of rational choice.

With respect to the theoretical significance of these findings, at the very least they support the demand of prospect theory to be acknowledged as a legitimate alternative for explaining decision-making behavior in the political context. They also show that in some cases it may be able to account for behavior which is puzzling for theories of rational choice.

Moreover, analyzing Roosevelt's decision-making behavior in the light of the predictions of prospect theory points to at least one area in which the theory would benefit from elaboration. That is to say, the finding that Roosevelt's change of frame was apparently triggered by strong emotion suggests a need for further research into the causes of frame changes, particularly with regard to the role of affect.

Finally, while supporting the idea that crisis-generated stress can affect decision-making in a number of areas, such as the cognitive appraisal of the decision-making problem and the evaluation and selection of alternatives, this study raises a question about Janis and Mann's account of the effects of stress. If Roosevelt experienced a level of stress sufficient to cause him to redefine the decision problem and reverse his policy preferences, why did the rest of his decision-making behavior not also manifest the kind of cognitive impairment under conditions of high stress predicted by the decisional-conflict model? If that model is to be of use in explaining political decision-making behavior, surely it requires clarification in this area.

The attempt to apply prospect theory to an historical case has thus had theoretical benefits in several areas. Not only has it suggested a possible direction for advancing the theory itself, it has also provoked some interesting questions about alternative explanations of decision-making behavior.

ACKNOWLEDGMENTS

I would like to thank Carol Dweck, Alexander George, Robert Jervis, Jack Levy, Rose McDermott, Eldar Shafir, and Janice Stein for their comments on this article. An earlier version was presented at the Thirteenth Annual Scientific Meeting of the International Society of Political Psychology, Washington, D.C., July 11–14, 1990.

REFERENCES

Alsop, J., & Kintner, R. (1940). *American white paper*. New York: Simon and Schuster.
Bazerman, M. H. (1983). Negotiator judgment. *American Behavioral Scientist, 27,* 211–228.
Berle, B. (Ed.), (1973). *Navigating the rapids, 1918–1971: From the papers of Adolph A. Berle.* New York: Harcourt, Brace, Jovanovich.
Bueno de Mesquita, B. (1981). *The war trap.* New Haven: Yale University Press.
Blum, J. M. (Ed.). (1965). *From the Morgenthau Diaries* (Vol. 1). Boston: Houghton Mifflin.
Bullitt, O. H. (Ed.). (1972). *For the President: Personal and secret—Correspondence between Franklin D. Roosevelt and William C. Bullitt.* Boston: Houghton Mifflin.
Butler, R., & Woodward, Sir, E. L. (Eds.). (1951). *Documents on British foreign policy, 1919–1939.* (3rd Series, Vol. 3). London: His Majesty's Stationery Office.
Cantril, H. (1940). *The invasion from Mars.* Princeton, NJ: Princeton University Press.
Cohen, R. (1979). *Threat perception in international crisis.* Madison, WI: University of Wisconsin Press.
Cole, W. (1983). *Roosevelt and the isolationists, 1932–45.* Lincoln, NE: University of Nebraska Press.
Dallek, R. (1979). *Franklin D. Roosevelt and American foreign policy, 1932–1945,* New York: Oxford University Press.
Davis, M. A., & Bobko, P. (1986). Contextual effects on escalation processes, *Organizational Behavior and Human Decision Processes, 37,* 121–138.
Divine, R. (1965). *The reluctant belligerent.* New York: John Wiley.
Divine, R. (1969). *Roosevelt and World War II.* Baltimore: Johns Hopkins Press.
Farnham, B. (1990). Political cognition and decision-making, *Political Psychology, 11,* 83–111.
Farnham, B. (1991). *Value conflict and decision-making: Franklin D. Roosevelt and the Munich crisis, 1938.* Unpublished doctoral dissertation, Columbia University, New York.
Fischoff, B. (1983). Strategic policy preferences: A behavioral decision theory perspective, *Journal of Social Issues, 39,* 133–160.
Haight, J. M. Jr. (1970). *American aid to France, 1938–1940.* New York: Atheneum.
Haight, J. M. Jr. (1960). France, the United States, and the Munich crisis, *Journal of Modern History, 32,* 340–358.
Hermann, C. F. (1972). Threat, time, and surprise: A simulation of international crisis. In C. F. Hermann (Ed.), *International crisis* (pp. 187–211). New York: Free Press.
Hoffman, M. L. (1986). Affect, cognition, and motivation, Sorrentino, R. M., & Higgins, E. T. (Eds.), *Handbook of motivation and cognition,* New York: Guilford Press.
Holsti, O. R. (1972). *Crisis, escalation, war,* Montreal: McGill-Queens University Press.
Holsti, O. R. (1971). Crisis, stress and decision-making, *International Social Science Journal, 23,* 53–67.
Holsti, O. R. & George, A. (1975). Effects of stress on the performance of foreign policy-makers. In C. Cotter (Ed.), *Political science annual* (Vol. 6, pp. 255–319). Indianapolis: Bobbs Merill.
Hooker, N. H. (Ed.) (1956). *The Moffat papers: Selections from the diplomatic papers of Jay Pierrepont Moffat, 1919–1943.* Cambridge, MA: Harvard University Press.
Hull, C. (1958). *Memoirs.* New York: MacMillan.
Ickes, H. (1954). *Secret diary* (Vol. 2). New York: Simon and Schuster.
Janis, I. (1959). Decisional conflicts: A theoretical analysis, *Journal of Conflict Resolution, 3,* 6–27.
Janis, I., & Mann, L. (1977). *Decisionmaking: A psychological analysis of conflict, choice, and commitment.* New York: Free Press.
Jervis, R. (1989). *Political implications of loss aversion,* Unpublished manuscript.
Kahneman, D., & Tversky, A. (1984). Choices, values, and frames, *American Psychologist, 39,* 341–350.
Kahneman, D., & Tversky, A. (1979). Prospect theory: An analysis of decision under risk, *Econometrica, 47,* 263–291.
Kahneman, D., & Tversky, A. (1982). The psychology of preferences, *Scientific American, 246,* 160–173.

Kaufmann, W. W. (1963). Two American ambassadors: Bullitt and Kennedy, In G. A. Craig & F. G. Gilbert (Eds.) *The Diplomats, 1919–1939*. (Vol. 2) New York: Atheneum.

Klass, P. (October 30, 1988). Wells, Welles and the Martians, *New York Times Book Review*, p. 1.

Langer, W. L., & Gleason, E. S. (1952). *The challenge to isolation, 1937–1940*. New York: Harper and Brothers.

Lash, J. P. (1976). *Roosevelt and Churchill, 1939–1941: The partnership that saved the West*. New York: W. W. Norton.

Lazarus, R. S. (1982). Thoughts on the relations between emotion and cognition, *American Psychologist, 37*, 1019–1024.

Levi, A. & Tetlock, P. E. (1980). A cognitive analysis of Japan's 1941 decision for war, *Journal of Conflict Resolution, 24*, 195–211.

Levin, I. P., Johnson, R. D., Russo, C. P., & Deldin, P. J. (1985). Framing effects in judgment tasks with varying amounts of information, *Organizational Behavior and Human Decision Processes, 36*, 362–377.

McDermott, R. (1990). Prospect theory in international relations: the Iranian rescue mission. Unpublished manuscript.

Memo from Adolf Berle to the President. (September 1, 1938). President's Secretary's File, State Department, Berle Folder, Box 93, Roosevelt Library, Hyde Park, NY.

Morgan, P. (1977). *Deterrence: A conceptual analysis*, Beverly Hills, CA: Sage Library of Social Science.

Morgenthau Diary, (1938). Roosevelt Library, Hyde Park, NY.

Murray, A. (1946). *At close quarters*. London: John Murray.

Offner, A. A. (1969). *American appeasement: United States foreign policy and Germany, 1933–1938*, New York: W. W. Norton.

Quattrone, G. A., & Tversky, A. (1984). Causal versus diagnostic contingencies: On self-deception and on the voter's illusion, *Journal of personality and Social Psychology, 46*, 237–248.

Quattrone, G. A., & Tversky, A. (1988). Contrasting rational and psychological analyses of political choice, *American Political Science Review, 82*, 719–736.

Shapira, Z. (1981). Making trade-offs between job attributes, *Organizational Behavior and Human Performance, 28*, 331–355.

Schewe, D. B. (1979). *Franklin D. Roosevelt and foreign affairs, January 1937–August 1939* (Vols. 4–8). New York: Garland Publishing.

Sorrentino, R. M., & Higgins, E. T. (1986). Motivation and cognition, In R. M. Sorrentino and E. T. Higgins (Eds.) *Handbook of motivation and cognition*. New York: Guilford Press.

Stein, J. G. & Tanter, R. (1980). *Rational decision-making*. Columbus, OH: Ohio State University Press.

Steinbruner, J. (1974). *Cybernetic theory of decision*, Princeton, NJ: Princeton University Press

Taylor, T. (1979). *Munich*. New York: Doubleday.

Tetlock, P. E. (1985). Accountability: The neglected social context of judgment and choice. *Research in Organizational Behavior, 7*, 297–332.

Tversky, A., & Kahneman, D. (1981). The framing of decisions and the psychology of choice, *Science, 211*, 453–458.

Tversky, A., & Kahneman, D. (1986). Rational choice and the framing of decisions. *Journal of Business, 59*, S251–S278.

United States, Department of State. (1938). *Foreign Relations of the United States* (Vol. 1).

Zajonc, R. B. (1980). Feeling and thinking: Preferences need no inferences, *American Psychologist, 35*, 151–175.

Prospect Theory in International Relations: The Iranian Hostage Rescue Mission

Rose McDermott[1]

INTRODUCTION

The renewed controversy surrounding the involvement of the Reagan campaign in the Iranian hostage crisis fuels new interest in the activities of the Carter administration to secure the hostages' release. After exhausting all diplomatic channels for achieving this goal for over six months, President Carter undertook a dramatic military rescue attempt in April of 1980. Carter's action was not only completely contrary to his humanitarian emphasis in world politics but was a highly risky prospect from a military standpoint as well.

How can Carter's actions be explained in light of his predilection for the peaceful resolution of conflict? How is it possible to understand the nature of the risks Carter was willing to run, both militarily and politically, in order to force the release of the hostages from Iranian control? This article argues that prospect

---

[1]New School for Social Research, 313 West 4th St., New York, New York 10014.

theory provides the best way to understand these seemingly anomalous and incomprehensible events in the Carter administration.

Prospect theory encompasses two elements. The first is a framing phase, during which information is received and processed in a way that places emphasis on particular aspects of a problem, such as whether or not it takes place in a situation of gains or losses. Gains or losses are judged relative to the reference point. In most cases, this is the status quo. However, in many important circumstances, a leader will refuse to accept a new status quo as the reference point and thus will cling to the old status quo as the "appropriate" reference point. The second evaluative segment argues, in short, that people tend to be risk-seeking in the domain of losses and risk-averse in the domain of gains (Tversky & Kahneman, 1984).

The application of prospect theory to any case in the international environment thus necessitates a two-stage analysis. The beginning stage corresponds to the first, editing, phase of the theory. In this part, the particular framing of the relevant issues and questions are investigated at a substantive level in order to discern differences in the political emphases and goals of various players. The second phase consists of the evaluation phase, whereby the specific domain of gains or losses, and relative risk propensity, either acceptant or averse, is discussed and analyzed.

This process allows for a comparison between the predictions of the theory and the outcomes of actual events. The critical variable here is the subjective assessments of domain and risk. While these are clearly tied to, and often derivative of, objective assessments, they are not always, or necessarily, totally analogous.

The framing and evaluation of President Jimmy Carter's decision to undertake a rescue mission of the American hostages in Iran in April of 1980 is investigated here. The hope is to use the flashlight of prospect theory to help illuminate a case that might otherwise prove inexplicable using more dominant paradigms in political science.

The failed rescue mission of the hostages is inexplicable from the perspective of a structuralist paradigm. Structuralism would suggest that it is highly unlikely for a superpower like the United States to get caught in a hostage relationship with a small power like Iran. But once engaged, structuralism would predict that the power discrepancy in the international system would play to the advantage of the United States. The United States should have been able to find a way to use its power to coerce the Iranians into returning the hostages. However, the United States did not go into Iran with a large show of force; indeed, Carter was widely criticized in the press at the time for rendering America impotent in the face of the Islamic students. Why didn't the Carter administration respond to Iran with more direct force from the outset? Structuralism provides no adequate response.

The rescue attempt took place at the very nadir of the crisis, following the collapse of negotiations with Iranian moderates like Bani-Sadr through French legal intermediaries (Sick, 1986). As a result, it offers a superb case for investigation from the perspective of prospect theory because it takes place exclusively in the domain of losses. Prospect theory can offer both explanation and analysis for an action that is seemingly incomprehensible from a more structural perspective. Indeed, no other theory would predict this behavior as accurately as prospect theory.

DOMAIN

One of the most dramatic events that occurred during Carter's tenure as president was the Iranian hostage crisis. On November 4, 1979, in the context of a broader Islamic revolution, as many as 3,000 Iranian students seized the U.S. embassy in Tehran, taking 66 Americans hostage in the process. The students themselves undertook this attack as a symbolic gesture, and expected the takeover to last only a matter of days; they were quite surprised when they received the vociferous blessings and benedictions of the Imam and proceeded to settle in for a longer episode than originally anticipated (Sick, 1986). Thirteen of the hostages, all either black or female, were subsequently released on November 18 and 19 (Sick, 1986). The remaining 53[2] were kept for 444 days until their negotiated release on January 20, 1980, about two minutes into the Reagan presidency.[3]

The Carter administration consistently sought to negotiate diplomatically for the release of the hostages, although they simultaneously developed contingency plans for military action (Brzezinski, 1985). The actual rescue mission itself took place on April 24, 1980. This mission resulted in the deaths of eight American soldiers, with four additional American injuries, and failed to bring about the release of any of the hostages.

---

[2]One of the hostages, Richard Queen, was released on July 11, 1980, for medical reasons that were later diagnosed as multiple sclerosis.

[3]Gary Sick has recently claimed that the Reagan campaign was independently negotiating with the Iranian Revolutionary Council over the timing of the hostages' release. He argues that the Carter administration was unaware of these illicit negotiations involving the exchange of hostages for arms through Israeli intermediaries. See Gary Sick, "The Election Story of the Decade," *New York Times*, April 15, 1991. ABC News *Nightline*, in collaboration with the *Financial Times* of London, has conducted a series of investigations on these allegations. Although much of the evidence in support of Sick's claims is circumstantial, there are many indications that the basis of his argument may be correct. In a classic case of underestimating the base rate, much of the discussion has focused on the whereabouts of William Casey, Reagan's campaign chief, and later head of the CIA. The problem with this focus is that it fails to investigate how frequently Casey's location was unknown; there is no base rate information on his absence from the public eye. To the extent that having an unknown location was a rare event for Casey, it becomes more diagnostic information.

In applying prospect theory to any case in the international arena, it is crucial to first establish the operative domain as one of either gains or losses. While it may be impossible to actually get inside the head of the relevant decision-maker to assess his subjective perspective, it is possible to use other indicators to determine the most likely domain of action. To take a simple example, if an investigator wanted to know whether a decision-maker felt hot or cold and wasn't able to ask directly, he could look at a thermometer to make a best guess. If the temperature was 100 degrees, chances are the decision-maker felt hot. If the thermometer read 32 degrees, chances are the person felt cold. In a similar way, it is possible to use external indicators to determine, in general, how a president assessed his domain of action.

Carter was clearly operating in a domain of losses at the time of the decision to go ahead with the rescue mission, confronting a situation where things were bad and clearly continuing to get worse with the passage of time. This is obvious from every indicator: Carter faced a revolutionary Islamic power that refused to negotiate directly with him, an increasingly frustrated and hostile American public, a growing sense of desperation among numerous members of Congress and other governmental officials about the safety and release of the hostages, and declining international prestige and credibility. Carter could only have seen himself operating in a domain of losses, both domestically and internationally.

On the domestic front, Carter's popularity was declining rapidly. One poll from June 1979, even before the hostage crisis began, reported that only 20% of the population approved of Carter's foreign policy (*New York Times*, June 25, 1979). More to the point, according to a *Time* poll conducted during the last two weeks of March, 60% of the American public felt that Carter was too soft on Iran.

Moreover, Carter's reelection campaign was going badly. During the last week of March, just prior to the rescue mission, Carter had sustained two large losses in the New York and Connecticut primaries to Senator Edward Kennedy. Although he won the Wisconsin primary on April 1, there were press reports that he used the hostage crisis to manipulate that victory by prematurely announcing good news about their impending release. According to both Hamilton Jordan's and Jody Powell's reports, the president's statement on April 1 had been prompted by what was viewed as a genuine breakthrough in the negotiations and was not related to the primaries in Wisconsin and Kansas that day. Indeed, the polls prior to April 1 showed the president with a solid 15-point lead in Wisconsin even before the announcement was made concerning the hostages.

In addition, it was the first time that Carter had slipped below Reagan in the election polls; Carter had held a 2 to 1 lead over Reagan in December. By March, however, almost half of the people who supported Carter did so "without enthusiasm." Moreover, 81% of the population said they felt that America was in serious trouble, and about 70% said they thought it was time for a change in the presidency (*Time,* April 14, 1980).

Carter's relationship with Congress was deteriorating as well. Presidential victories on votes in Congress declined from 81.4 to 73.3 percent in the Senate alone between 1979 and 1980. Moreover, Republican support in the Senate for Carter's positions fell below 50% (Ornstein, 1984).

Pierre Salinger, who covered the hostage crisis for ABC News from Paris, provides a good summary of the situation:

> Other factors were weighing on the President. Better than anyone, Carter knew how the hostage crisis had paralyzed his administration's efforts in other fields, if only because it diverted his own attention and energies so greatly. Politically, therefore, he was twice wounded—first by the crisis, and again by its impact on his programs. His campaign for reelection registered the frustrations of the American public. While his political fortunes had risen after the taking of the hostages, he was beginning to slip in the polls and had lost a key primary in New York to Senator Edward Kennedy. Jimmy Carter was now in the midst of a fight for his life, and it looked as if he was losing. A military option that freed the hostages would dramatically alter the odds. (Salinger, 1981)

It is significant that Salinger notes here that a military option that freed the hostages could somehow rectify all the losses and perhaps even restore or improve the previous status quo. In other words, it appeared that things would continue to get worse unless something was actively done to rectify the situation.

The view from inside the administration was equally bleak, as National Security Advisor Gary Sick commented:

> The image of U.S. weakness generated by months of humiliating setbacks and frustrations was not healthy for relations with allies or adversaries. In domestic politics, continued passivity not only condemned the President to self-immolation in the polls but it risked generating a popular backlash in favor of forces who opposed everything Vance and Carter represented. (Sick, 1986)

As Sick mentions, the international impact of the hostage crisis was as problematic for Carter as were the domestic pressures. Secretary of State Cyrus Vance had had great difficulty in trying to get the allies to cooperate with the United States in joining and enforcing economic sanctions against Iran. For example, a U.N. Security Council resolution against Iran had been vetoed by the Soviets earlier in the year. Grievances brought against Iran by the U.S. in the World Court were slow to reach fruition. Even after the Iranians were convicted in this Court, there was no real mechanism to enforce the penalties imposed. Moreover, Carter had been warned by President Anwar Sadat of Egypt that America's "international standing" was being damaged by "excessive passivity" (Brzezinski, 1985).

Thus, Carter was man who had sustained tremendous losses to personal popularity, national honor, and international interests when the hostages were taken. By the time of the rescue mission, Carter was a leader ready to take a gamble to return things to the status quo, with the hostages safely at home, national pride and international honor restored, and his political fortunes turned upward. He was not willing to define the new status quo as an acceptable reference point because that concession might cost him his reelection, among other calamities. In terms of prospect theory, he was a man operating in the domain of losses.

THE FRAMING OF OPTIONS

In seeking to apply prospect theory to the Iranian hostage crisis, it is necessary to analyze the options that were considered by the relevant players, in order to determine the perceived relative riskiness of each. Assessments of risk can involve either calculations of the probability of success for a particular choice and/or the utility of each option.

The way these options were framed for President Carter by his advisors is an important element. According to Gary Sick, there was a consensus within the administration on the hierarchy of risk presented by the various options. Risk here meant both the likelihood of success as well as the costs and benefits involved. The main disagreement among advisors and decision-makers surrounded which level of risk was an acceptable one for the United States to take. In the end, the choice that was made was the highest level of risk that President Carter himself was willing to accept (Sick, personal communication).

From the outset, five basic options were considered for bringing about the release of the hostages and ending the diplomatic stalemate. From the lowest to the highest level of risk, these options were to do nothing; engage in minimal political and diplomatic sanctions; undertake a rescue mission; mine the harbors; and engage in an all-out military strike.

The relative benefits and risks involved in each option will be discussed in turn. As National Security Advisor Zbigniew Brzezinski (1990) comments, it is crucial to keep in mind the distinction between military and political risks throughout this analysis. In many cases, these risks are inversely related. Moreover, there is often a trade-off between domestic and international costs and benefits as well.

The first option was to do nothing and wait for the internal situation in Iran to stabilize and resolve the crisis by itself. This was the option that Vance supported. The strategy here was to continue with political and military pressure but not to offer any new initiatives until after the Iranians had formulated their new political system into a coherent structure. The benefit of this strategy was that it did not risk antagonizing the Iranians any further. In Vance's view, this approach was most likely to protect the hostages from further harm.

The political risks of this policy from a domestic perspective are obvious. Carter would be charged with ineffectiveness and be accused of being pushed around by the Ayatollah. More importantly, the personal sense of anger at the Iranians in the administration was running very high at the time. From the perspective of central decision-makers, it was virtually impossible to conceive of accepting deliberate international humiliation in the face of such abominable Iranian action without doing something in response. In short, there was a universal sense that the situation was intolerable. Deep anger and frustration added to the belief that there was no strategic or political reason why the United States should allow itself to be pushed around by a third-rate fanatical religious state in the Middle East. Thus, while the military risks of doing nothing were relatively low, the domestic political risks were high.

The second option was to up the ante slightly but only through diplomatic means. This meant breaking political and economic relations with the Iranians, placing an embargo on shipments of military sales, expelling Iranian citizens from the United States and so on. Everyone assumed that these things would be done, as they all were eventually, and they were not regarded as particularly risky from either a political or a military standpoint. In fact, these actions amounted to more show than substance. The real goal in undertaking these actions was to bring pressure on the Europeans to join in the sanctions against Iran.

This policy amounted to a balancing act between American interests in Iran and U.S. relationships with reluctant European allies. The diplomatic measures were somewhat successful in gaining European cooperation. However, European accommodation to the American position was more a result of the implicit threat of the use of U.S. military force than of genuine interest in sanctioning the Iranians. After the rescue mission took place, the Europeans felt betrayed, although these diplomatic initiatives did serve as a good cover for the rescue mission preparations.

The third option that was seriously considered was the rescue mission itself. This was really an intermediate option in terms of political riskiness, but it was the riskiest option that could be taken militarily without engaging in an outright act of war. The mission was intended to work by stealth, and the goal was to minimize casualties and bring about the release of the hostages. Everyone involved in the planning considered it to be a clever and carefully thought out plan. Even those who now have the benefit of hindsight, such as Sick and Brzezinski, consider the plan to have been subtle, sophisticated, and likely to have succeeded.

According to Sick, all the decision-makers understood the serious military risks involved in undertaking the mission, but it still offered the only real possibility of rescuing most of the hostages alive. The planners knew that the possibility of success was not 100%, but they believed that the risks were manageable. In other words, the risks here were seen as being more about the probability of military success than about the political costs and benefits of undertaking the mission, which seemed more acceptable.

The key factor here is that the rescue mission was the best balance of political and military risk. If it worked, the hostages would be free, Carter would be a hero, and America's international credibility would be salvaged. Theoretically, a success would have amounted to a return to the old status quo as the reference point. However, everyone agreed that the military risks were admittedly high, and the probability of complete success relatively low.

However, military planning was designed to minimize these military risks as much as possible. The strategy was to enter Iran on a holiday weekend; the rescuers were to hit hard and quickly under cover of darkness. The American embassy itself is surrounded by large grounds, and no one expected enough noise would travel outside the compound to arouse suspicion, especially with the use of silencers on all weapons. The rescuers knew where the hostages were being held within the building, and they expected the students to be unprepared and unskilled in combat. Although no one discussed Iranian losses openly, there was every expectation that large numbers of Iranian students would be killed in the course of the mission. However, the risks to American soldiers and hostages were more specific, and every effort was made to minimize these losses. Thus, the rescue mission seemed to be a particularly attractive option when the alternatives were perceived to amount to either letting the situation continue to fester or to go to all-out war.

The fourth option was to mine the harbors or to otherwise interrupt commerce. This was seen to be politically quite risky because it was the equivalent of an act of war. The United States had no intention of declaring war but wanted to prevent ships from going into Iran without having to physically stop them. Mining would constitute a passive sea blockade, and if well publicized, most ships wouldn't try to run the risk of entering the mined area. The goal was to have a significant negative impact on Iran's exports and imports.

Mining the harbors was viewed as a sharp escalation. The fear was that the Iranians would invite the Soviets into the region to help with mine-sweeping and that this offer would provide the Soviets with an opening in the region that the United States wanted to prevent. Thus, mining was seen as a significant, but not an overwhelming, international risk. This option was certainly viewed as manageable from a military perspective. Using mines with automatic self-destruct mechanisms would allow some flexibility and this option was seriously considered. However, there was a military risk of repeatedly losing planes and ships in such an action, and the other political risks involved by inflaming the region were seen to be quite high as well. Most importantly, this option would do nothing directly to further the primary goal of releasing the hostages.

The last option available was an all-out military attack. This was extremely risky from both a political and a military standpoint and was never seriously considered. As with the previous option, the main reason this option was abandoned was because it did nothing to get the hostages back. It would inflame the entire region and escalate the crisis without doing anything directly to bring about the release of the hostages. Basically, this option was rejected every step of the way because the adverse consequences were too great, and the risks were too high both politically and militarily, domestically and internationally.

The most important point regarding the options that were politically more risky than the rescue mission is that neither one offered the chance to return the situation to the former status quo by brining about the release of the hostages. Thus, while the military risks of the rescue mission might have been greater than mining the harbor, and the domestic political risks of a punitive strike might have been less risky, neither option offered an immediate solution to the central issue of contention.

As mentioned, the principal decision-makers agreed on the options that were available and their relative levels of military and political risk. However, it is also true that each advisor possessed a different threshold, or tolerance level, for what was acceptable. As a result, each framed his arguments to Carter in quite different ways. These perspectives are addressed below.

Framing

It was the collapse of the administration's negotiations with Prime Minister Bani-Sadr on April 1 that led to Carter's subsequent decision to undertake the rescue mission (Jordan, 1982; Powell, 1984). The possibility of undertaking a military option in response to the hostage crisis was raised a couple of days after the embassy was taken in November of 1979. Under the instigation of Brzezinski, through Secretary of Defense Harold Brown, the Joint Chiefs of Staff (JCS) put together a Joint Task Force and began planning for a rescue attempt at that time. It was not seriously considered as an option, however, until the following April, after the collapse of direct negotiations with the Iranians.

Because of the number of memoirs and official documents that are available, it is possible to examine a number of different arguments that were presented to President Carter prior to his decision to go ahead with the rescue mission. The main perspectives that will be examined are those espoused by Secretary of State Cyrus Vance, National Security Advisor Zbigniew Brzezinski, and presidential assistant Hamilton Jordan. In the end, Secretary of State Cyrus Vance resigned over this episode, because he believed that the mission could not work and should be pursued because it was too dangerous.

Prospect theory argues that choice can often be substantively affected by relatively trivial manipulations in the framing and construction of available options. For example, coding helps define the reference point, and the presentation of options defines the universe of contingencies that are considered.

One notable aspect of the Iranian rescue mission case is that each advisor drew on different historical analogies to make his point and press his position. These analogies offered a frame for defining the reference point, as well as instructing individual advisors about appropriate courses of action in a given situation. Such historical analogies can be quite influential, as Jervis suggests:

> What one learns from key events in international history is an important factor in determining the images that shape the interpretation of incoming information. . . .
> Previous international events provide a statesman with a range of imaginable situations and allow him to detect patterns and causal links that can help him understand his world. (Jervis, 1976)

In this case, each advisor, working from a different script, foresaw a different probable outcome based on his chosen historical analogy. In some sense, these analogies offered predictions about the most likely outcome of events for each advocate. Conclusions reached and the policies promoted varied according to the similarities that each advisor saw between present and past events. Therefore, it is important to examine these analogies and their proponent's advice to Carter.

One advisor whose analogies affected his advice to President Carter was Secretary of State Cyrus Vance. Vance was adamantly opposed to the rescue mission, seeing it as too risky from both a military and a political standpoint. The final decision to attempt the rescue mission was made by Carter and his principal advisors on April 11 in a meeting that took place without Vance (Brzezinski, 1985; Vance, 1982; Carter, 1983). Upon his return from what everyone involved described as a "well-earned" vacation, Vance expressed shock and concern that such a momentous decision had been made without his input. As a result, another meeting of the principals was called on April 15, at which time Secretary Vance outlined his objections. At that meeting, Vance:

> pointed out that we had made substantial progress in gaining allied support for effective sanctions . . . [I] pointed out further that the formation of the Majlis, to which Khomeini had given jurisdiction over the hostage crisis, could be a major step toward a functioning government with whom we could negotiate in Iran . . . Even if the raid were technically successful, the mission was almost certain to lead to a number of deaths among the hostages, not to mention the Iranians. The only justification in my mind for a rescue attempt was that the danger to the hostages was so great that it outweighed the risks of a military option. I did not believe that to be the case.
> I reminded the group that even if the rescue mission did free some of the embassy staff, the Iranians could simply take more hostages from among the American journalists still in Tehran. We would then be worse off than before, and the whole region would be severely inflamed by our action. Our national interests in the whole region would be inflamed by our action. Finally, I said there was a real chance that we would force the Iranians into the arms of the Soviets. (Vance, 1983)

In spite of Vance's objections, the decision to go ahead with the mission was reaffirmed. At this time, Secretary Vance tendered his resignation to President

Carter, who waited to announce Vance's decision until after the rescue mission had taken place. Vance explains his decision to resign as a matter of principle:

> I had disagreed with policy decision in the past, but accepting that men of forceful views would inevitably disagree from time to time, had acquiesced out of loyalty to the President knowing I could not win every battle. The decision to extract the hostages by force from the center of a city of over five million, more than six thousand miles from the United States, which could be reached only by flying over difficult terrain was different: I was convinced that the decision was wrong and that it carried great risks for the hostages and for our national interests . . .
>
> [I] knew that I could not honorably remain as Secretary of State when I so strongly disagreed with a Presidential decision that went against my judgment as to what was best for the country and for the hostages. Even if the mission worked perfectly, and I did not believe it would, I would have to say afterward that I had opposed it, give my reason for opposing it, and publicly criticize the President. That would be intolerable for the President and me. That day, I told Carter I would have to resign if the mission went forward. (Vance, 1983)

Of all his advisors, Secretary Vance was closest to President Carter, both personally and ideologically (Sick, 1986; Carter, 1982). Indeed, both Vance's and Carter's accounts of the interaction surrounding Vance's resignation are quite moving and almost reminiscent of the kind of tragedy associated with a failed love affair. It is thus particularly significant that President Carter decided to override Vance's arguments and pursue the military option when he knew that Vance objected strongly enough to resign over it.

Secretary Vance argued throughout the hostage crisis that the United States should use patience and negotiation in order to gain the release of the hostages safely. His overriding concern was the lives and safety of the hostages and, in the event of the rescue mission, the lives of the American soldiers as well. He framed options in terms of mortality, and everything was evaluated in terms of the likelihood that a particular action would lead to the death of a human being. He also appeared to be more concerned about gaining and keeping the support of the European allies than other advisors.

In terms of the options presented earlier, Vance's threshold for risk was really at the first stage. More specifically, he wanted to do nothing and wait for the internal situation in Iran to settle down. He believed that once this happened, the Iranians would no longer have use for the American hostages and would release them voluntarily without additional pressure from the U.S. From Vance's perspective, anything that America might do to bring about the hostages' release in the meantime could only serve to further antagonize the Iranians and thus risk the ultimate safety of the hostages. He also thought that military action would alienate the European allies he had worked so hard to reassure. He thus saw a rescue mission as unacceptably risky from both a political and military standpoint.

It is significant to note that the Agnus Ward incident was the historical analogy from which Vance operated. As Vance recalls:

> I also believed that the hostages would be released safely once they had served their political purpose in Iran. I found support for this conclusion in what had happened in two similar cases where Americans were held hostage. They were the Agnus Ward incident, involving the seizure of our consular staff in Mukden at the end of World War II, and the case of the USS Pueblo. The Ward case had many similarities to the seizure in Iran, as is clear from the memorandum of the Joint Chiefs of Staff to President Truman recommending against the use of military force. I had sent a copy of this memorandum to the President shortly after the hostages were taken. I was convinced as time passed the chances of physical harm to the hostages diminished. (Vance, 1983)

Thus, Vance used the Ward and Pueblo analogies to support his view that the hostages would remain safe and be released unharmed as long as the United States was patient, restrained in action, and willing to negotiate. In other words, Vance thought that the new status quo, while not optimal, was nonetheless acceptable as long as no one was killed. He feared that American action would lead to the loss of life and thus was not an advisable course of action. So, for Vance, any action that the United States took would be to make a gain and not to prevent a loss.

Vance believed any rescue mission was doomed to military, and thus political, failure from the outset because of the high risk of deaths, yet he refused to gloat when his predictions came true. Rather, he was the first to offer Carter the most heartfelt condolences following the announcement of the failed mission (Jordan, 1982).

Vance had held sway in most of the early foreign policy decisions of the Carter administration. However, he was not the only senior member of the decision-making team; Brzezinski was equally important politically. There is little doubt that Brzezinski's opinion was taken quite seriously by Carter. Indeed, Gary Sick characterizes his importance to the president in quite compelling fashion:

> Brzezinski was the very antithesis of Cyrus Vance. . . .
> This restless energy and persistent pursuit of fresh approaches made Brzezinski a natural alter ego to Jimmy Carter's activism. Although the two men were psychologically very different and never really became personally close, they complemented each other in very special ways. Carter was dissatisfied with things as they were and was determined to use his Presidency to generate change. Brzezinski sparked new ideas at a dazzling rate and refused to be constrained by the status quo in devising his strategies. Although Carter probably rejected more of Brzezinski's ideas that he accepted, he obviously valued the irreverent inventiveness that Brzezinski brought to any subject. (Sick, 1986)

According to Gary Sick, the real shift in Carter's policy allegiance from Vance to Brzezinski came after the Soviet invasion of Afghanistan in late 1979. It is clear from Carter's much-publicized statements that he was deeply shocked and personally offended by the Soviet action. Indeed, it was after the Soviet invasion of Afghanistan that Vance announced that he would not stay in office beyond the election. It was following this event that Carter's policy changed from an emphasis on patience and negotiation to one based more on confrontation and competition. Indeed, a change in frame at this time from gains to losses regarding U.S.-Soviet relations resulted in a noticeable change in policy from appeasement to deterrence. It was within this context that the decision about the rescue mission was made (Sick, 1986).

Brzezinski was a powerful force in the decision to proceed with the mission. However, Brzezinski had quite a different agenda than Vance. His frame encompassed national power and prestige as well as the hostages' welfare. As Harold Saunders, Assistant Secretary of State for Near East and South Asia, notes, "Zbig Brzezinski was more concerned with national interest and honor, while Cy Vance emphasized humane values" (Saunders, 1985). In short, Vance was the idealist to Brzezinski's more classical realist position.

Brzezinski favored some kind of military rescue mission from the outset, even though, like Vance, he knew that military risks were involved in the rescue mission:

> My view was that casualties in the rescue mission would be unavoidable; but we also had to face the possibility that the attempt might fail altogether. (Brzezinski, 1982)

The difference was that Brzezinski was more willing to accept these risks than Vance and saw them as more unavoidable (Brzezinski, 1985). His threshold of risk on the list of options was the highest of the central decision-makers. Indeed, he went so far as to support a punitive military raid against Iran, in the face of universal opposition. Brzezinski was also the one who began to plan for a second rescue mission, two days after the first failure (Brzezinski, 1985). As noted, Brzezinski's interest was broader than the lives and safety of the hostages:

> In effect, I felt that the question of the lives of the hostages should not be our only focus but that we should examine as well what needed to be done to protect our vital interests. I was painfully aware that at some point perhaps a choice between the two might even have to be made. (Brzezinski, 1985)

Indeed, it was Brzezinski who phoned Brown on November 6 to get the JCS to work on a rescue mission. Brzezinski was the one who questioned whether or not the mission should go ahead with five helicopters after the hydraulic leak was discovered in the crucial sixth during the course of the rescue mission itself. Indeed, his commentary on this event provides singular insight into the conscious use of framing to influence a decision-maker:

> I stood in front to his desk with my mind racing: Should I press the president to go ahead with only five helicopters? Here I was, alone with the President. Perhaps I could convince him to abandon military prudence, to go in a daring single stroke for the big prize, to take the historic chance. And at the same time, a contrary thought flashed through my mind: would I not be abusing my office by pressing this man into such a quick decision after months of meticulous planning? Would I not be giving into a romantic idea?
> I had decided to urge going ahead with five only if Colonel Beckwith was prepared to do it, but not to press for it without the field commander's concurrence. (Brzezinski, 1985)

In this sequence, Brzezinski demonstrates a conscious awareness of an advisor's ability to persuade and manipulate a decision-maker, even one so powerful as the president, through the framing of options.

The evidence suggests that Brzezinski had a great impact on Carter's thinking with regard to the hostage rescue mission. In the memo he wrote to the president the day before Carter approved the mission, after demonstrating much reluctance earlier, Brzezinski argued:

> In short, unless something is done to change the nature of the game, we must resign ourselves to the continued imprisonment of the hostages throughout the summer or even later. However, we have to think beyond the fate of the fifty Americans and consider the deleterious effects of a protracted stalemate, growing public frustration, and international humiliation of the U.S. (Brzezinski, 1985)

Thus, it is evident that Brzezinski started from a different set of assumptions than Vance. Brzezinski believed that things would get worse without drastic American action, while Vance believed exactly the opposite. At the meeting the following day, Brzezinski argued that

> We ought to attempt the rescue as early as possible because the nights are getting shorter; that we should consider taking prisoners back with us, so that we would have bargaining leverage in the event that the Iranians seized other Americans as hostages; and that we should consider a simultaneous retaliatory strike in the event the rescue failed. (Brzezinski, 1985)

It is interesting to note that Brzezinski was influenced by a quite different historical analogy than Vance. Brzezinski's model for the rescue mission was the Israeli raid on Entebbe. One of the reasons he supported a smaller American helicopter force grew out of this experience:

> Some have argued subsequently that the mission should have been composed of, say, twice as many helicopters; but if the Iranians had discovered the mission as a result of the size of the air armada penetrating their airspace, we all would have doubtless been charged with typically excessive American redundancy, with unwillingness to go in hard and lean—the way, for example, the Israelis did at Entebbe. (Brzezinski, 1985)

Indeed, during the operational aspects of the planning, Brzezinski was quite aware of a second powerful analogy with the Bay of Pigs. He was careful to steer Carter clear of the mistakes that Kennedy had made at that time. As Brzezinski describes it:

> He and I had earlier discussed John Kennedy's interference with the military planning for the Bay of Pigs operation, and Carter was clearly determined to make certain that his personal concerns did not interfere with the mission's chances of success. (Brzezinski, 1985)

The Bay of Pigs analogy indeed became quite a salient analogy for Carter. According to Sick,

> John F. Kennedy was widely criticized, especially within military circles, for insisting on civilian control over military operations in the Cuban Missile Crisis down to the most minute detail. [Later Sick notes: "presumably it was due to his disastrous experience at the Bay of Pigs that led President Kennedy to insist on civilian control of every detail during the Cuban Missile crisis."] Lyndon Johnson was similarly criticized for asserting Presidential control down to the unit level during operations in Vietnam. Jimmy Carter consciously attempted to avoid these extremes. (Sick, 1985)

Brzezinski's historical analogies may have contributed to Carter's conscious decision to give control of the operational plans for the rescue mission over to the military. This strategy may have hurt chances for the success of the mission because problems with the chain of command that might have emerged earlier with stricter civilian control didn't become salient until the execution of the mission itself. (This analogy is particularly ironic given that Carter requested a copy of Kennedy's speech following the Bay of Pigs debacle from Cody Powell after the failure of the rescue mission, in order to help him prepare his own speech for the public. See Jordan, 1982.)

A third important advisor to Carter during the hostage rescue mission, at least partly because of his emphasis on domestic political considerations, was Hamilton Jordan, the presidential advisor. His memoirs seem to be the most psychologically candid of the plethora of books written by Carter administration officials. For example, Jordan wrote of Brzezinski's comments, following the April 15 meeting during which Vance raised his objections, that "Cy is the ultimate example of a good man who has been traumatized by his Vietnam experience" (Jordan, 1982). This comment was obviously made in reference to Vance's service both as secretary of the army and deputy secretary of defense during the Vietnam war.

In fact, Jordan is quite open about his anger at Vance for not believing early that the rescue would succeed, and also for abandoning Carter in his time of greatest need after it had failed. His book seems less affected by hindsight, in this way, than the others.

Jordan tended to frame things in terms of its impact on the reelection campaign. He made arguments based on how particular actions would affect the president's domestic appeal and popularity. Jordan's perspective is interesting especially in light of Brzezinski's claims that domestic considerations were irrelevant to Carter during this time:

> Perhaps surprisingly, there was never any explicit discussion of the relationship between what we might do in Iran and domestic politics: neither the President nor his political advisor ever discussed with me the question of whether one or another of our Iranian options would have a better or worse domestic political effect. (Brzezinski, 1985)

This recollection lacks self-awareness in the way best exemplified by the story of the man who didn't like parties because he had never been to one where he wasn't in attendance. In other words, it is difficult for someone to discount sufficiently for the impact of his own presence on a situation. No one may have talked about domestic politics around Brzezinski perhaps because they knew he wasn't concerned about the subject. Nonetheless, it is clear from Jordan's memoirs that the reelection campaign was far from an insignificant concern during this period, particularly given Carter's pledge not to campaign on the road because of the crisis.

Jordan presents his own hopes concerning the rescue mission as follows:

> As I listened to General Pustay's presentation (on March 24, 1980), I began to be convinced that maybe it would work. After months of waiting and hoping, negotiating and failing, here was a way to go in and snatch our people up and have the whole damned thing over! Not to mention what it would do for the President and the nation. It would prove to the columnists and our political opponents that Carter was not an indecisive Chief Executive who had failed to act. It would bolster a world community that was increasingly skeptical about American power. A daring mission would right the great wrong done to our country and its citizens. (Jordan, 1982)

Jordan's sentiments are particularly notable for their emphasis on righting a wrong, or somehow trying to get back to normal, or restore the former status quo as the appropriate reference point. Once again, the goal of recouping all of the personal, national, and international losses in one great daring gamble emerges as highly appealing, from both a political as well as a psychological standpoint. This is exactly what prospect theory would predict in such a situation.

THE DECISION

The most important decision-maker, of course, was President Carter himself. Carter's memoirs, although containing diary entries, are not notable for their level of cognitive or emotional introspection. It is painfully evident throughout, however, that Carter was a man who deeply experienced the personal burden of his global responsibilities. He emerges as a sincerely moral, genuinely kind and caring man whose leadership abilities were seriously challenged by the enormity of the crises he faced. Given the complexity of the problem, and the diversity of opinions that Carter received, it is challenging to understand how he reached the decision that he made concerning the rescue mission.

A framing analysis allows an examination into how all the information and options were assimilated by President Carter. Carter faced a situation that clearly militated against the impact of a deleterious groupthink-type effect;[4] the president's mindset can be examined in light of the different frames that his advisors presented. His mindset is assumed to include his own perception of broader domestic and geopolitical considerations.

Prospect Theory would predict that, in the domain of losses, Carter would opt for a risky gamble that might return the situation to the former status quo.

---

[4]For more on the Groupthink effect, see Irving Janis (1982), who describes the phenomenon of groupthink as a "quick and easy way to refer to a mode of thinking that people engage in when they are deeply involved in a cohesive ingroup, when the members' strivings for unanimity override their motivation to realistically appraise alternative course of action" (p. 9). This clearly *didn't* happen in the Carter administration, as evidenced by the drastic differences in opinions espoused by Vance and Brzezinski, among others. The reasons for this are no doubt many but are certainly due in part to deeply held personal animosities between these participants, as well as the personal styles of some participants, such as Brzezinski, who did not shy away from confrontation.

Such a risky gamble is characterized by a situation where the probability of success is lower than that offered by other options, but the utility of the outcome is higher. If the rescue mission had been a success, Carter would have gained the release of the hostages, the respect of his allies and adversaries, and the votes of his constituency. In other words, he could have recouped all his losses, and made some gains as well. No other option available offered this possibility.

What is surprising, however, given the debate among his advisors, was Carter's confidence in the likelihood of the plan's success. Even after the mission failed, he insisted on its viability in the April 24-25 diary entry:

> The cancellation of our mission was caused by a strange series of mishaps—almost completely unpredictable. The operation itself was well planned. The men were well trained. We had every possibility of success, because no Iranian alarm was raised until two or three hours after our people left Iran. (Carter, 1982)

Carter's retrospective confidence is surprising because of the complexity and enormity of the task as well as the low estimates of success offered by the JCS and others prior to the mission. At this point, however, Carter's confidence is a central issue because it clearly helped to promote his decision to go ahead with the mission.

There are several possible reasons, both cognitive and motivational, for this confidence. From the cognitive point of view, it could have been a classic case of the conjunctive fallacy, which demonstrates that people think the probability of total success for an event that requires the combination of a number of smaller events is greater than the likelihood that any one of those events alone will succeed. This notion is psychologically appealing because people think the possibility of any one of a number of different things happening is greater than the chance of only one of those things occurring; they fail to realize that all the events in the cumulative sequence must occur for the larger event to succeed. In events requiring such a combination, complete success is only as likely as the least likely event. That is because if one link fails, the entire chain fails as well.

The conjunctive fallacy provides a compelling explanation for the overconfidence that led to the failure of the space shuttle Challenger in January of 1986, for example. In the Iranian situation, Carter may have thought that the number of contingency plans and back-up supplies ensured a higher probability of success than was realistic, especially given the sheer number of contingencies that had to succeed in order for the entire plan to work.

This type of confidence is also reminiscent of Jervis's argument that an irrational pursuit of consistency often leads to the avoidance of value trade-offs. As Jervis notes,

> [P]eople who favor a policy usually believe that it is supported by many logically independent reasons. When a person believes a policy contributes to one value, he is likely to believe that it also contributes to several other values, even though there is no reason why the world should be constructed in such a neat and helpful manner. This would not be irrational if in order to agree with a proposition a person had to affirm a number of

> necessary conditions. But often the person holds a number of beliefs, each of which would be sufficient to justify his policy preference. (Jervis, 1976)

This avoidance of value trade-offs characterized the positions of both Brzezinski and Vance as well as Carter in the case of the rescue mission in Iran. Vance believed the mission was likely to fail, would alienate European allies, inflame the Islamic world, result in more American hostages being taken, and throw the Iranians into the Soviet camp, although these views were not logically related. Brzezinski and Carter believed the mission would succeed, engender the gratitude, however subdued, of allied and Arab leaders, would not lead to Soviet infiltration of the area, and not harm other Americans in the region.

Other possible explanations for Carter's confidence are more motivational in nature. One might be simple wishful thinking. Carter may have believed that the mission would succeed because he wanted it to succeed. However, there is evidence to refute this view. Carter was aware of the military risks involved in attempting to rescue the hostages because Vance had objected to the mission precisely on the grounds of the high probability of failure and lost lives. Given Carter's awareness of the risks involved, it is difficult to sustain an argument that he believed it would succeed solely because he wanted it to work.

Another explanation for confidence in the plan after the decision was made may have had to do with justification. This is similar to the phenomenon that occurs in dissonance experiments, when the "spreading apart" of the alternatives makes the chosen option much more attractive than the rejected one, no matter how close in value they were evaluated prior to actual choice (Festinger, 1957; Festigner & Carlsmith, 1959; Wicklund & Brehm, 1976). In this way, dissonance reduction works to justify the superiority of the chosen option after the decision. This helps to reduce regret, even long after the decision has proved to be suboptimal.

Carter's belief perseverance in the likelihood of the mission's success, even after its failure, is also highly reminiscent of the findings of Festinger, Riecken, and Schacter (Festigner et al., 1956). They tell the story of a religious cult led by a woman who preached and prepared all her followers for the imminent end of the world. Proselytizing for the group took place only *after* the original predictions had failed to come true. Festinger, et al. suggested that such post-failure belief is generated to justify all the costs incurred in espousing the original belief system. Moreover, proselytizing provides consensual reality testing for such beliefs. It is plausible to argue that Carter was affectively motivated to believe in the likelihood of the mission's success, even after its failure, in order to justify the lives lost in its pursuit.

Carter's confidence in the probability of success is important because it flies in the face of the estimated risk, both in terms of lives and material lost, as well as estimates of the likelihood that the hostages would be released. This is important because it is precisely this confidence, which was greater than more objective estimates of the likelihood of success, that allowed Carter to decide to go ahead with a mission he knew to be risky. He understood the risk, but had confidence that it was worth taking because of the possibility of restoring the former status quo as reference point.

In making his decision, Carter attempted to assimilate and integrate the opinions that had been offered to him by his advisors. He may not have been aware, however, of the way in which this advice was skewed by the way in which their assessments of the operative domain differed from his own.

In terms of prospect theory, Vance did not see himself as being so obviously in the domain of losses. As is clear from his statements, he did not think that things would get drastically worse unless America took positive steps to prevent that happening. As his earlier quotes indicate, he believed that as long as the United States was patient and did not use force, things would resolve themselves in America's best interest over time. Moreover, Vance did not see the entire political situation as deteriorating in quite the same way as Brzezinski did. Thus, while Vance knew things were worse than they had been before the hostages were taken, he seemed to have accepted and indeed "renormalized" the hostage situation as a new status quo "reference point" in a way that Brzezinski, Jordan, and Carter did not. This may have been because he thought of things in terms of lives lost, and since no lives had been lost prior to the rescue mission, he saw the situation as still being relatively neutral. Thus he was not prepared to take risks, because he did not see himself as acting in the domain of losses.

Brzezinski perceived himself as confronting an entirely different situation. He clearly viewed himself and the country to be in the realm of serious losses. Again, this may be because he framed things in terms of threats to national prestige and honor, rather than in terms of lives lost. The United States was certainly in a worse situation according to these values than it had been before the hostages were taken. Thus, in a classic case of loss aversion, he did not assimilate his losses quickly or easily. Rather, Brzezinski was prepared to take great risks to return to the former status quo and to increase America's standing by bringing about the release of the hostages. He believed that the situation was bound to get significantly worse unless America took drastic action to prevent further deterioration right away. As a result, Brzezinski argued against Vance's predictions. Moreover, Brzezinski believed the mission would succeed, albeit with casualties:

> A very comprehensive review of the rescue plan by Brown, Jones, and myself in mid-March led me to the conclusions that the plan had a reasonably good chance of success, though there would probably be casualties . .
> [W]e could undertake the admittedly risky but increasingly feasible rescue mission . . . With the passage of time, we were all becoming more confident that possible kinks were being worked out of the rescue plan and that the probability of success was increasing. . . . (Brzezinski, 1982)

By and large, Carter agreed with Brzezinski and took issue with almost all of Vance's concerns. Indeed, in response to Vance's objections on April 15, Carter replied:

> I understand and am not unconcerned about their welfare. But my obligation is to those hostages, who represent me, you, and our country! . . .
> I disagree with your assessment of the reaction to the rescue mission. It if works, our friends all over the world will breathe a sigh of relief that it's over and that they won't have to impose further sanctions. The Moslem countries may make a few public statements for the sake of Islamic unity, but you know as well as I do that they despise and fear Khomeini and will be snickering at him behind his back. (Jordan, 1982)

Carter was also in the realm of losses, although not to the same extent as Brzezinski. Carter's primary concern was really the safety of the hostages, more than the international prestige of America. Indeed, Carter described this goal in a diary entry of November 10:

> We want it to be quick, incisive, surgical, no loss of American lives, not involve any other country, minimal suffering of the Iranian people themselves, to increase their reliance on imports, sure of success and unpredictable. (Carter, 1982)

Carter kept these as his basic goals throughout the crisis, and, in fact, the rescue mission came closer to meeting these specific goals than any of the other options. It is clear from his comments that Carter's explicit goal was to bring the hostages home, not to punish the Iranians. This is at least part of the reason why the rescue mission, even though more risky in terms of probability of success, was chosen over the other military options, such as mining the harbor or launching a punitive strike. In fact, Carter's threshold of risk on the earlier list of options *was* at the level of the rescue mission itself. He was a man who found the use of force repugnant. He felt pressure to do something to free the hostages. However, he could not bring himself to engage in an act of war such as mining the harbors, especially if it would do little to directly bring about the release of the hostages.

Thus, Carter made a decision on April 11, following the final collapse of negotiations on April 1, to proceed with a rescue mission he believed would succeed in releasing the hostages without alienating allies, inflaming the Islamic world, pushing Iran into the Soviet camp, or resulting in the taking of additional American hostages. In other words, he took a gamble he understood to be militarily risky in order to grab a chance at recouping previous losses and re-establishing the earlier status quo.

Riskiness of Chosen Option

The relative riskiness of undertaking the rescue mission is best evaluated relative to the other options considered at the time. These include the diplomatic and military options discussed above. By April, almost all political, economic and diplomatic sanctions possible had been unilaterally imposed on the Iranian government by the U.S. These included expelling Iranian diplomats and students from the U.S.; breaking diplomatic relations; imposing an embargo on all exported material, including weapons paid for by the shah but never delivered; freezing Iranian assets in the U.S.; and making financial transactions in Iran illegal in order to prevent U.S. citizens, including the press, from traveling there.

From the start, Carter believed that military options should only be pursued if there was an immediate threat to the hostages' lives, if, for example, the Iranians put them on trial and condemned them, as threatened, or if all negotiating channels failed. This failure of negotiations is in fact what occurred in April of 1980.

At that time, the rescue mission was the option that offered the greatest prospect of recouping all previous losses and returning to the status quo that existed before the hostages had been taken in November. It was understood that the political risks of undertaking a rescue mission were high, especially if it failed. However, as mentioned, Brzezinski and Carter felt that doing nothing was even more risky politically, especially given the widespread criticisms of presidential incompetence that were floating around the press at the time. Everyone believed that a successful mission could redeem all losses. However, the political risk of a failed mission was difficult to assess in advance. Unfortunately, the outcome of events proved just how politically risky a failed mission could be: Carter lost the election; the hostages were dispersed all over Iran and not released for another nine months; and America's international stature diminished even further.

From a military perspective, it is clear from the principals' memoirs that the rescue mission was understood to be the riskiest option that was seriously considered, both in terms of likelihood of success, as well as in terms of lives and material that could be lost.

The military itself knew of the high risks it was undertaking in planning the rescue mission. Indeed, the JCS report on the mission states explicitly that "the rescue mission was a high risk operation. People and equipment were called on to perform at the upper limits of human capacity and equipment capability" (U.S. Defense Dept., 1980). Indeed, Admiral Holloway judged the likelihood of success to have been about 60% to 70% (Ryan, 1985).

Hamilton Jordan tells a story about a query from the JCS's General Jones to Charles Beckwith, the man who eventually led the mission, at the outset of planning. Beckwith was asked the probability of success and the risks involved; he responded," 'Sir,' I said, 'the probability of success is zero and the risks are high.' " (Jordan, 1982).

However, as mentioned earlier, the confidence of the principals in the success of the rescue mission increased after the decision was made. Even after the mission failed, Secretary Brown rates the probability of success as high as 70%, arguing that the mission was well-planned (Jordan, 1982).

It is interesting to note, however, that the intelligence estimates of success may have been lower than understood by the military planners. Salinger describes an alleged CIA report given to Stansfield Turner on March 16 that evaluated the prospects for rescue mission success as follows:

> 6. The estimated percent of loss among the Amembassy hostages during each of the five major phases was:
>
> (a) Entry/Staging : 0%
> Assumes no loss of cover
>
> (b) Initial assault :20%
> Assumes . . . immediate loss of those under State FSR and FSS cover and others
>
> (c) Location/Identification :25%
> Loss of State personnel before full suppression of resistance Problem accentuated since Amembassy hostage not collocated
>
> (d) Evacuation to RH-53D's :15%
> Assumes loss from snipers, inside and outside Amembassy compound, and from AT and Apers mines.
>
> (e) Transfer-RH-53s to C-130s : 0%
> Assume maintenance of site security
>
> 7. The estimate of loss rate of 60% for the Amembassy hostages represents the best estimate of CA and M & P staff.
>
> 8. It is presumed to be equally likely that the Amembassy rescue attempt would be a complete success (100% of the Amembassy hostages rescued), as it would be a complete failure (0% of the Amembassy hostages rescued).
>
> 9. Of special note is the fact that no analogous large-scale rescue attempts have been mounted in heavily populated urban areas within hostile territory during the past 15 years. The only roughly similar attempts (Son Toy—Nov. 1970; Mayaguez—May 1975; Entebbe—July 1976) were all made in lightly populated rural areas of hostile territory (Salinger, 1981).

The story of this supposedly secret report was originally leaked to George Wilson at the *Washington Post* in August 1980 but was denied by Frank Carlucci, then deputy director of the CIA. According to Jody Powell, Carlucci's response to Wilson was as follows: "I have been unable to find anything in the alleged CIA document that is either accurate or which approximates any memorandum we prepared." Wilson refused to print the story, but a similar one was published by Jack Anderson several months later (Powell, 1984).

However, a *Time* report the week after the rescue mission stated that

> Pentagon officials have adamantly denied reports in Washington of a CIA estimate that 60% of the 53 hostages would probably have been killed in the rescue attempt. But *Time* has learned that initial casualty estimates once ran as high as 200 fatalities, including both hostages and rescuers. The final plan did, indeed, envision the possibility of losing from 15 to 20 hostages. (*Time*, May 12, 1980)

Whether or not the CIA document was a forgery, the question of historical analogy is again highlighted, albeit in a slightly different context. The fact of the matter is that rescue raids have a high historical (base rate) failure rate; the Iran rescue mission may offer an almost classical example of the representativeness heuristic in foreign policy, where base rates were underestimated in light of a salient successful case. In this instance that notable case was Entebbe, a rescue raid which was successful, although it took place in quite a different terrain.

In the case of American rescue attempts, the historical track record is dismal at best. The Son Toy raid on a Vietnamese prisoner-of-war camp, which included soldiers who later participated in the Iran mission, failed because the prisoners had been moved to another location prior to the arrival of the rescue team. The raid on the Palestinians who took nine Israeli athletes hostages during the 1972 Munich Olympics resulted in the deaths of all the hostages and five of the right-wing terrorists. The 39 hostages in the Mayaguez incident were indeed freed, but it appears that their release was underway *prior* to the rescue mission.[5] Even so, that mission cost the lives of 41 American soldiers, and wounded another 50. Another relatively similar case, that of the Hammelburg raid to release prisoners of war in Germany during World War II was only partly successful as well because fighting with German forces subsequent to the raid was heavy.

In fact, Entebbe and Mogadishu stand as relative anomalies in the history of these kinds of missions, both for their success and their lack of casualties: three hostages and one Israeli officer were killed at Entebbe; and three terrorists were killed by the West Germans in Somalia. The key to both these successful raids was total surprise combined with a relatively isolated area of attack. In spite of the critical geographical differences, Entebbe was the operative analogy for most of the principals involved in the Iranian rescue mission (Christopher et al., 1953; *Time,* May 5, 1980; Ryan, 1985).

THE IRANIAN RESCUE MISSION

The actual outcome of the decision to rescue the hostages in Iran highlights the reality of the huge military risk that was involved in the undertaking. Indeed, the overwhelming complexity of the plan is a critical part of any assessment of the risk involved in the decision to undertake the rescue mission.

The rescue attempt, codenamed Operation Eagle Claw (the planning phase was called Rice Bowl), was a highly complex undertaking (Ryan, 1985; U.S. Defense Dept., 1980). The plan was for eight RH-53D helicopters to be launched off the aircraft carrier Nimitz from the Arabian sea and fly 600 miles to a landing field designated as Desert One, near a town called Tabas. These helicopters had to fly under total radio silence at a low altitude to avoid Iranian radar detection, using only visual navigation, and very limited inertial guidance. At the designated site, the helicopters were to meet with six C-130 transport planes that were

---

[5] I am grateful to Robert Jervis for clarification on the specifics of this mission.

to fly in from Masirah Island, off the coast of Oman. Three C-130s carried the assault force of about 120 men; the other three carried fuel for the helicopters.

After meeting, the C-130s were to refuel the helicopters, transfer the special operations men to them, and return to base. The helicopters were then to fly on to another location in the hills about 100 miles southeast of Tehran, called Desert Two, where the men were going to hide out during the day until the surprise attack on the embassy, which was planned for the following night. Local sympathizers had arranged ground transportation to the embassy. After the ground attack on the embassy, the helicopters were going to pick up the soldiers and the hostages at a stadium across the street from the embassy compound, fly them to a nearby abandoned airfield, at Manzariyeh, and fly them out of the country on C-141s that were to meet them there. Each phase was timed to coincide.

Every stage of the plan was acknowledged to be risky, both in terms of the probability of success, as well as the likelihood of lives and material lost. The initial phase of inserting the aircraft into the country without detection was considered by members of the rescue team to be the most difficult aspect of the plan (Jordan, 1982). The advanced stages of the plan never came to fruition because the mission was aborted at Desert One because there were too few helicopters to carry out the rest of the mission. Planners judged that the mission required a minimum of six helicopters in order to complete the task; eight helicopters were considered by all to be sufficiently redundant for the success of the mission. However, this number proved to be inadequate and the mission was aborted because only five operational helicopters reached Desert One.

Following the decision to abort the mission, the accident that resulted in the American casualties occurred. A helicopter was refueling for the return flight, kicked up a blinding amount of sand, and accidentally flew into the nose of a C-130 and instantly exploded. Eight men were killed, four were badly burned, and the rest were quickly evacuated, leaving six helicopters, three with sensitive classified material, on the ground for the Iranians to find. The Iranian police later bombed these helicopters and took pictures of them for propaganda purposes. Evidence suggests, however, that the Iranians were not aware of the attempted mission, or of its failure, until informed of it by the Carter administration at 1 a.m. Washington time on April 26 (Carter, 1982).

CONCLUSIONS

The failure of the rescue mission in Iran in April of 1980 was a tragedy whose failure weighed heavily on the principle decision-makers involved in its planning and execution. While Carter may not have believed that the costs associated with the mission were high, he was wrong objectively. The failure of the rescue mission did make things worse for him. From a political standpoint, the failure cost Carter valuable political capital. He was criticized in the press for inadequate planning, as well as for not making a stronger military move from the start. Moreover, the failure of the mission made any subsequent attempt more difficult. In short, Carter's plan failed to release the hostages and reaffirmed his growing domestic image of impotence. From a more personal perspective, the death of the eight American soldiers was particularly difficult for President Carter. In a statement issued on April 26, President Carter accepted full responsibility for the episode:

> Our rescue team knew, and I knew, that the operation was certain to be dangerous. We were all convinced that if and when the rescue phase of the operation had been commenced, it had an excellent chance of success. They were all volunteers; they were all highly trained. . . . (Carter and Trimble, 1989)

The decision to undertake the rescue mission in Iran was made during a time of extreme difficulty for the Carter administration. Indeed, there is no question that it took place during a domain of loss for the administration in general and for Carter in particular. This was true on both a domestic and on an international level. The taking of the hostages was a severe blow to American power, prestige, and credibility on the international scene. The lack of allied and U.N. support for sanctions was considered an insult. Moreover, Carter was facing an increasingly arduous reelection campaign at home. In a classic example of operating in the domain of losses, it seemed that he had little to lose in launching the rescue mission and everything to gain should it succeed. In fact, had the mission succeeded, history might look quite different because it is easily conceivable that Carter could have won reelection on the crest of popularity that would certainly have followed such a courageous rescue, successfully completed.

The choice of the rescue mission was indeed the riskiest military option seriously considered. This is true both in terms of likelihood of success as well as in terms of personnel and material costs. Other military options were uniequivocally rejected by Carter because they offered little probability of success for releasing the hostages and involved overt acts of war. Nevertheless, Carter felt that he had to do something to return the hostages home.

Ex post facto, an analyst can see that the best option had been offered by Secretary Vance. The hostages were released essentially unharmed by the Iranians when they no longer served any function. Once the revolutionary government was secure, the hostages were allowed to leave, although there may have been some other factors involved in releasing them only a few minutes after Carter was no longer officially the president. However, Carter was clearly unaware of these other factors. In some sense, Carter received the "right" advice—to do nothing—from Vance; he chose to ignore it, however, and take the more risky military option. Even if he didn't think of the rescue mission as risky, he knew that objectively it was *more* risky than other options that were available to him. He knew the mission carried greater potential costs than the other options; it also promised greater benefits. In this sense, he took the gamble in an attempt to win the prize.

Throughout the crisis, it was difficult for any of the participants to assess the balance of political and military risks. This was especially the case because national and international political risks were often as inversely related as were political and military risks. Nonetheless, it is clear that Carter made a risk-seeking choice. He had other choices that were both militarily less risky, like mining the harbors, or politically less risky, like seeking additional indirect diplomatic negotiating channels. However, he took the one gamble that offered a chance of recouping all the losses he had previously sustained to regain the former status quo. Had he succeeded, the payoff would certainly have been great. However, the probability of success was low, and the mission failed. While other options, such as negotiating, may not have offered the same potential payoff, they proved more likely, and more profitable, in the end.

This finding is perfectly consistent with, and even predictable, based on prospect theory. Moreover, prospect theory provides insight which makes little sense from a structural perspective. Indeed, no other theory would predict such risky behavior in a bad situation. Contrary to his inclinations against the use of force, Carter ordered a military mission to rescue the hostages. He saw himself confronting a bad situation and took a seemingly irrational gamble in order to recoup his losses and regain the previous status quo. Thus the failed rescue of the hostages in Iran provides a superb illustration of the operation of prospect theory in the international realm.

REFERENCES

Brzezinski, Zbigniew (1982). The failed rescue mission. *New York Times Magazine,* April 18, p. 28–42.
Brzezinski, Zbigniew (1985) *Power and principle.* New York: Farrar, Strauss, and Giroux.
Brzezinski, Zbigniew (1990). Personal communication.
Carter, Jimmy (1982). *Keeping faith.* New York: Bantam.
Carter, Barry E. & Trimble P. (1989). *International law casebook,* forthcoming.
Christopher, Warren et al. (1985). *American hostages in Iran.* New Haven, CT: Yale University Press.
Festinger, L., Riecken, H. W., & Schachter, S. (1956). *When prophecy fails.* Minneapolis, MN: University of Minnesota Press.
Festinger, Leon (1957). *A theory of cognitive dissonance.* Stanford, CA: Stanford University Press.
Festinger, Leon & Carlsmith, M. (1959). Cognitive consequences on forced compliance. *Journal of Abnormal and Social Psychology,* 58, 203–211.
Janis, Irving (1982). *Groupthink.* Boston: Houghton Mifflin Company.
Jervis, Robert (1976). *Perception and misperception in international politics.* Princeton, NJ: Princeton University Press.
Jordan, Hamilton (1982). *Crisis.* New York: Putnam.
Kahneman, Daniel & Tversky, A. (1984). Values, choices and frames. *American Psychologist,* April.
New York Times, June 25, 1979, p. 1.

Ornstein, Norman et. al. (1984–5), *Vital statistics on Congress, 194–5*. Washington, American Enterprise Institute for Public Policy Research 84.
Powell, Jody (1984). *The other side of the story*. New York: William Morrow and Company, Inc.
Ryan, Paul (1985). *The Iranian rescue mission*. Annapolis, MD: Naval Institute Press.
Salinger, Pierre (1981). *American held hostage*. Garden City, New York: Doubleday and Company.
Saunders, Harold (1985). Beginning of the end. In Warren Christopher et al., *American hostages in Iran*. New Haven, Ct: Yale University Press.
Sick, Gary (1985). Military options and constraints. In Warren Christopher et al., *American hostages in Iran*. New Haven, Ct: Yale University Press.
Sick, Gary (1986). *All fall down*. New York: Penguin Books.
Sick, Gary, Personal communication by phone, July 1990.
Sick, Gary (1991). The election story of the decade. *New York Times*, April 15.
Time, April 14, 1980.
Time, May 5, 1980.
Time, May 12, 1980.
U.S. Defense Department. (1980). The rescue mission report, August. Typescript.
Vance, Cyrus (1983). *Hard choices*. New York: Simon and Schuster.
Wicklund & Brehm, J. *Perspective on cognitive dissonance*. Hillsdale, NJ: Erlbaum.

Prospect Theory and Soviet Policy Towards Syria, 1966–1967

Audrey McInerney[1]

INTRODUCTION

The Six Day War in June 1967 struck a devastating blow to the Soviet Union's Arab clients and risked a U.S.-Soviet confrontation. It was a war the Soviets did not want and had sought to avoid. But, in fact, Soviet rhetoric and behavior just prior to the June War was inflammatory and reckless in such a way that they helped provoke an Arab-Israeli confrontation. In the months prior to the war, the Soviets became more willing to accept the risk of war in order to defend the existence of the neo-Baath regime in Syria. This paper argues that prospect theory provides a plausible explanation as to why the Soviet leadership took a foreign policy risk to defend the Syrian regime from an Israeli attack.

Evidence suggests that during the period of intense East-West rivalry Soviet leaders behaved in a manner similar to Tversky and Kahneman's subjects when faced with similar situations. This perspective is interesting because it differs from standard expected utility explanations and those based on unique Soviet experiences or ideological biases. For example, Nathan Leites's operational code of the Bolsheviks, based on a psychological analysis of Soviet leaders, suggests

[1]Columbia University, New York, New York 10027.

they "know when to retreat" and accept small setbacks knowing that they will bounce back when conditions are ripe. The failure to retreat in the face of overwhelming odds is, according to the operational code, considered adventurism (Leites, 1953; George, 1969). Hannes Adomeit (1982) has also drawn on Soviet ideology and the operational code to explain Soviet risk-taking. Prospect theory, on the other hand, suggests that the Soviets would be less willing to retreat if it meant accepting a loss to the status quo.

Common cognitive processes, such as those identified by prospect theory, can better explain instances of Soviet risk-taking. The Soviet leadership has reacted to foreign policy dilemmas in much the same way as other states' leaders, even though defining the status quo involves the interaction of cognitive processes with uniquely Soviet characteristics involving ideological concerns and political culture.

The most interesting question this argument raises is how the Soviets decided whether they were faced with potential gain or potential loss. This, in turn, raises the question of how the Soviet leadership has defined the status quo, the standard against which gain and loss must necessarily be measured.

STARTING A WAR TO DEFEND THE STATUS QUO?: THE SOVIET UNION AND SYRIA

In April and May of 1967, the Soviets circulated what is generally agreed to be incorrect information about Israeli troop concentrations on the Syrian border. According to the Soviets, Israel's purpose was an imminent assault on Syria with a view to overthrowing the incumbent neo-Baath regime. In April and early May the Soviets privately conveyed false information about Israeli troop concentrations to Egyptian leaders. In May the Soviets began publishing their accusations in the press. The purpose in making these statements about Israel was to cement the defensive unity of Egypt and Syria and to encourage Nasser to more vigorously support Syria in general and to move against Israel in particular.

To the Soviets, an Israeli attack must have appeared plausible in view of events in the region. Israel was seen as an agent of U.S. imperialism and hostile to the Soviet presence in the region. Additionally, in 1966 and 1967 there was a significant increase in U.S. economic and military aid to Israel (Neff, 1984), making Israel more capable of fighting the Soviet Union's Arab clients. Finally, the Soviets may have seen the April 1967 military coup in Greece as part of a larger imperialist design (Samoilov, 1967; Bragin, 1967). The Soviets could easily believe Israel was a U.S. tool in instigating a coup in Syria that would bring to power a pro-Western regime.

In the immediate Middle East scenario, there had been several recent armed conflicts between Israel and Syria, including a dramatic air battle on April 7 in which six Syrian MiGs were shot down and which demonstrated that Syria could not fight Israel on its own. As the conflict between Israel and Syria rapidly escalated, bellicose statements emanated from the Israeli government, including threats to overthrow the Damascus regime if terrorist activities directed toward Israel did not cease. In view of the above, if the Soviets did not fully believe their claims about Israeli troop concentrations, they did appear to have good reasons to make them.

The effect of the Soviet warnings was that Nasser was handed the opportunity to take action against Israel by focusing on the need to defend his Arab ally, Syria. Nasser, sensitive to criticism that he had not aided Syria on April 7 or Jordan when attacked the previous November, and concerned for his slipping prestige in the Arab world, decided to use the information provided by the Soviets to demand the withdrawal of United Nations forces from the Sinai and subsequently to occupy Sharm el-Sheik and close the Tiran Straits to Israeli shipping. The Israelis had previously made it known that they considered closure of the straits a *casus belli* (Golan, 1990; Stein and Tanter, 1980) and the United States had publicly guaranteed free shipping in the Gulf of Aqaba (Johnson, 1971). Thus, the Soviets knew that Nasser's actions created a real possibility of war, one that, in fact, materialized. Evidently, this was not what the Soviets wanted (Heikal, 1978). During the course of Nasser's actions in the Sinai, the Soviet leaders sent him several messages requesting that he exercise caution and not antagonize Israel. The Soviets belatedly became concerned about the risk of a Middle East war, which, of course, brought with it potential confrontation between the United States and the Soviet Union. Perhaps of even greater concern to the Soviets—because they knew it more likely—was that war could topple the Syrian regime. This was the very outcome the Soviets had sought to prevent with their earlier warnings.

Immediately upon the outbreak of hostilities, the Soviets began working toward a ceasefire, cooperating with the United States and the U.N. Security Council. The only instance of Soviet militancy came on June 10 when Kosygin threatened via the hotline to intervene unilaterally and militarily in the war if Israel did not stop its advance into Syria and toward Damascus (Johnson, 1971). When the ceasefire did go into effect, the Soviet Union returned to a more cooperative stance on resolving the issues, one that its Arab allies believed to be too favorable to Israel. It seems clear that at least some of the Soviet leadership could see no benefit in an Arab-Israeli war and were fearful of one starting once Nasser moved his troops into the Sinai. Yet Soviet decision-makers had been willing to engage in the reckless tactic of originating and spreading the story of an imminent Israeli attack on Syria.

THE PUZZLE

Why did the Soviet leadership choose to risk war in the Middle East? The standard explanation is that the Soviets sought to enhance their prestige in the region, and particularly to decrease Western influence. The way to do so was via an anti-Western anti-imperialist coalition of Arab regimes. To that end, Soviet policy emphasized Arab unity among "socially progressive" regimes like that of the Baath Party in Syria. Jon Glassman writes:

> . . . in the weeks before the Six-Day War Soviet diplomacy played a dangerous game that had backfired. The Soviets had apparently wished to fortify Syria's "progressive" regime and the Arab "anti-imperialist" front by stirring the Arabs into a common stand against the military threat supposedly posed by Israel. The retreat of Israel in the face of Soviet-inspired Arab unity, and particularly in the face of the Soviet-supplied Egyptian army, Moscow apparently thought would surely improve the prestige and political position of the Soviet Union in the Middle East. (Glassman, 1975, p. 43)

The question then becomes: why did the Soviets need to engage in such reckless behavior to promote its goal of Arab unity and, in particular, to prop up the Syrian regime? Writing about the June War, former President Johnson noted "the Soviet Union was extremely sensitive about Syria, which it appeared to regard as a rather special protege" (Johnson, 1971, p. 301).

Why was this particular Syrian government a "special protege" to the Soviets? The Soviet Union had had good relations with Syria since the late 1950s and with the moderate wing of the Baath Party until February 1966 when the neo-Baaths took power in a bloody coup. While there was much instability in Syria under the moderate Baaths (eight coups between 1961 and 1966), "the Soviets remained uninvolved in these domestic upheavals" (Golan, 1990, p. 141). The main Soviet concern had always been Arab unity in the face of Western intrusion and both moderate and radical Baaths supported unity as part of their ideology. The moderate Baaths were socialist in orientation and "progressive" enough to be acceptable to the Soviets. And while the neo-Baaths proclaimed a transformation of Syria based on "scientific socialism," they were more extreme and doctrinaire than the Soviets themselves and quickly developed a reputation for ruthless repression of opposition. Thus, on the surface, there should have been nothing particularly appealing to the Soviets about the post-February 1966 Syrian regime. Additionally, while Syrian-Egyptian relations had deteriorated with the breakup of their union in 1961, by the end of 1966 Egypt and Syria had repaired their relationship, going so far as to sign a mutual defense pact in November of that year. To the Soviets, Arab unity should have been progressing nicely.

SOVIET-SYRIAN RELATIONS, 1966–67

From the outset, the neo-Baath regime made clear its left-wing orientation. Immediately after the coup the party press published accusations that the former premier, Salah el-Bitar, had been contemplating the denationalization of industry and showed "secret sympathy" for "American imperialist aggression" (Brady, 1966d). The neo-Baath newspaper, *Al Baath*, also announced that, in order to deepen the socialist experience, it was making the army an ideological instrument for the transition to socialism. This gesture made it easier for the Soviet leadership to deal with a military regime, usually considered a reactionary force.

In April Syrian Prime Minister Yusuf Zayen traveled to the Soviet Union and secured development assistance that included $150 million to build a hydroelectric station on the Euphrates River. By this time the Soviet Union was "showering praise on the new Syrian leaders," and *Pravda* noted with approval that Zayen was accompanied to the Soviet Union by representatives of "patriotic forces of Syria," meaning communists and other leftists (*New York Times*, 1966d). *Izvestia* wrote in early May 1966 that "the new government of Syria is firmly and confidently setting its course on a noncapitalist path of development, leading to socialism" (Ivanov, 1966b). Kosygin traveled to Egypt and encouraged the Egyptians to show support for the left-wing Baaths in Syria, who had, incidentally, called for Arab unity under socialism, but free of domination by Nasser (Brady, 1966b).

With increasingly warm relations between the Soviet Union and Syria and increasingly hostile relations between Israel and Syria came numerous Soviet references to the dangers faced by the fledgling Syrian regime. Soon after the coup, in early May 1966, Syrian Foreign Minister Ibrahim Makhous announced that there were suspicious concentrations of Israeli troops on Syria's borders and expressed concern about a possible assault (*New York Times*, 1966a and b). During that month the Soviet press repeated these accusations (*Pravda* and *Izvestia*, May 28, 1966). *Izvestia* indicated that Israel's intention was to overthrow the regime (*New York Times*, 1966b). Although the Soviet press spread the alarm, they were careful to indicate the information was from other "reports." There is no evidence of any private, and thus more authoritative, accusations made before April 1967. Aside from declaring that the U.S.S.R. could not remain indifferent to attempts to disturb the peace, this was the extent of Soviet action on the Israeli-Syrian conflict.

The Soviet press did not become active again on the issue of Syria's defense until the fall of 1966 when there emerged serious internal threats to the Syrian regime. Political instability was generated by tensions among the ruling elites and between them and the population. On September 6 there was an attempted military coup led by Colonel Salim Hatoum who had supported the neo-Baath coup in February but had been denied a share in power by Major General Salah Jadid (vice-president and de facto head of the Baath Regional Command and the real strong man of the regime). The coup failed in part because air support promised by Defense Minister Hafiz el-Asad never materialized.

Following the coup attempt, a smoldering conflict between Jadid and Asad came increasingly into the open. Between September 6 and October 22, 1966, the neo-Baaths called for volunteers for a national guard to protect the regime. "Opposition to the regime increased instead, in part because a number of people suspected of loyalty to the previous regime were arrested by workers' armed platoons. Religious leaders also stepped up their campaign against the neo-Baath at this point because of the regime's collaboration with the Communist Party" (Bar-Siman-Tov, 1983). Indeed, "armed workers" of the General Federation of Labor under Khalid al-Jundi (cousin of Cabinet Minister Abd al-Karim al-Jundi) took to the streets, summarily arresting people and holding trials on the spot (Bar-Siman-Tov, 1983). The federation issued a communique stating that workers should stay alert "to purge state administrations, business and industrial organizations of the public sector of all reactionary and conspiratorial elements hostile to the revolution and its socialist experience" (Brady, 1966a).

Interestingly, *Isvestia* gently criticized the Syrian regime in early September, indicating that the coup attempt was a response to overzealous expropriations:

> Some instances of "putting the cart before the horse" occurred in the Syrian Arab Republic when certain small enterprises were hastily nationalized. Reaction immediately magnified these mistakes and took advantage of them. The present government is definitely an advocate of the principle of the safeguarding of the interests of the petty and middle entrepreneurs. (Tuganova, 1966)

In September 1966 the main danger to the Syrian regime appeared to be from domestic infighting, as the frontier between Israel and Syria was relatively quiet for the time being. Hardline Deputy Soviet Foreign Minister Vladimir Semyonov said in Damascus on September 29 that "the Soviet Union's attitude towards external dangers confronting Syria is clear and very firm, we are on Syria's side. We have warned the imperialist aggressor that the Soviet Union is close to the region. The warnings of the Soviet Union are well-known and I repeat them today." Semyonov was probably referring, at least in part, to Colonel Hatoum and other Syrian officers who failed in the coup attempt and were in exile in Jordan announcing their intention to try again.

In addition to political instability within Syria, tensions between Israel and Syria did increase dramatically in the autumn of 1966. During October there were a number of cross-border clashes. Several Israeli civilians and military personnel were killed and wounded by Al Fatah landmines, bombs, and ambushes. On October 12 *Al Baath*, the Syrian government newspaper, announced that Syria was ready to counter any aggression from Israel or elsewhere and that "the 'People's Army,' a newly formed workers' and peasants' militia, was mobilized on October 19 to 'protect the revolution against its enemies at home and abroad' " (*Keesings*, Vol. 16, p. 21817). As a result of the increasing clashes, on November 13 the Israeli army engaged in one of its biggest reprisal raids in Jordan.

Concerned about the instability in Syria, the Soviet press on October 3 presented a preview of its tocsins of the following spring. The danger of an Israeli attack was a good issue on which to focus since the eradication of Israel appeared to be the only issue the various factions in the Syrian government could agree on and the government's only source of support among the Syrian population at large. Again, unlike later accusations, the Soviets were merely repeating what had been heard elsewhere:

> The foreign press reports that troops are being concentrated on the Israeli side of the [Syrian] border, air force maneuvers are being held, and large numbers of paratroopers equipped with light field guns and large-caliber mortars are being moved there. A partial mobilization of reservists is underway in Israel. . . . Apparently no longer content with provoking border incidents, the reactionary militarist circles of Israel are hatching plans for an armed invasion deep into Syrian territory with the aim of overthrowing the present government of that country. (Petrov, 1966)

Pravda pointed out that Rabin, Israel's chief of staff, said in an interview with the Israeli military magazine *Bamahane* that Israeli armed forces "are directed at the present political regime in Syria." *Pravda* also claimed to be repeating what has been written in the Lebanese newspaper *Al Muharir* (Petrov, 1966).

The Soviets also heard warnings from the Syrians themselves in this period. For example, in response to an Israeli complaint to the United Nations Security Council, George Tomeh, head of Syria's delegation to the U.N., sent a note to the Security Council on October 3 which "said the Israeli accusations were being used as a pretext for a possible Israeli attack on Syria" (Kosut, 1968, p. 24).

Unlike the situation in the following May, the Soviet leaders apparently did not make any behind-the-scenes statements or exhortations about the threat to the Syrians, except to urge Egypt to draw closer to Syria in defense against Israel (Neff, 1984). For its part, the Soviet Union indicated it was doing nothing but "vigilantly following the development of the situation in the Near and Middle East . . ." (Petrov, 1966). Once more, in early November, the Soviet press accused Israel of preparing to attack Syria and warned that the Soviet Union was "carefully observing" events there (Ivanov, 1966b). This caveat coincides with the signing of the mutual defense pact between Syria and Egypt on November 3, 1966 and the restoration of diplomatic relations, severed in 1961 (Kosut, 1968).

In January 1967 there was a rise in Syrian complaints about Israel. Six notes were sent to the U.N. Security Council warning of an imminent Israeli attack, and announcements were broadcast about Israeli troop concentrations on the border. In early January, just prior to a visit from Jadid, the Soviet press sought to justify the role of the Syrian army in politics, arguing that the army was truly revolutionary and was leading the country onto the "path of social progress in the interests of the broad working masses" (Iskenderov, 1967). The next day *Pravda* printed another accusation about Israel's intentions: "Evidently those who are artificially creating an uneasy atmosphere on the Israeli-Syrian border want to intimidate Syria and to topple the progressive regime that exists there" (Belyayev, 1967).

On Jadid's visit, *Pravda* reported "an exchange of opinions" regarding "the activities of the two parties and the further development of relations between them" (*Pravda*, February 12, 1967). These phrases indicated disagreement between Jadid and his benefactors over their relationship. Nevertheless, on Jadid's return there were reports in the pro-Cairo newspaper, *Al Anwar*, that opposition to Jadid was brewing because he was allying Syria with Moscow against Peking. At least some of Syria's leadership felt that maintaining impartiality over the Sino-Soviet split was in Syria's best interests (Brady, 1967a).

During the spring of 1967, things became progressively more difficult for the Syrian regime. First, popular "resistance to the neo-Baath increased during February and March with the distribution of an anti-government manifesto and a number of bomb-throwing incidents in Damascus, Aleppo and Hama. The regime reacted with a series of arrests aimed at curbing further outbreaks of anti-government violence" (Bar-Siman-Tov, 1983, p. 156). Jadid and Asad apparently set aside their differences to deal with the conflict between rulers and ruled and the conflict with Israel, both of which were intensifying (Bar-Siman-Tov, 1983). In early February Israeli government officials were openly speaking of "an armed thrust [into Syria] in relatively large force" (Neff, 1984, p. 56). Syria's President Atassi responded on February 22 by declaring that "it is the duty of all of us now to move from defensive positions to offensive positions and enter the battle to liberate the usurped land" (Neff, 1984, p. 56).

Indeed, Syrian-Israeli clashes intensified in this period and in April 1967 the conflict between Israel and Syria took a serious turn for the worse. On April 7 the Israeli and Syrian air forces engaged in an air battle in which six Syrian planes were shot down. The Soviets did not respond to the incident until April 21, and when they finally did, their words were nonspecific and the reaction rather mild. The Israeli ambassador to the Soviet Union was called to the foreign ministry and told that Israel was "playing with fire," that its policy was "fraught with dangers" and that Israel would bear "full responsibility for the consequences of its actions" (Glassman, 1975, pp. 38–39). Shelepin's hardline pro-Arab ally, First Secretary of the Moscow Party Committee Nikolai Yegorychev, was in Cairo on April 20. Michel Tatu (1970) speculated that his talks with Egyptian leaders prompted the Soviet protest to Israel and press comment on the following day.

On April 25 the Israeli ambassador was again summoned to the foreign ministry and given a note asserting "the Soviet government is in possession of information about Israeli troop concentrations on the Israeli-Arab borders at the present time. These concentrations are assuming a dangerous character, coinciding as they do with the hostile campaign in Israel against Syria" (Glassman, 1975, p. 39). When the Syrians complained to the Soviet military about the extended silence, the military reportedly told the Syrians that they agreed with Syria's policy toward Israel but the civilian leadership did not (Glassman, 1975; Laqueur, 1968). This is consistent with other evidence about Soviet Defense Minister Grechko's attitude toward supporting the Arabs more vigorously in their conflict with Israel and, by extension, the United States.

Finally, the April 27 issue of *Pravda* published an account of the April 21 protest note delivered to the Israeli ambassador but did not mention Israeli troop formations near Syria's border (Glassman, 1975). However, it is at this time that the Soviet leadership began to exacerbate the situation in the Middle East. At the end of April the Soviets reportedly conveyed to the Egyptians an Israeli general staff document. They argued it showed the Israelis definitely planned an attack on Syria. According to Nadav Safran (1969), the document was probably a contingency plan for such an attack. At the same time, popular riots against the Syrian government were taking place, adding another source of instability.

From April 27 to May 16, 1967 Anwar Sadat, in his capacity as president of Egypt's national assembly, visited the Soviet Union. On the 29th Kosygin told Sadat in a private conversation that Israel had massed two brigades on the Syrian border (Heikal, 1973). On the same day, the Soviet Foreign Ministry called the Israeli ambassador to its offices to protest the alleged presence of the troops (Dawisha, 1979; Glassman, 1975). On May 11 both Soviet President Podgorny and Deputy Foreign Minister Semyonov told Sadat that Israeli forces were at the Syrian border and that an attack was planned for some time between May 18 and May 22 (Golan, 1990; Gelman, 1984, Heikal, 1978, and Safran, 1969). Sadat telegraphed this information back to Nasser. According to Mohammed Heikal (1978), the Syrians had already passed similar information to the Egyptians.

In May the Soviet press began publishing their reports of Israeli troop concentrations. On May 18, the day U.N. Emergency Forces (UNEF) left the Sinai at Egypt's request, *Izvestia* wrote that "the Arab countries are seriously disturbed by reports coming in to the effect that Israel is making intensive preparations for an armed attack on Syria." Israel, according to *Izvestia*, was working at the behest of British and American imperialists who "are interested in the overthrow of the present government in Syria" (Tuma, 1967).

In early May more political troubles developed for the Syrian regime. Bar-Siman-Tov writes that "the internal conflict that developed in Syria between 5–15 May 1967 was the most serious in the history of the neo-Baath regime" (Bar-Siman-Tov, 1983, p. 156). On May 6 a merchants' strike began in Syria to protest the arrest of a Moslem religious leader who had criticized the regime as godless. (The accusation was based on an article, "The New Arab Man," attacking belief in God and published in the army newspaper [Bar-Siman-Tov, 1983; Laqueur, 1968]). Khalid al-Jundi announced that his armed workers battalion would open the shops by force. He argued that there should be no neutralism between socialism and capitalism in the world struggle and that Syria should be completely wedded to the socialist camp (Brady, 1967b). Meanwhile, the Syrian government announced that all businesses would be nationalized, with the exception of construction and retail trade (Pace, 1967). The regime also conducted a wave of arrests throughout Syria which culminated on May 15 in a violent clash at an Aleppo mosque followed by the arrest of 300 people (Bar-Siman-Tov, 1983).

On May 14 Nasser sent his chief of staff, General Mohammed Fawzi, to Syria to verify claims of the Israeli troop buildup, but Fawzi could not do so (Golan, 1990; Safran, 1969). Nevertheless, on May 16 Nasser asked that UNEF forces be removed from the Sinai Peninsula. During this time, Israel invited the Soviet ambassador in Israel to the Syrian border to point out the alleged troop concentrations, an offer he refused three times (Yost, 1968; Golan, 1990). Additionally, Egypt asked the Soviet ambassador in Cairo for information from Soviet satellites on the disposition and strength of Israeli forces on the Syrian border. The ambassador replied that the U.S.S.R. could not determine whether Israeli concentrations were a deliberate provocation or a precautionary measure to guard against an attempt by Syria to take advantage of Israel's National Day (May 15) to launch an attack (Heikal, 1978).

On May 18, 1967, General Secretary U Thant agreed to remove all UNEF forces from the Sinai, Israel mobilized, and interestingly, the KGB chief, Vladimir Semichastny, was fired (Laqueur, 1968). (It is possible that Semichastny lost his job in part because his intelligence information provoked an unwanted crisis in the Middle East.) It is at this point that the Soviets started to back away from their encouragement of Egyptian and Arab militancy. For example, on May 24 while the Egyptian minister of war, Badran, was visiting Moscow, Kosygin told him that the Egyptians had made their point and achieved their objectives (i.e., the thinning out of Israeli troops on the Syrian frontier, the withdrawal of U.N. troops from the Sinai, and Egyptian control of the Gulf of Aqaba). He said that the Soviet Union would back Egypt, but now was the time for compromise, to work politically and not to provoke Israel into an armed conflict (Heikal, 1973 and 1978).

Kosygin's intention was to defuse the situation in the Middle East. But, according to Heikal, Badran conveyed to Nasser Kosygin's expression of support without stressing that Kosygin meant support for political rather than military objectives (Heikal, 1973). Badran's impression was reinforced by a conversation he had at the Moscow airport with Defense Minister Marshal Grechko in which Grechko said, "stand firm, whatever you have to face, you will find us with you. Don't let yourselves be blackmailed by the Americans or anyone else." According to Heikal, after Badran left, Egyptian Ambassador Ghaleb asked Grechko about his remarks. Grechko replied, "I just wanted to give him one for the road." The ambassador's letter to Nasser about this remark did not reach him until after the start of the June War. Heikal's general impression of Soviet signals at this time was that they wanted Nasser to de-escalate (Heikal, 1978).

Badran was in Moscow in the first place because Nasser insisted to the Soviets that arrangements for military aid against Israel be made. When Nasser learned that Israeli troops were being moved from positions in the north near Syria, to the south, Nasser told the Soviet ambassador in Cairo, "you are responsible to me for all this. Your people in Moscow must understand that politically, and on the military plane, I want this to be translated into material aid as quickly as possible" (Heikal, 1978, p. 178). The Soviets told the Egyptians that they would not help Egypt if it attacked Israel or if Egypt were attacked by Israel alone (Dawisha, 1979). Concerned about reports of an imminent Egyptian attack, the Soviet ambassador awakened Nasser with a visit at 3:00 a.m. on May 26, 1967. According to Heikal, he said that if the reports were true, "the Soviet Union urged the President not to go ahead with his plans because whoever fired the first shot would be in an untenable political position. As friends, they advised Egypt not to fire that shot" (Heikal, 1973, p. 244).

During the war the Egyptians asked for a resupply of weapons, but arms were not forthcoming (Heikal, 1978) because the Soviets were actively trying to end the conflict. However, continuing Soviet concern for the Syrian regime was still evident. The Soviet press wrote that Israel was "seizing Syrian territory and advancing in the direction of Damascus" (*Pravda* and *Izvestia,* June 11, 1967). While the public Soviet response was mild in that only "sanctions" were threatened, Kosygin's message to Johnson over the hotline threatened military action. Once the ceasefire was in place, the Soviets appeared to have been satisfied. They were left with the task, however, of repairing relations with their Arab clients. While the Soviet leadership urged compromises on the Arabs based on their military inferiority, at the war's end they began a massive resupply of weapons and a training program, both designed to make the Arabs fit to attain their goals against Israel.

ANALYSIS

1. Why Risk War?

How is prospect theory useful in explaining these events? Following prospect theory, the Soviets were risk-acceptant in order to maintain the status quo in the Middle East. Because the Soviets sought to save Syria's neo-Baath government, they promoted a war scare and helped to precipitate the very war they had been warning against. The Soviets used the war scare to activate the Syrian-Egyptian defense treaty and promote unity among Arabs and within the Syrian regime.

Why did the Soviets fear a collapse of the Syrian regime? Given the internal instability in Syria and its vulnerability to an Israeli incursion, this eventuality seemed quite certain. Here the *certainty effect* seems to have been operative. The certainty effect means that in order to increase the chance of avoiding any loss at all, people are willing to accept the danger of even greater sacrifice. For example, in a choice between a 100% chance of losing $10 and a 20% chance of losing $55, most people opt for the latter gamble. Most people shy away from the *certainty* of losing even a little and opt for the lower chance of losing much more. The Soviets thought the neo-Baath regime would indeed topple if they did not do anything about it, and they were willing to take a gamble (war) that could mean a large loss.

For the Soviets, the risk of doing nothing in the face of Israeli threats and deadly skirmishes between Syria and Israel was that the Syrian regime would fall. The risk of war, on the other hand, was that their clients in both Egypt and Syria would be badly beaten and the governing regimes would fall. The ultimate risk was U.S. involvement that might draw in the Soviet Union. But the Soviets thought it less likely there would be a war in the Middle East—even with the activation of the Egyptian-Syrian defense treaty and the removal of UNEF from the Sinai—than that the Syrian government would fall.

In January 1960 a similar episode between Egypt and Israel occurred with little consequence. Nasser asked for the withdrawal of U.N. troops from the Sinai and massed troops along Israel's frontier, ostensibly to help protect Syria. There was a stalemate between the two armies for two months, after which both withdrew and Nasser successfully claimed credit for deterring the Israelis from attacking Syria (Neff, 1984; Quandt, 1977). In the Soviet view, their warnings about Israeli troops in the fall of 1966 helped avert an Israeli confrontation with Syria and successfully brought Egypt and Syria together. The possibility of war became more real when Nasser closed Sharm el-Sheik, and this was when the Soviets began to change course and promote the exercise of caution.

Why was the Soviet Union so attached to the Syrian regime? Here the *reference effect* is important. The Soviet leadership apparently considered the status quo or reference point to be the rule of the pro-Soviet Provisional Command in Syria, even though this status quo was a recent occurrence. The neo-Baath regime was only a year old and its governing Provisional Command was a newfound friend for the Soviets.

Why did the Soviets use this faction as its reference point, as opposed to other Syrians vying for power (such as the recently-ousted moderate Baaths)? The concept of the *endowment effect* helps provide an answer. The endowment effect posits that once an individual obtains a good, he will consider its possession part of his status quo. There is evidence that the endowment effect is virtually instantaneous; the individual will immediately change his reference point. One reason why people adjust so quickly to a new status quo is suggested by the concept's name. In the new status quo, one is "endowed" with a new possession; one is better off than before. The endowment effect works only for gain; there is no endowment effect for loss.

Why, then, would the Soviets feel "endowed" by this particular Syrian leadership? Among the so-called progressive Arab regimes, Syria appears to have been ideologically closest to the Soviet Union. In foreign policy matters, Asad's strategy of unifying the Arab nations via an all-out assault on Israel was predominant and in domestic matters his rival Jadid's radical socialist strategy was predominant, making for a thoroughly radical regime. Not only did the new leadership proclaim the socialist transformation of Syrian society and enact a Marxist program of rapid economic development, but it was the only regime in the Middle East that tolerated the operation of the Communist Party, going so far as to include one of its members in the Syrian government cabinet. (This was Minister of Communications Samih Attiyah. Two other members of the cabinet were known as "fellow travelers." [Pace, 1967; Karsh, 1988]) Additionally, the Communist Party newspaper was permitted to resume publication and Khalid Bakhdash, head of the Communist Party, was permitted to return to Syria after the February coup (Karsh, 1988). Although the activities of the paper and of Bakhdash were circumscribed, Syria's was a far more "progressive" attitude than any of the other so-called radical regimes on the road to socialist development. In fact, the Soviets told Nasser in May 1967 that the Syrian regime was more progressive than his (Sadat, 1978), a "taunt" that was probably designed, in concert with the warning of an Israeli attack, to goad Nasser into action.

The Soviets, then, viewed their new relationship with the Syrians not as a recent gain that could be sacrificed to preserve the peace, but as their reference point from which they did not wish to move.

2. Defining the Status Quo

For the Soviets the status quo in the Middle East meant not losing their influence in Syria either to the United States or to the People's Republic of China. While the Soviets were concerned with forging anti-Western, anti-imperialist coalitions in the Third World, they were also concerned with keeping communist parties and progressive forces on their side of the Sino-Soviet split. They went to great lengths to have these groups state unequivocally their support for Moscow's position as leader of the world communist movement.

There is evidence that the situation in Syria may have provided a cause for Soviet concern because China was courting Arab regimes and pro-Chinese elements existed within the Baath party. The evidence can be divided into two categories. The first is the ideological disposition of the Provisional Regional Command of the Baath Party. The second concerns the internal maneuvering for power within this neo-Baath movement. First, in several respects, the neo-

Baaths seemed ideologically more akin to the Chinese point of view, and more extreme than the Soviet communists. As Patrick Seale writes, the Syrian chief of staff, Ahmad al-Suwanydam, "had served as military attache in Peking where he had absorbed a powerful dose of Maoist doctrine" (Seale, 1988, p. 107). Under Khalid al-Jundi a General Labor Federation was formed which operated in the same fashion as the Red Guards. Armed "workers battalions" ferreted out "counterrevolutionaries" and intimated and beat shopkeepers, state administrators, and any potential dissenters. Finally, upon ascending to power, the Provisional Command called for a Chinese-style war of liberation for the Palestinian people (and began support for al-Fatah guerrilla raids on Israel) (Dawisha, 1979).

The second source of Soviet concern was the continuing instability within the ranks of the Provisional Command itself. One of the controversies centered on how ideologically close they should be to the Soviet Union. There seems to have been no question that Syria should be allied with the Soviet Union against Israel and the West, but many in the neo-Baath leadership wanted to follow a more independent line and remain neutral with regard to the Sino-Soviet split (Karsh, 1988). At the outset, Prime Minister Zayen indicated that his party was neither pro-Moscow nor pro-Chinese (Brady, 1966c), nonetheless he made overtures to the Soviet Union. When Major General Salah Jadid (de facto leader of the Syrian cabinet) returned from a trip to Moscow in January 1967, he was accused (by Asad) of aligning Syria with Moscow against Peking. This incident caused a crisis within the leadership (Brady, 1967a).

Noteworthy is the resolution of the June 1967 plenum of the Central Committee (in which Nikolai Yegorychev lost his job, ostensibly for criticizing Soviet policy in the Six-Day War) which included the following: "[It is necessary] to resist the slander campaign and splitting activities of Mao Tse Tung's group aimed at disuniting the anti-imperialist forces and undermining the trust between the peoples of the Arab states and the peoples of the socialist countries." Jon Glassman (1975) notes that by criticizing the PRC, the Soviet leadership could have been obliquely criticizing domestic hardliners like Yegorychev.

The Chinese occasionally included the Middle East in their verbal assaults against Soviet policy in the Third World. For example, in a broadcast about the various imperialist plots against the Arab world, the Chinese included the following barb at the Soviet Union:

> Working hand in glove with the US imperialists in the past year, the Soviet revisionists have been playing a contemptible role of betraying the national interest of the Arab peoples. They have revealed themselves more and more as an accomplice of US imperialism, as they gave sham support to the Arab people but actually betrayed them. Early last year, the Soviet revisionist leading cliques advertised among Palestinian Arabs a "Tashkent spirit" in relation to Israel, a tool for aggression in the hands of US imperialism. (Peking New China News Agency, 1967)

On January 4, 1966, Kosygin had sponsored the Tashkent meeting between Pakistan and India to discuss a settlement of their differences. By referring to a

"Tashkent spirit," the Chinese meant that the Soviets wanted the Arabs to negotiate a compromise with Israel rather than continue their struggle for a Palestinian state. The Soviet leadership had to take care that this kind of challenge from the Chinese did not weaken its position in the Middle East. To this end the Soviets sought to show their Arab clients that they supported them in their efforts against Israel, but at the same time the Soviets sought to discourage Syria and Egypt from starting a war, thus introducing a certain inconsistency in their foreign policy goals in the region. During the Six-Day War and in the months following it, the Soviets left themselves open to more Chinese accusations of betrayal as they promoted a ceasefire and negotiations with Israel. However, with the war fresh in their minds, the Soviets realized the danger of going too far to counter Chinese criticism.

With the near-complete destruction of its clients' armed forces and the invasion of Syria by Israel, the "reality constraint" brought to light the inconsistency between Moscow's goals. Rosenberg and Abelson (1960) have proposed that individuals making decisions often do not integrate their values, that is, arrange them hierarchically from most important or most desirable to least important or least desirable. When values are not prioritized, one might give equal weight to two values (for example, promoting militancy among Arabs to answer Chinese accusations versus promoting negotiations in the face of military defeat) that are mutually exclusive and, moreover, negate or jeopardize one another. One can hold two irreconcilable values, especially if they relate to different immediate tasks. This cognitive inconsistency is known as value separation. The inconsistency between values will not be confronted unless the "reality constraint" is strong, that is, unless the individual is motivated by an event or highly structured external situation to think about the topic and in fact does so (Rosenberg & Abelson, 1960, p. 121; Steinbruner, 1974, p. 108). Until the June War, the Soviets were able to ignore the inconsistency between the goal of promoting Arab unity and Syria's policies through confrontation with Israel and the goal of avoiding war in the Middle East because the reality constraint was weak. According to John Steinbruner, the reality constraint is weak and value separation tends to take place under conditions of intense uncertainty (as is the case in foreign policy decision-making) (Steinbruner, 1974).

The Soviets could not both fend off the Chinese accusations and promote Arab-Israeli negotiations that were deemed necessary in light of the Israeli victory. The Soviets were forced to move toward a more moderate stance on the Arab-Israeli conflict, at least temporarily. At the same time they compensated by massively rebuilding the Arab armies. The Soviets have a quite flexible doctrine of "correlation of forces." When the correlation of forces shifts out of Soviet favor, they fairly easily accept a tactical retreat.

The Chinese challenge for ideological leadership in the Middle East makes it plausible that the status quo the Soviet Union was defending in the Middle East included not only a pro-Soviet anti-Western coalition, but also a pro-Soviet anti-Chinese coalition. The Soviets wanted to make sure that Jadid and the other pro-Soviet neo-Baaths remained at the helm in Syria.

The socialist orientation of Syria was probably particularly pleasing to Soviet ideologues such as Suslov and Shelepin. Marxist-Leninist ideology can be seen as an "intrinsic interest" which at least some Soviet leaders may have been compelled to defend. (For a discussion of the distinction between intrinsic and strategic interests, see Stein, 1985.) Indeed, the line drawn on Soviet policy toward the Middle East seems to be the standard one between the ideologues and reformers. Grechko, Semichastny, and Yegorychev have been associated with a hardline policy orientation in the Middle East and Aleksandr Shelepin has been identified as an ardent supporter of a pro-Baath Soviet policy. Galia Golan writes, "Shelepin had been close to the Egyptians and, reportedly, even more so to the Syrian Ba'athists. French journalist Michel Tatu has associated both Shelepin and Vladimir Semichastny [head of the KGB] . . . with a strong pro-Ba'athist, militantly anti-Zionist position which may have prompted them to urge greater Soviet involvement on behalf of the Arabs" (Golan, 1990, p. 65). Additionally, Golan cites a former Israeli intelligence source as claiming "the KGB and military elements favoured a more active Soviet role and assistance to the Egyptians and, especially, the Syrians" (Golan, 1990, p. 63).

It is plausible that these hardliners, attached to a Marxist-Leninist and Soviet great power worldview, had a motivated bias to frame the status quo in terms of dominant Soviet influence in the Middle East, to see losses to Soviet interests there, especially in Syria, and thus argue for a more active foreign policy. In contrast, Kosygin and Gromyko who counseled caution to the Egyptians, tended to take a more benign view of international relations and thus perhaps had a motivated bias to accept the status quo as one in which the Soviets had a more limited hold on regimes in Egypt and Syria and to see the risk of achieving further gains as unnecessary.

The differences between factions in the Soviet leadership in willingness to run risks to save the Syrian regime suggests the potential importance of framing in choosing policy alternatives. Additionally, it suggests everyone does not frame situations in the same way; that is, there is not an objective status quo or objective situation that is clear to everyone.

CONCLUSIONS

Prospect theory can help explain a puzzling episode in Soviet foreign policy in the Middle East. The Soviet leadership appears to have behaved recklessly in encouraging Nasser to "do something" to protect Syria. By utilizing a cognitive explanation, we can understand why the Soviet leadership behaved in this way.

The Soviets framed the situation in the Middle East by identifying a status quo—Arab unity and an ideologically acceptable regime in Syria. When those circumstances were threatened and the Soviet leaders felt they might lose what they had, they were driven to take risks in order to save the status quo. On the other hand, the Soviets may not have consciously acknowledged they were taking a risk. Rather than accepting a known risk to avert loss, as prospect theory would suggest, the Soviet leadership may have seen itself as merely committed to a policy of preserving the Syrian regime. The Soviets knew, however, a war in the Middle East was not in their interests, and they were willing to gamble to avoid what they considered an almost certain loss.

REFERENCES

Adomeit, H. (1982). *Soviet risk taking and crisis behavior.* London: George Allen and Unwin.
Antiregime moves pointed by Syria. (1966a). *The New York Times.* May 10, 1966.
Arab anti-imperialism struggle develops. (1967). Peking New China News Agency International Service in English, January 6, 1967.
Bar-Siman-Tov, Y. (1983). *Linkage politics in the Middle East: Syria between domestic and external conflict, 1961–1970.* Boulder, CO: Westview Press.
Belyayev, I. (1967). Commentators column: To the roar of gunfire. *Pravda,* January 18, 1967.
Brady, T. (1967a). Dissension reported among Syrian leftist leaders. *The New York Times,* February 2, 1967.
Brady, T. (1966a). Leftist Syrian workers oust officials. *The New York Times,* September 8, 1966.
Brady, T. (1966b). Some army units defy Syrian coup. *The New York Times,* February 24, 1966.
Brady, T. (1966c). Syria to pursue own left policy. *The New York Times,* March 6, 1966.
Brady, T. (1966d). Syrian junta seems to be in control. *The New York Times,* March 6, 1966.
Brady, T. (1967b). Syrians using force to break a protest strike by merchants. *The New York Times,* May 9, 1967.
Bragin, N. (1967). Plot against Cyprus. *Pravda,* June 7, 1967.
Dawisha, K. (1979). *Soviet foreign policy toward Egypt.* New York: St. Martin's Press.
Fleishman, J. (1988). The effects of decision framing and other's behavior on cooperation in a social dilemma. *Journal of Conflict Resolution, 32,* 162–180.
Gelman, H. (1984). *The Brezhnev politburo and the decline of detente.* Ithaca, NY: Cornell University Press.
George, A. (1969). The operational code: A neglected approach to the study of politics. *International Studies Quarterly, 13,* 190–222.
Glassman, J. (1975). *Arms for the Arabs: The Soviet Union and war in the Middle East.* Baltimore: The Johns Hopkins University Press.
Golan, G. (1990). *Soviet policies in the Middle East.* New York: Cambridge University Press.
Heikal, M. (1973). *The Cairo documents.* New York: Doubleday.
Heikal, M. (1978). *The sphinx and the commissar: The rise and fall of Soviet influence in the Middle East.* New York: Harper & Row.
Hopwood, D. (1988). *Syria 1945–1986: Politics and society.* London: Unwin Hyman.
Iskenderov, A. (1967). Problems and judgments: The army, politics and the people. *Izvestia,* January 17, 1967.
Ivanov, K. (1966a). Notes to the point: Is it not time to think better of it? *Izvestia,* November 7, 1966.
Ivanov, K. (1966b). Problems and judgments: Around Damascus. *Izvestia,* May 2, 1966.
Izvestia is critical of Israel on Syria. (1966b). *The New York Times,* May 8, 1966.
Johnson, L. B. (1971). *The vantage point: Perspectives of the presidency, 1963–1969.* New York: Holt, Rinehart & Winston.

Kahneman, D., & Tversky, A. (1989). Choices, values, frames. *American Psychologist, 39,* 341–350.
Keesings Contemporary Archives, Vols. 15 and 16, 1965–1966 and 1966–1967.
Karsh, E. (1988). *The Soviet Union and Syria: The Asad years.* London: Royal Institute of International Affairs.
Kosut, H. (Ed.) (1968). *Israel and the Arabs.* New York: Facts on File, Inc.
Laqueur, W. (1968). *The road to Jerusalem: The origins of the Arab-Israeli conflict, 1967.* New York: Macmillan.
Leites, N. (1953). *A study of bolshevism.* Glencoe, IL: Free Press.
Maoz, Z. (1990). Framing the national interest: The manipulation of foreign policy decisions in group settings. *World Politics, 43,* 77–110.
Neff, D. (1984). *Warriors for Jerusalem: Six days that shook the Middle East.* New York: Simon & Schuster.
Pace, E. (1967). Syria, reiterating hostility to Israel, ready to "struggle." *The New York Times,* May 19, 1967.
Petrov, R. (1966). General Rabin rattles his saber. *Pravda,* October 3, 1966.
Quandt, W. (1977). *Decade of decisions: American policy toward the Arab-Israeli conflict, 1967–1976.* Berkeley, CA: University of California Press.
Quattrone, G., & Tversky, A. Contrasting rational psychological analysis of political choice. *American Political Science Review, 82,* 719–736.
Rosenberg, M., & Abelson, R. (1960). An analysis of cognitive balancing. In M. Rosenberg et al. (Eds.), *Attitude organization and change* (pp. 112–163). New Haven, CT: Yale University Press.
el-Sadat, A. (1978). *In search of identity: An autobiography.* New York: Harper Colophon Books.
Safran, N. (1969). *From war to war: The Arab-Israeli confrontation 1948–1967.* Indianapolis, IN: Bobbs-Merrill.
Samoilov, S. (1967). Shadow of the CIA over Greece. *Pravda,* June 5, 1967.
Seale, P. (1988). *Asad: The struggle for the Middle East.* Berkeley, CA: University of California Press.
Soviet government note to the government of Israel. (1967). *Pravda* and *Izvestia,* June 11, 1967.
Stein, J. G. (1985). Calculation, miscalculation and conventional deterrence I: The view from Cairo. In R. Jervis et al. (Eds.), *Psychology and deterrence* (pp. 34–59). Baltimore: The Johns Hopkins University Press.
Stein, J. G., & Tanter, R. (1980). *Rational decision making: Israel's security choices, 1967.* Columbus, OH: Ohio State University Press.
Steinbruner, J. (1974). *The cybernetic theory of decision.* Princeton, NJ: Princeton University Press.
Syria threatens to cut pipelines. (1966c). *The New York Times,* May 7, 1966.
Syrian communist leader back from self exile. (1966d). *The New York Times,* April 24, 1966.
TASS statement. (1966). *Pravda* and *Izvestia,* May 28, 1966.
Tatu, M. (1970). *Power in the Kremlin from Khrushchev to Kosygin.* New York: Viking Press.
Tuganova, O. (1966). Problems and judgments: Search for a path. *Izvestia,* September 3, 1966.
Tuma, E. (1967). On a dangerous course. *Izvestia,* May 18, 1967.
Tversky, A. (1977). On the elicitation of preferences: Descriptive and prescriptive considerations. In D. E. Bell, R. L. Keaney & H. Raiffa (Eds.), *Conflicting objectives in decisions* (pp. 209–219). New York: Wiley.
Tversky, A., & Kahneman, D. (1986a). The framing of decisions and the psychology of choice. In J. Elster (Ed.), *Rational choice* (pp. 123–141). New York: New York University Press. Originally published in *Science* (1981), No. 211, 453–458.
Tversky, A., and Kahneman, D. (1986b). Rational choice and the framing of decisions. *Journal of Business, 59,* S251–S258.
United forces of Progress—On stay in the Soviet Union of Arab Socialist Renaissance Party delegation. (1967). *Pravda,* February 12, 1967.
Yost, C. (1968). The Arab-Israeli war: How it began. *Foreign Affairs, 46,* 304–320.

Prospect Theory and International Relations: Theoretical Applications and Analytical Problems

Jack S. Levy[1]

INTRODUCTION

My earlier summary of prospect theory (1992) identified some apparent empirical anomalies of expected utility theory and demonstrated how Kahneman and Tversky (1979) have incorporated these anomalies into an alternative theory of risky choice. Prospect theory has enormous potential for explaining a wide range of international behavior and, on the face of it, a number of its hypotheses appear to provide reasonable explanations for observed behavior. But there are a number of conceptual and methodological problems which must be overcome before hypotheses based on prospect theory can be constructed and tested against

[1]Department of Political Science, Rutgers University, New Brunswick, New Jersey 08903-0270.

the empirical evidence. I begin with some of the implications of prospect theory for international relations and then consider some of the difficult analytical problems which arise.

SOME IMPLICATIONS OF PROSPECT THEORY FOR INTERNATIONAL RELATIONS

The Status Quo Bias

One implication of prospect theory is that people have a tendency to remain at the status quo. The status quo is probably the most common reference point for states as well as for individuals in their framing of a decision problem, and the endowment effect (Thaler, 1980) and the loss-aversion properties of the value function imply that the disadvantages of leaving the status quo are over-weighted relative to the corresponding advantages. One manifestation of this is the tendency for selling prices to exceed buying prices by a substantial amount (Knetsch and Sinden, 1984), which results in undertrading. Samuelson and Zeckhauser (1988) label this tendency the *status quo bias*. It has been demonstrated in a number of experimental and field studies of consumer and investment behavior which show that people adhere to status quo choices more frequently than a standard expected-utility model predicts (Samuelson & Zeckhauser, 1988; Hausman, 1979; Hartman, Doane, & Woo, 1991; Kahneman, Knetsch, & Thaler, 1991). The marketing failure associated with the introduction of the "new" Coca Cola in 1985, for example, is explained in part by the status quo bias.

Our intuitive sense of international politics suggests that states are also likely to share a status quo bias (Jervis, 1989, pp. 29–35), though demonstrating this rigorously may not always be easy. States seem to make greater efforts to preserve the status quo against a threatened loss than to improve their position by a comparable amount. A state might be willing, for example, to fight to defend the same territory that it would not have been willing to fight to acquire, or to accept greater costs in order to maintain an international regime than to create it in the first place (Keohane, 1984).

As Jervis (1989, pp. 29–35; 1992) notes, there may be other explanations for the tendency for states to try harder to maintain the status quo than to change it in their favor. First, there may be an asymmetry of interests favoring the side defending the status quo. The distribution of values and territory which make up the status quo in international politics is not random or accidental but may reflect the fact that states "have generally achieved dominant influence in the areas that are most important to them" (Jervis, 1989, p. 30). Consequently, the defense of the status quo might be the defense of what the state defines as important quite independently of any inherent status quo bias. Although this should serve as a useful caution in making inferences about international politics, we must recall that the above-cited experiments on consumer behavior are very careful to control for disparities in perceived values yet still find strong status quo effects.

The status quo might also be preferred because of its salience in tacit bargaining (Schelling, 1960; Jervis, 1989, p. 31) or because of the reputational and domestic political costs that might follow from retreats from the status quo. But these other variables may not be entirely unrelated to prospect theory, as Jervis acknowledges. Although the salience of the status quo may be important in itself, it also contributes to the tendency to define the status quo as the reference point around which to frame gains and losses, so that the salience of the status quo might affect outcomes through its impact on framing, loss aversion, and the status quo bias.

Loss aversion also helps to explain why states are more concerned to prevent a decline in their reputation or credibility than to increase it by a comparable amount, or why they worry more about falling dominoes than anticipate the benefits of states bandwagoning in their favor (Jervis, 1991). Reputation affects future utilities, and future losses hurt more than future gains gratify. Moreover, even if it were the case that the domestic political calculations of decision-makers could be better explained by expected-utility theory than prospect theory, there may be an underlying tendency for domestic publics to react more strongly to strategic or economic losses than to comparable gains, and to punish their leaders more for the former than to reward them for the latter. Loss aversion and the status quo bias would still have an impact but through their effect on public opinion rather than on political leaders directly.

Prospect theory implies that all of these effects would be reinforced if the threat of loss were perceived to be certain in the absence of corrective action, for the over-weighting of certain outcomes relative to others would further increase the incentive to undertake excessive risks in order to avoid that loss. More generally, whenever we find perceptions of certain losses, whether defined in terms of the status quo or in terms of an alternative aspiration point, prospect theory predicts particularly risky behavior (that is, greater than that predicted by an expected-value calculus) in order to avoid those losses.

Downward Trends, Framing, and Risk-Seeking Propensities

The tendency towards risk aversion in the domain of gains,[2] and the dampening effect this has on aggressive behavior to improve one's position, presum-

---

[2]For the sake of simplicity, I assume that the probabilities involved in risky choices are in the moderate range (above .10 or so) and ignore for now the greater unpredictability of risk attitudes for extremely small probabilities.

ably contributes to stability in international politics. Risk-acceptant propensities in the domain of losses, however, might have the opposite effect and contribute to instability under certain conditions. A state which perceives itself to be in a deteriorating situation might be willing to take excessively risky actions in order to maintain the status quo against further deterioration, even if a standard probability calculus based on expected value would lead to a preference for restraint. This would be particularly likely if the state perceived that the further deterioration in its position were certain, or if its position had already deteriorated and the state wanted to recover those losses. These possibilities are not examined in the experimental literature, which deals almost exclusively with static-choice problems.

There are numerous examples in which states appear to adopt risk-seeking behavior in order to prevent the deterioration of their international positions, although demonstrating this empirically is not always easy, as I argue later. Loss aversion might lead states in a crisis situation to take preemptive action and accept the risks inherent in war if they were nearly certain that the adversary was about to initiate a first strike, even though a standard probability-utility calculus might call for restraint (Jervis, 1989, p. 171). States may also take disproportionately risky action short of war. Ross (1984, p. 247) concludes that although Soviet leaders tend to be risk-averse,[3] they are willing to engage in the "use of decisive and perhaps risky action far more readily for *defending* as opposed to *extending* Soviet gains." McInerney (1992) provides support for this hypothesis in her case study of Soviet efforts to maintain their position in the Middle East in 1966–1967.

Loss aversion and risk-seeking also help explain why states frequently find themselves continuing to follow failing policies far longer than a standard cost-benefit calculus might predict (Jervis, 1992), in the desperate hope that they might recover their sunken costs. Examples of futile military interventions or prolonged wars (Vietnam and Afghanistan, for example) come immediately to mind. This parallels the familiar tendency in economics for individuals to hesitate to sell at a loss because of a psychological entitlement to a formerly prevailing price—as evidenced both in declining real estate markets and in stock markets (Sherrin & Statman, 1985; Kahneman, Knetsch, & Thaler, 1990, p. 1345).

Gains and losses need not be defined exclusively, or even primarily, in terms of a state's international security and influence, for state officials are also concerned about their domestic political positions. They may be tempted to engage in forceful action against external enemies in order to secure a diplomatic or military victory that might pacify their domestic enemies or otherwise distract

---

[3]This conventional wisdom regarding Soviet risk orientation is reflected by Pipes's (1973, p. 11) argument that "Soviet leaders act according to the proverb, 'If you don't know the ford, don't step into the river. . . .' They rarely gamble."

attention from domestic problems. The temptation toward such diversionary action may be enhanced by risk-acceptant attitudes in the domain of losses created by a deteriorating domestic situation (Levy, 1989a, p. 274). This hypothesis is reflected in Mayer's (1977, pp. 220–21) argument that beleaguered political elites often adopt a "fortress mentality [and] are particularly inclined to advocate external war for the purpose of domestic crisis management even if chances for victory are very doubtful." The combination of perceived external decline and internal insecurity may be particularly conducive to risk-seeking, as McDermott (1992) shows in her case study of the U.S. decision to attempt a hostage rescue mission in Iran in 1979. In other situations, however, there may be difficult trade-offs between military/strategic/diplomatic risks and domestic political risks (Lamborn, 1985).

Prospect theory implies that the magnitudes of the losses involved need not be that large in order to induce risk-seeking behavior, particularly if the losses were perceived to be certain. A setback might be minor compared to a state's overall position, but because it is evaluated with respect to the current reference point rather than one's net asset position, its effects tend to be evaluated in absolute rather than relative (to total assets) terms. More importantly, because of the anticipation that any such setback will involve significant reputational costs, falling dominoes, and a disproportionate domestic political reaction, even small losses appear to have significant consequences.

These considerations lead Jervis (1989, p. 170) to suggest that the very fact of a loss is often more important than the magnitude of the loss and that large losses may not be that much worse than smaller ones. (This depends, of course, on the precise shape of the loss curve and the metric that is used.) Consequently, political leaders may be inclined to engage in relatively risky behavior in order to avoid or recoup even small losses or retreats from the status quo. This tendency is all the greater for a state which perceives itself to be in a zero-sum relationship with its adversary, which might occur for the two leading states in a bipolar system or for an enduring rivalry.

The destabilizing tendencies of loss aversion might be particularly great if two adversaries both perceived themselves to be in a deteriorating situation. This could occur either because one set of political leaders focused on their state's relative external decline while the other focused on its deteriorating domestic situation, because they focused on different dimensions of power, or because one misperceived the situation. If any of these situations occurred, loss aversion might drive both toward riskier strategies than warranted by straightforward cost-benefit calculations. I have suggested that this may have been the situation for France and Germany in 1870, and perhaps for the United States and Japan in 1941 (Levy, 1987, p. 93). It might also have been true for the United States and Iraq in 1990–1991: the U.S. feared Iraq's acquisition of nuclear and biological weapons, and Iraq may have feared a deterioration of its position in the context of

Soviet decline, unconstrained American hegemony and its hostility toward Iraq, and the possibility of a diplomatic realignment in the Middle East.

The simultaneous perception by each of two states that it faces a domain of losses, and the mutual risk-seeking tendencies which are likely to follow from it, can also be induced by the effects of framing in a changing situation. States might identify different reference points to frame their respective decisions, and this might lead both to perceive that they are defending the status quo. Consider a situation in which state A has just made a tangible gain at state B's expense, say through the seizure of territory or control over a vital operational area. The endowment effect suggests that A will accommodate its gains much more quickly than B will accommodate its losses. Consequently, B will attempt to recover its losses and restore the old status quo, and A will attempt to maintain the new status quo against B's encroachments. Each will accept larger-than-normal risks in order to maintain its version of the status quo.

In such a situation it is likely that instability will be further fueled by misperceptions. If B perceives that A is thinking in terms of gains rather than losses, B might underestimate A's resolve because B will erroneously expect A to be risk-averse. B will then see A's unexpectedly aggressive stance as an indicator of hostile intent rather than as a defense of the new status quo, and this will help fuel the conflict spiral and increase the likelihood of miscalculated escalation (Jervis, 1976, ch. 3).

This behavior leads Jervis (1989, p. 171) to suggest that a fait accompli strategy is more dangerous than George and Smoke (1974, pp. 536–40) imply, because the target will make a greater effort to recover its loss than one might expect on the basis of a straightforward calculation of costs and benefits. Possible illustrations of this might include Britain's resolve to recover the Falklands after their seizure by Argentina in 1982 and the American determination to roll back Iraq's invasion of Kuwait in 1990–1991. It is also interesting in this regard to consider whether the Argentines saw a possible withdrawal from the Malvinas (or whether Saddam saw a possible withdrawal from Kuwait) as a return to the status quo or a retreat from it. The former would have been easier psychologically in each case. Of course, if the initiator conceives of its fait accompli as an attempt to recover old possessions rather than make new acquisitions, its resolve will be all the greater, as evidenced by Argentina's determination to recover the Malvinas.

The timing of an attempt to reverse a fait accompli might also be an important variable. The longer a fait accompli is allowed to stand before action is taken to reverse it, the greater the likelihood that the initiator has accommodated to the new status quo, and the greater its resistance to any reversal. The time factor might be even more important for third-party accommodation to the new status quo over time and consequently for the diplomatic costs associated with any action. Because of the status quo bias, immediate action is more likely to be perceived as a legitimate defense of the status quo than action which is delayed. Thus Austria-Hungary's delay in responding to the assassination at Sarajevo decreased the perceived legitimacy of its action against Serbia in the eyes of Europe and made great power intervention and a general war more likely (Levy, 1990/91).

The changes which induce these framing effects may be gradual rather than sudden. Consider a situation in which A is gradually gaining in power at the expense of B, and the two states try to negotiate a settlement over a conflict between them. It is possible that A might frame his reference point at some future asset level based on the assumption of the continued improvement in his position, treat any point short of that aspiration level as a loss, and be willing to undertake inordinately risky actions to reach his target position. (Recall, however, that the endowment effect appears to be stronger for actual possession of a good than for a property right to future possession, much less a chance for future possession [Levy, 1992].) Meanwhile, B is likely to use the current status quo as the reference point and to be risk-seeking in order to maintain it.

This logic is fully consistent with, and in fact helps to reinforce, the theory of relative deprivation and the phenomenon of the revolution of rising expectations. The argument is that the likelihood of violence is greatest not under conditions of greatest suffering, but instead when the level of material benefits or rate of improvement falls behind expectations (Davies, 1962; Gurr, 1970). Given rising expectations, whether based on the extrapolation of past trends or on conceptions of justice, people define their reference point at some future and higher level of satisfaction, frame any point short of that as a loss (regardless of recent accomplishments), and are willing to take excessively risky actions to reach that aspiration level. The situation is not symmetrical, however, and falling expectations do not have a comparable effect because people are much slower to accommodate to losses than they are to gains. Similar arguments apply to theories of status inconsistency or rank disequilibrium in international politics (Galtung, 1964; Midlarsky, 1975).

Deterrence and Bargaining

The framing of a decision problem can also affect behavior with respect to deterrence and other forms of bargaining. Influence attempts based on coercion are more likely to be successful if the adversary one is attempting to influence sees itself in the domain of gains, and is contemplating an effort to improve its position, than if the adversary sees itself in the domain of losses and is considering how to prevent its position from deteriorating further. The loss aversion hypothesis would suggest that the adversary is likely to be more willing to take excessive risks in the second situation than in the first. This helps explain why it is generally easier to deter an adversary from initiating an action she has not yet taken than to compel her to undo what she has already done or to undertake actions which she would prefer not to do (Schelling, 1966, pp. 69–91; Jervis, 1989, p. 29).

This does not imply, of course, that deterrence is always easy. Potential initiators do not always define their reference point in terms of the existing status quo, and consequently they do not always see themselves in the domain of gains. Moreover, they might see the target as particularly attractive or the status quo as particularly unattractive. Lebow and Stein (1987), for example, argue that deterrence often fails because initiators are often driven to aggressive external behavior by a deteriorating domestic political environment.

The issue of deterrence leads to another interesting question relating to framing. Consider a situation in which one state threatens military action against another. This initial threat of military action in itself changes the status quo in terms of utilities because of the reputational and perhaps domestic political costs involved (Levy, 1989b, pp. 126–27). What happens if the state making the threat is then confronted by a deterrent threat from the target or the target's protector? Does the first state frame a possible withdrawal of the threat (or failure to implement it) as a retreat *to* the old status quo or a retreat *from* the new status quo? The second frame is more likely to induce risk-seeking behavior and the escalation of the conflict.

These types of behavior are a manifestation of a more general tendency created by the endowment effect, the irreversibility of indifference curves, and loss aversion. If actors in a bargaining situation treat their own concessions as losses and the concessions they receive from their adversary as gains, they will overvalue the concessions they make to the adversary relative to the concessions they receive from the adversary. This leads to a greater tendency of both parties to risk the negative consequences of a possible deadlock in order to minimize their concessions. This can result in a reduction in the size of the bargaining space of mutually advantageous exchanges (Knetsch, 1989, p. 1283). This leads Kahneman, Knetsch, and Thaler (1990, p. 1345) to suggest a "concession aversion," or a reluctance to accept a loss on any dimension of an agreement in multi-attribute negotiations. If true, this would further undercut the possibility of compromise based on issue linkages (Morgan, 1990).

There is some evidence to support this hypothesis (Tversky & Kahneman, 1986, p. S262). Bazerman (1983) found that subjects who bargained over the allocation of losses more often failed to reach agreement and more often failed to find a Pareto-optimal solution than subjects who bargained over gains. Morgan and Wilson (1989) find a similar pattern in their experimental test of a spatial model of crisis bargaining in international relations: subjects sought agreements when the payoffs were positive but were more likely to risk war to avoid a loss when the payoffs were negative, even though in each case the preferred option was the one with the lower expected value.

This asymmetry in bargaining over gains and losses is likely to be minimal, in routine economic transactions (Kahneman & Tversky, 1984, pp. 348–49), or where goods are acquired for later sale rather than use (Kahneman, Knetsch, & Thaler, 1991, p. 200). This implies that if concessions involve a "bargaining chip," and especially if the items or resources involved were acquired or created with that purpose in mind, the asymmetry of value attached to concessions given and compensation received is likely to be much less. As a result, the bargaining space, and the likelihood of a successful compromise, would be larger.

These considerations lead Janice Stein (1992) to argue that recent theories of cooperation in international politics are biased because they generally deal only with situations characterized by cooperation in the distribution of gains. Stein hypothesizes that cooperation should be more difficult when the situation involves cooperation in the distribution of losses, and she has initiated a research program to test this hypothesis.

In the preceding discussion I have considered some of the consequences for international relations of the conditional hypothesis that *if* actors perceive themselves to be in the domain of losses, they tend to engage in riskier forms of behavior than might be predicted by a probability calculus based on expected utility. Prospect theory suggests another hypothesis as well: actors perceive themselves to be in the domain of losses more often than we would normally expect. What an "objective" analyst might see as a domain of gains, the actor in question might define in terms of losses. This makes it imperative that the analyst attempt to determine the definition of the situation and the framing of choice in the eyes of the actor. This is a complex and demanding task, but it is made somewhat easier by the fact that political leaders often speak explicitly in terms of gains or losses, as evidenced by the McInerney (1992), McDermott (1992), and Farnham (1992) case studies in this issue.

As noted above, little research has been done on the framing process itself, and we have no well-developed theory to guide us. It is useful to note, however, that it might be necessary to go beyond the actor in question to understand how he/she frames a particular choice problem. Because of the importance of framing, one actor might try to influence the behavior of another by influencing how the second frames a particular choice problem—in particular, how he/she defines his/her reference point, and whether a possible outcome is seen as a gain or as a foregone loss.

The manipulation of frames applies to internal actors as well as external adversaries. An individual or organizational unit within a state might try to influence foreign policy behavior in this manner, as Maoz (1990) recognizes in his study of "framing the national interest." It might be easier to influence a strategy choice by manipulating how a decision problem is framed than to influence that strategy directly. If one prefers a cautious approach, for example, one might try to frame the problem as a choice between foregone gains rather than between actual losses. Note also that framing is not restricted to the identification of a reference point. One might also affect choice through the manipulation of the agenda, redefinition of the issue-area (as primarily political, economic, military, etc.), or in other ways, which might in turn affect perceptions of losses or gains.

It is often difficult to demonstrate empirically that actors attempt to manipulate the framing of a decision or that this manipulation has a causal impact. In order to avoid the danger of circular reasoning, it is necessary to measure manipulation independently of the policy outcomes one is trying to explain. It is particularly hard to assess the causal effects of manipulation, because it is difficult to demonstrate the counterfactual of what would have been done in the absence of manipulation (Maoz, 1990).

ANALYTICAL PROBLEMS IN THE APPLICATION OF PROSPECT THEORY TO INTERNATIONAL RELATIONS

Can We Generalize from Laboratory Experiments?

We can see that prospect theory has some intriguing implications for international relations. But the application of the theory also raises difficult conceptual and methodological issues which are not always given adequate recognition, and it would be useful to consider some of these problems here. An understanding of these potential problems will suggest how we might construct research designs to overcome them and thus facilitate the rigorous application of prospect theory to international relations.

First of all, we must recognize that the findings upon which prospect theory is based emerge from highly structured conditions generated by simple but ingenious research designs. Subjects are generally given a choice between a certain outcome and a lottery which involves two or more possible outcomes, the values and probabilities of which are known. The two prospects or alternatives have expected values which are known and easily compared. The evaluation of prospects is facilitated by the use of monetary outcomes—or in some cases mortality or survival rates or inflation and unemployment rates—which are measurable on an interval scale and which can be roughly scaled into utilities. The possible effects of extraneous variables are minimized by strict experimental controls and by the randomization of those effects over a large number of subjects, so that threats to the validity of causal inferences are minimal.

The experiments are designed in order to eliminate the possibility that a preference for one prospect over another is due to the fact that one was inherently more valuable than another in terms of a straightforward expected value calculation. More specifically, the experimental designs are such that expected-utility theory and prospect theory give different predictions as to likely choices. This facilitates a test of the hypothesis that the combination of the value function and probability-weighting function lead individuals to prefer a prospect in spite of its lower expected value than the alternative. Moreover, subjects are generally given a one-time choice, and outcomes are not affected by choices made by an adversary. The framing of the choice problem is usually inherent in the problem presented by the experimenter, and when framing itself is a variable it is usually clear how the subject frames an outcome and why he does so in that manner.

Few of these conditions are satisfied in the highly unstructured choice problems which foreign policy decision-makers typically face. These choices rarely involve one riskless and one risky option, but rather two risky options, and which is more risky is often difficult to define conceptually or measure empirically. The utilities of the payoffs for each outcome are not given but instead are highly subjective. Factors such as power and territory are notoriously resistant to the type of interval-level measurement required by either expected-utility theory or prospect theory, and the fact that the net value of an outcome is affected by bureaucratic and domestic political as well as international considerations compounds the problem of constructing a one-dimensional utility or value function. The probabilities for each of these outcomes are not given, but must be estimated by the decision-maker. Technically, most choices in international relations are made under conditions of uncertainty rather than risk.[4]

The choice problem is compounded by the fact that outcomes are determined not only by one state's choice, but also by the choices of others and by random shocks. It is also complicated by the fact that current choices have future consequences which are themselves risky or uncertain and which need to be incorporated into one's current risk calculus. This is particularly true for international behavior, which is so concerned with future power, wealth, influence, and reputation. The uncertainty surrounding both the value of outcomes and their probabilities means that it is extraordinarily difficult to evaluate and compare prospects, and to rule out the alternative explanation that one prospect is chosen over another not because of framing, loss aversion, and the overweighting of certain outcomes, but rather because it is more valuable in terms of a standard cost-benefit calculus for a risk-neutral actor.

---

[4]There is considerable controversy over the meaning and measurement of uncertainty and the distinction between uncertainty and risk (Kahneman & Tversky, 1982). For the sake of simplicity in this study, I assume that decision-makers make some form of subjective probability assessment. Decision-makers' degree of confidence or *ambiguity* about their subjective probability assessments is potentially an important variable in itself. Ambiguity includes both the amount of ambiguity and one's attitude toward it (comparable to attitudes toward risk) (Ellsberg, 1961; Einhorn & Hogarth, 1985), but for the sake of simplicity I do not deal with that issue here.

The Analysis of Framing

Unlike laboratory situations in which the experimenter sets the frame, framing in international relations is much more problematic. The status quo itself is continuously changing along several dimensions, so aspiration levels and extrapolations of current trends compete with the status quo itself as a reference point around which decision-makers might code a choice problem. Consequently, questions of accommodation or renormalization become more important. Cancellation, combination, and other editing operations are also less predictable. Thus the framing of the choice problem is as critical to decision-making as is the evaluation of prospects, and requires intensive examination by the analyst. Evidence regarding precisely how an actor frames a choice problem must be independent of the outcomes the analyst wants to explain, of course, in order to avoid circular reasoning.

In addition, the question of *why* an actor frames a choice problem in a particular way is also important if we are to make causal inferences. One of our central hypotheses is that framing around a reference point shifts the value function, which, in conjunction with the probability-weighting function, causally determines preference and choice. If the same underlying conditions influence both the framing of a choice problem and the behavior we want to explain, an inference that framing and loss aversion causally determine choice might be spurious. For example, if internal and external decline lead decision-makers to frame their alternatives as losses, and if their deteriorating situation also leads them to risky policies in an attempt to reverse their fortunes, it is not necessarily the case that framing causally influences behavior (unless one could show that the behavior was riskier than predicted by a standard cost-benefit calculus). These considerations lead Jervis (1992) to note that it is necessary to rule out the possibility that the same forces which determine the reference point also lead directly to the risky behavior.

The empirical demonstration of how foreign policy decision-makers frame a choice problem is one of the strengths of recent case studies in which apply prospect theory to international relations. McInerney (in this issue) shows convincingly that Soviet leaders accommodated to the new status quo in Syria in 1965–1966 (the pro-Soviet provisional command); perceived that threats to their position (external threats from Israel, internal threats to the stability of the Syrian regime, and Chinese challenges to Soviet legitimacy in the Third World) created a situation of nearly certain losses; and believed that they faced a choice between two alternatives that were each unattractive relative to the status quo. Because Soviet leaders saw themselves in the domain of losses, McInerney argues, they were willing to pursue a policy that involved considerable risks of a regional war in an attempt to avoid what they regarded as the virtually certain costs of inaction.

McDermott's analysis elsewhere in this issue of how the Carter administration framed its decision regarding the Iranian hostage rescue mission is also fairly persuasive. She effectively uses memoirs and some interview material to show that different expectations about the future by Vance, Brzezinski, and Carter led each of them to frame the issue in slightly different ways; that Carter believed that he faced unattractive alternatives in the context of a deteriorating international and domestic political context; and that he wanted to recoup his losses. McDermott acknowledges, however, that Carter believed that a successful rescue mission might not only allow him to recover his losses but also bring some domestic political gains as well.

This possibility raises an interesting question. The experimental literature focuses primarily on choices involving either the domain of losses or the domain of gains but not a combination of the two. That is, it focuses on "pure lotteries"—where either all possible outcomes are negative, or all possible outcomes are positive—but not on "mixed lotteries," where there are both positive and negative outcomes. There is little evidence as to whether loss aversion and the reflection effect are equally strong for "mixed lotteries" as for "pure lotteries" (for an exception see Fischer et al., 1986).

Farnham also provides here a convincing analysis of framing in the case of Roosevelt's perception of and response to the Munich crisis in September 1938. She uses an impressive set of primary sources to demonstrate that Roosevelt perceived that the international situation had deteriorated from one period to the next, that by the second phase of the crisis he perceived that war was certain, and that he faced two relatively unattractive options. She makes a very strong case that Roosevelt's emotional response to the likelihood of an imminent war led to a fundamental change in his representation of the crisis, quite independently of any change in the objective situation.

Farnham's analysis of framing is particularly useful because it contributes to the meager literature on the sources of framing. She argues that Roosevelt's change in frames was due to affective rather than strictly cognitive variables—to his emotional reaction to the prospect of war and to Hitler's apparent eagerness for it. Farnham also provides a useful analysis of the possibility of reciprocal relationships between affect and framing: not only does one's emotional state affect how one frames a decision, but how one frames a decision might affect one's emotional response as well. McDermott also contributes in this issue to the theoretical literature on framing by providing a useful discussion of the impact of historical analogies on the framing of a decision problem.

I have discussed these studies of framing appearing in this issue in order to demonstrate that the successful analysis of framing is a time-consuming task and one which requires a significant amount of data regarding the perceptions of actors. Unlike laboratory experiments, empirical studies cannot take framing for

Ruling Out Alternative Explanations: Expected Value and Rational Choice

Now let us turn to the evaluation phase of the choice problem. Technically, in order to explain a choice in terms of prospect theory one would have to identify how the actor (1) defines the reference point, (2) identifies the available options, and assesses the (3) value and (4) probability of each outcome. The analyst would then have to (5) modify the subjective probabilities by an appropriate probability-weighting function, and, finally, (6) show that the resulting value of the preferred prospect or option exceeds the value of alternative prospects. Needless to say, these are very demanding tasks because utilities, expected probabilities, and these other variables are extremely difficult to measure empirically.[5] It is largely for this reason that social psychologists adopt the method of hypothetical choices in highly structured laboratory conditions so that other variables can be strictly controlled (Kahneman & Tversky, 1979, p. 265).

Of course, the resistance of utilities, probabilities, and related variables to direct and easy empirical measurement also affects the empirical test of expected-utility theories of foreign policy (Stein & Tanter, 1980). But expected-utility theory has slightly less stringent data requirements than does prospect theory. Although expected utility requires information on the actor's perception of available options, the possible outcomes associated with each option and the subjective probability attached to each, and assessment of relative value, it requires no information on framing (because it assumes that a single utility function is valid across the full range of situations or "frames") and requires no additional weighting of subjective probabilities. Moreover, expected-utility theory can be derived from a small set of assumptions which are normatively appealing, whereas prospect theory makes no normative claims (Tversky & Kahneman, 1986, p. S272) and includes an editing component which has not been theoretically developed, much less formalized. Thus expected-utility theory is more parsimonious than prospect theory.

In evaluating the relative merits of an explanation of a particular case based

---

[5]Objective measures of state utilities for war and nonwar outcomes have been constructed from systemic patterns of formal alliances (which presumably reflect the similarities of state interests) and have been very useful for large-n statistical studies of international conflict behavior (Bueno de Mesquita, 1981). They have also been used by Huth et al. (1992) to analyze whether risk-seeking in the domain of losses affects conflict behavior. Although the use of the objective indicators of state utilities makes it easier for Huth et al. (1992) to control for the expected value of alternative choices, the gain in statistical controls and generalizability admittedly comes at some cost in terms of the construct validity of the empirical measures of utility.

on prospect theory with one based on a conventional rational choice or expected-utility model, the primary criterion must be one of empirical fit. Is the empirical evidence more consistent with one theory than another? But if observed behavior were equally consistent (or approximately so) with both expected-utility theory and prospect theory, the expected-utility explanation would be preferable on grounds of its greater parsimony and normative appeal.

This suggests that it is not enough for the analyst to demonstrate that the observed behavior is consistent with prospect theory. It is also necessary to demonstrate that prospect theory provides a *better* explanation of that behavior than does expected-utility theory.[6] That is, the analyst must come to terms with an important alternative explanation: the decision is made, not because of framing, loss aversion, and the over-weighting of certain outcomes, but instead because it is more highly valued in terms of a straightforward expected value calculation or perhaps an expected utility calculation based on a relatively simple utility function (preferably one without an inflection point).[7]

There are no obvious operational criteria to specify the point at which the data favors one theory over another. Recall, however, that experimental and empirical research on prospect theory suggests that the *magnitude* of risk-seeking tendencies in the domain of losses or risk aversion with respect to gains is fairly substantial. That is, individuals are often willing to tolerate a prospect which is significantly lower in expected value than an alternative in order to avoid a certain loss or secure a certain gain. This, in conjunction with the parsimony argument, suggests that the burden of proof is on prospect theory to demonstrate

---

[6]These criteria for the evaluation of theory are consistent with the familiar argument that theories are to be evaluated with respect to other theories as well as with respect to the empirical evidence (Lakatos, 1970). Empirical data alone is insufficient to falsify or test a theory. Other relevant criteria include the logical coherence of a theory, the degree of its empirical confirmation in a number and variety of other cases, and whether it can be subsumed under another well-confirmed theory (Hempel, 1966).

[7]One rather intractable analytic problem which complicates the task of comparing a prospect theory explanation based on risk attitude and a straightforward expected-value explanation is the fact that risk is conventionally defined in terms of marginal utility, that is, in terms of the curvature of the utility function. Decreasing marginal value is equivalent to risk aversion and increasing marginal value is equivalent to risk acceptance.

This means that an actor's *intensity of preference* for an outcome is conceptually impossible to distinguish from his or her *intrinsic risk aversion*, or "nervousness" (Bell & Raiffa, 1988, p. 384) deriving from uncertainty itself. The preference for $50 with certainty over a 50/50 lottery between 0 and $100, for example, might simply reflect the fact that the difference between 0 and $50 has a greater value than the difference between $50 and $100, quite independently of the nervousness one feels about taking a gamble. Thus Rhodes (1989, pp. 54–55) distinguishes attitudes toward "surprise," which reflect how much one "worries" about the consequences of uncertainty, from risk attitudes.

This problem has led some analysts to decompose the standard Von Neumann-Morgenstern utility function into a riskless measurable value function and a risky utility function (Dyer & Sarin, 1979; Bell & Raiffa, 1981; Fischer et al., 1986). These theoretical advances have not become part of the dominant paradigm in utility theories, however, and I will not deal with them here.

that because of framing, loss aversion, and probability weighting decision-makers pursue policies characterized by noticeably lower expected utilities than their alternatives.

On the conceptual level, this criterion requires that we qualify our theoretical arguments and evaluate predictions based on prospect theory not in absolute terms, but relative to a rational choice model based on a straightforward expected-value calculus. We should say, for example, not that an actor pursued a risky policy because she was in the domain of losses, but that because of risk-seeking with respect to loses she adopted a more risky alternative than predicted by a standard expected-value calculation. Jervis (1989, 1992) is very careful about this and consistently qualifies his arguments with such statements as a certain option "would not seem as attractive as standard utility maximization theory implies" or that the risky option might be taken "even if the standard probability-utility calculus calls for restraint." Similarly, Quattrone and Tversky (1988, p. 724) distinguish their risk-based explanation of the incumbency bias in voting behavior from the alternative explanation that one candidate is perceived to be better than another. Huth et al. (1992) are careful to control for expected value in their large-n statistical study of risk propensity in great power conflict behavior, though some may question their empirical measures.

Others have been less sensitive to this problem in their applications of prospect theory to international relations, though admittedly it is more difficult to compare the predictions of the two theories in empirical studies than to acknowledge the problem in conceptual treatments. Consider McDermott's (1992) explanation for Carter's decision to select the risky rescue mission rather than the certainty of the continued deterioration of his domestic and international positions. She argues that Carter believed that a successful rescue would not only recoup his losses, but that it might also generate some gains, and that he perceived that the chances of success were fairly high. (CIA estimates were lower, suggesting that cognitive or motivational biases may have led Carter to exaggerate the chances of success.) But if the expected probability (and value) of such a positive outcome were high enough for Carter, and if the downside risks tolerable, then the decision for the rescue mission might be satisfactorily explained by a standard cost-benefit calculus, quite independently of risk orientation. McDermott's interpretation may be correct, but it would be more compelling if she made an explicit effort to come to terms with this plausible alternative explanation.

Such an effort can be found in Farnham's (1992) study of Roosevelt's change from a policy of nonintervention to diplomatic intervention in the Munich crisis. Farnham goes to considerable lengths to argue that a rational choice model cannot account for the variations in Roosevelt's behavior. Her controlled comparison of successive phases of the crisis demonstrates that a sudden increase in Roosevelt's assessment of the probability of war did not lead to a change in policy to avoid that war. She also demonstrates that Roosevelt did not change his assessment of the relative costs of intervention and nonintervention outcomes for the United States. He continued to perceive that intervention could bring significant domestic costs as well as diplomatic costs if it was ineffective, and he was still convinced that Britain and France would win any war and that the United States would not be directly threatened by the war. What did change was Roosevelt's emotional state. Farnham argues persuasively the idea of war became emotionally compelling to Roosevelt in the second phase of the crisis, and this led him to change the way he framed the problem. This frame change led to a change in Roosevelt's risk propensities and consequently to a preference for a risky interventionist policy in an attempt to avoid the certain losses that would follow from nonintervention.

Thus Farnham demonstrates that an explanation of Roosevelt's policy change based on framing and loss aversion is more persuasive than one based on a strict maximization of expected value. By demonstrating that an explanation based on prospect theory is not only consistent with the empirical evidence, but that it is also superior to a leading alternative explanation, Farnham provides a useful model of how applications of prospect theory to international relations ought to proceed.

The success of Farnham's study should not conceal the fact, however, that foreign policy decisionmakers rarely evaluate various policy outcomes along anything approximating an interval-level scale in order to make the tradeoffs required by an expected utility or prospect theory framework. Or if they do, they leave few empirical traces, so that it is extremely difficult to reconstruct their utility or value functions from the empirical evidence.

The Assessment of Probability and Risk

Although decision-makers rarely articulate their assessments of value with any degree of precision, they are sometimes more explicit about their subjective probability assessments. (McDermott's analysis of the Carter administration's estimates of the likelihood of success of various phases of the proposed rescue mission provides a good example of this.) Political leaders are frequently clear as to whether they perceive outcomes in terms of gains or losses, and this is often reflected in their language. This suggests an alternative, though somewhat weaker, set of criteria by which the empirical validity of prospect theory might be evaluated. This alternative would focus on the question of framing and on probability assessments rather than weighted utilities (Stein, 1992). Because of the certainty effect, outcomes perceived as certain should be over-weighted relative to risky outcomes. Risk-seeking in the domain of losses should lead decisionmakers to take disproportionate risks to avoid certain losses, and risk aversion in the domain of gains should lead decision-makers to be excessively eager to secure certain gains.

This approach directs the analyst toward the following questions: (1) In terms of *framing*, do decision-makers perceive their options to involve losses or gains (or a mixed lottery of losses and gains)? Do they appear to dwell more on potential losses than potential gains and possibly exaggerate the dangers through psychological bolstering (Janis and Mann, 1977)? Do they consider alternative frames, and why is one selected over another? (2) In terms of *probability assessments*, do any of these assessments approach certainty?[8] If so, is there evidence that they give disproportionate weight to these outcomes? Do they take excessive risks to avoid certain losses? Are they surprisingly cautious when they have the opportunity to secure a certain gain?

If no outcome is perceived as certain, this criterion cannot be applied. If an outcome is expected with near certainty, and if the observed behavior is not in the predicted direction, that should be sufficient for us to conclude that behavior is inconsistent with prospect theory. If the predicted behavior is observed in the context of expectations of certainty, one could conclude that it was consistent with prospect theory. It is still possible, of course, that the prospect selected is also the more preferred one on the basis of a straightforward probability calculus, and the analysis should still do as much as possible to rule out that possibility.

These criteria may sound simple enough, but they give rise to several additional problems. Unlike laboratory experiments in which one option is guaranteed to lead to a certain outcome, political leaders rarely perceive that any given policy option leads to a particular outcome with certainty (unless, through editing operations, they do not differentiate among the possible outcomes of a particular policy option, but instead collapse them into a single outcome, treat it as a certain gain or loss without attaching to it a more specific value, and evaluate the transformed prospects). Instead, each policy option involves some degree of risk and uncertainty, both in its immediate effects and its future consequences.

This raises the extremely difficult problems of defining what we mean when we say that one prospect is riskier than another and determining how decision-makers actually compare relative risks among options. If actors evaluate probabilities and values along an interval scale, then an expected utility calculation provides the optimal criteria for evaluating risky choices. In the absence of cardinal (or interval) utilities, however, there are a number of alternative decision criteria that an actor might utilize. Does a risk-averse actor adopt a minimax criteria and act to minimize the maximum loss she might suffer? Or does she select the option which minimizes the range or variance in possible outcomes? Or

---

[8]It is striking how often decision-makers speak explicitly in terms of the inevitability (and not just high probability) of war. This tendency can be explained by a number of cognitive and motivational biases (Jervis, 1976: Janis & Mann, 1977).

does she adopt a minimax risk (regret) or some alternative criteria (Luce & Raiffa, 1957, pp. 278–86). It is not always clear which prospect or strategy involves the greatest risks or how the actor evaluates the relative risks.

The problem would be simplified under the following conditions: An actor sees herself in a mixed domain of losses and gains, with one option which could lead only to negative outcomes and another which could lead to either negative or positive outcomes. (Note that we cannot specify which is preferable on expected-value terms in the absence of information of how extreme each of these outcomes is.) If the decision criterion is to avoid a certain loss, the actor might then choose the second option. This is a plausible interpretation of Carter's decision to approve the rescue mission, in that inaction could only lead to losses, whereas the rescue mission held out the possibility of gains. (Recall that McDermott assumes a domain of losses rather than a mixed lottery involving both losses and gains.)

Many cases in international politics involve the additional complexity of trade-offs between immediate and future risks (and uncertainties). This raises a difficult theoretical problem and one which has not received much attention in the literature on prospect theory. In the formal decision-theoretic literature, future utilities are discounted and then combined with present utility into a single utility function and hence a single-risk attitude. George (1969, pp. 214–15) questions the validity of this assumption in international relations, suggests that risk orientation is a multidimensional concept, and argues that political leaders often evaluate risks sequentially. Decision-makers not only focus on the level of risk, but also assess when the risky outcomes are likely to arise, and the extent to which they (decision-makers) will be able to control the sequence of events leading to those risky outcomes (see also George & Smoke, 1974, pp. 527–30).

Thus the assessment of which options involve the greatest risks, and by how much, is rarely easy, either for the actor or for the analyst. Some analysts might assume that war, or the use of force short of war, always carries the largest risks, perhaps because of the "fog of war" and the inherent danger that war might escalate. This might be consistent with a minimax criterion, for a devastating defeat in war is reasonably regarded as the worst possible outcome, however small its probability of occurrence might be.

But nonaction and the continued deterioration of the status quo also involves substantial risks, and in some situations these may be perceived to be greater than the risks of war. Political leaders are often quite confident that they can achieve a rapid and complete victory with minimal costs (White, 1968; Jervis, 1976; Levy, 1983) and thus underestimate the risks involved in the use of force. At the same time, they may exaggerate the possible internal and external threats that might arise from their failure to act (Mayer, 1977). Exactly how decision-makers will evaluate and compare these risks is highly uncertain, and consequently it is difficult to predict how a risk-seeking (or risk-averse) actor will behave.

It not at all clear, for example, that U.S. decision-makers regarded the military, diplomatic, and domestic political risks of military action in the Persian Gulf in 1991 as greater than the risks involved in continuing economic sanctions, holding the diplomatic coalition together, and allowing Saddam Hussein more time to acquire nuclear and biological weapons. Nor is it clear, returning to the McDermott study, that Carter, given his high estimates of success of a rescue mission, perceived that a rescue mission involved more risks than did allowing the hostage crisis to continue, with all of its unpredictable consequences for his own upcoming reelection campaign as well as for the image and influence of the United States in the world. If this were true, it is not clear whether the decision for the rescue mission is best explained in terms of (1) risk-seeking behavior to avoid the certain losses inherent in the continued deterioration of the status quo, (2) risk-averse behavior to avoid the enormous risks and uncertainties inherent in the continued deterioration of the status quo, or (3) the maximization of expected value based in part on Carter's expectation of a successful rescue mission.

The problem of evaluating perceptions of relative risks also applies to crisis bargaining. "Spiral theorists" generally believe that the uncompromising demonstration of resolve through threats is the riskiest (in terms of the probability of escalation to war) strategy in a crisis because of the security dilemma and the psychological dynamics associated with it. "Deterrence theorists," on the other hand, believe that a policy of firm deterrent threats is the least risky strategy because it clarifies commitments, demonstrates resolve, and minimizes the likelihood of miscalculation (Jervis, 1976). Decision makers may also have different ideas (in terms of risks) as to whether hardline bargaining tactics (and conciliatory gestures) ought to come early or later in the negotiating process, as Rogers (1991) shows in his analysis of images of escalatory dynamics and optimum bargaining tactics.

The Preventive War Problem

The complexities of relative risk assessment are also evident for a state which is in relative decline and which faces a decision whether (1) to initiate preventive military action against a rising challenger while the opportunity is still available, or (2) to accept the continued deterioration of its international position (along with the domestic costs that it might entail).

As I noted in an earlier study (Levy, 1987, pp. 101–3), war now involves uncertainties regarding the probability of victory (presumably over 50% for a declining but still stronger state in a bilateral war), its costs, and the likelihood and costs of escalation or the intervention of third states. Delay involves uncertainties regarding whether and how far one's position will continue to deteriorate, what the adversary will do once it achieves a position of superiority (or before), the feasibility of securing diplomatic support to contain the adversary, the possibility of appeasing it, and particularly the likelihood and costs of a future war. In domestic terms, war now could generate for the elite in power either the domestic benefits of a victorious war or the potentially fatal costs of defeat, whereas delay might generate a gradually increasing discontent but the opportunity to pass the potential costs of war onto the elites' political successors. A further complication for prospect theory is that the possibility of gains from war creates a situation of mixed losses and gains rather than a domain of pure losses for the declining state. (I assume here that the declining state defines the present status quo as its reference point. The rising challenger might focus on a higher—that is, future—aspiration level.)

It is difficult to say which of these two prospects—preventive war or continued decline—involves the greatest risks, at least in the eyes of decision-makers, and therefore which way a risk-seeking actor in the domain of losses would be inclined if the decision were not compelling on expected-value grounds alone. Assessment all depends on the criterion decision-makers use to compare relative risks. If decision-makers adopt a minimax criteria, they might prefer to delay and avoid the worst possible outcome, defeat in a preventive war. Alternatively, because war might bring gains as well as losses and thus involve a mixed lottery, decision-makers who want to avoid the near-certain losses inherent in the continued deterioration of their position might prefer war now, given their perception that inaction would lead to continued decline. This second interpretation might be reinforced by another consideration which follows from the endowment effect: states will probably try to hang onto their current entitlements longer than they should on the basis of a rational calculus.

A criterion based on the range or variance of possible negative outcomes, on the other hand, might led to a different result. It would suggest that the risks of delay are greater than the risks of war now, for the number and magnitude of negative outcomes presumably increases as one's relative power declines. This would create an incentive for a risk-acceptant actor to delay but for a risk-averse actor to prefer preventive action now. This tendency for risk-acceptant dominant states to prefer inaction, but for risk-averse states to prefer war now, is precisely what Kim and Morrow (1991) derive from their formal theoretical model of war decisions during power transitions; moreover, this hypothesis receives some support form their empirical analysis for the period since 1815.

Unfortunately, neither the theoretical nor experimental literature proves much guidance for an analysis of the trade-offs between risks now and risks later. No analysis of this kind can be definitive in the absence of auxiliary assumptions about the decision criteria adopted by policy-makers and the extent to which they discount future utilities.

Risk Propensities When Probabilities Are Small

Another problem (though perhaps a lesser one) with nearly all applications of prospect theory to international relations is that they treat as unconditional the hypothesis that actors are risk-averse with respect to gains and risk-acceptant with respect to losses. But recall that risk orientation is determined not only by the value function but also by the probability-weighting function. For small probabilities the over-weighting of probabilities works in the opposite direction as the value function and encourages risk-seeking in the domain of gains and risk aversion in the domain of losses. Which of these counteracting tendencies will dominate depends on the precise shapes of these functions over this range of small probabilities.

This indeterminacy is further compounded for prospects involving extremely small probabilities, where observed behavior is quite erratic and where the probability-weighting function is therefore indeterminate. The problem is compounded also in situations which involve catastrophic losses (which presumably involve very small probabilities), where studies have shown that the tendency toward risk-seeking may be reversed (Payne et al., 1981; Tversky & Kahneman, 1986, p. S258).

Thus we must be very cautious in making assumptions about risk attitudes in situations involving small probabilities and/or catastrophic losses. Such situations may be fairly common in international relations, particularly those involving decisions on war and peace, and particularly in the nuclear age. It may be true that states would be less likely to risk a nuclear war to improve their position than a standard-probability calculus might suggest, or more likely to risk one if they thought the adversary was about to attack and that there was a small chance they could escape unscathed by preempting (Jervis, 1989, p. 171), but we should remember that under some conditions prospect theory would make the opposite predictions. Similarly, the argument that deterrence against an expansionist adversary is reinforced by the presumed aggressor's risk aversion with respect to gains may not be true, for the over-weighting of a small probability of a large gain might (depending on the respective shapes of the value and weighting functions) lead to risk-acceptant behavior.

What this means is that analysts who apply prospect theory need to be quite sensitive to the probabilities which decision-makers attach to various outcomes. If probabilities are in the moderate range, the standard prospect theory hypotheses based on the value function can be applied. But if probabilities are small, one cannot apply these hypotheses directly without making assumptions about the respective shapes of the value and probability-weighting functions. The analyst's task is complicated further by uncertainty regarding the transition point from over-weighting to under-weighting of probabilities, particularly for the more complex choice problems typically found in international relations.

Other Determinants of Risk Propensity

Most of our discussion, along with most applications of prospect theory to international relations, assumes that the risk orientation of decision-makers is determined primarily by the framing of losses or gains around a reference point.

But this is a very strong assumption, and probably not a very reasonable one, for attitudes toward risk can also be affected by idiosyncratic, cultural, political, ideological, and other decision-making variables as well as framing effects. Recall that the reflection effect found in laboratory experiments typically applies to about 60% to 80% of the subjects. Although this consistency level is quite high by any social science standards, and although these findings have been found to be valid for a wide variety of subjects, including business executives (MacCrimmon & Wehrung, 1986) and the medical community, it does raise the questions of who the other 20% to 40% are and why they behave differently.

Nonconforming behavior of this order of magnitude may be of lesser significance than majority tendencies in situations which involve large numbers of individuals in market situations, but it can have enormous impact in international relations. General Tojo's remark a few weeks before Pearl Harbor is reminder enough: "There are times when we must have the courage to do extraordinary things—like jumping, with eyes closed, off the veranda of the Kiyomizu Temple" (quoted in Morgan, 1977, p. 153). The behavior of the deviant 20% to 40% is itself a critical issue for research in international relations.

It is clear that individual characteristics such as personality, age, race, gender, education, income, and profession can all have an impact on risk attitude, as a number of empirical studies have shown (for sources see MacCrimmon & Wehrung, 1986, p. 49). The influence of most individual-level attributes may be effectively randomized in large-n laboratory studies so that we can reasonably assume that risk orientation in those studies derives exclusively from framing around a reference point. But there is good reason to believe that attitudes toward risk are one factor which distinguish political leaders from the population at large and which facilitate their rise to high-level political positions, so that we cannot dismiss these other sources of risk orientation in the analysis of foreign policy behavior.

The question of the risk attitudes of political leaders is a complex issue, for recruitment processes in some political systems may be more biased than others toward risk-seeking individuals (Morgan, 1977, pp. 153–64). Highly bureaucratized systems might reward individuals with risk-averse attitudes, whereas dictatorial or revolutionary regimes might be more conducive to risk-seeking leaders. As Mussolini asked, perhaps with some exaggeration, "have you ever known a prudent calculating dictator?" (quoted in Morgan, 1977, p. 153). These possible effects of political structure may be tempered by those deriving from small group dynamics: the "risky shift" hypothesis suggests that risk-seeking propensities tend to increase in the context of group decision-making, although more recent literature is more balanced on the question of the magnitude and direction of choice shifts (Pruitt, 1971; Kirkpatrick et al., 1976; Janis, 1982).

Political culture may also influence risk attitudes. Nearly all experimental work on framing, the reflection effect, and loss aversion has been conducted on American subjects, frequently college students. It would be interesting to examine whether observed tendencies are as prominent in European, Latin, Middle Eastern, or Eastern cultures. Ideological variables may also be significant. George (1969) argues that individual approaches to risk are an important component of operational code belief systems and that because of the Bolshevik operational code Soviet leaders have a different (and more differentiated) approach to risk than U.S. leaders. Adomeit (1982, p. 56) also emphasizes ideological factors and argues that Soviet risk-taking tends to occur in leftist periods in Soviet history and risk avoidance in rightist periods.

Thus it is quite possible that individual, institutional, cultural, and other variables have a significant influence on risk orientation. An analysis of the role of risk propensities in international relations should not be confined to framing around a reference point but should be expanded to include other variables as well.

The analysis of other influences on risk propensity is admittedly a data-intensive task, but it is particularly important for individual case studies, where it is more difficult to control systematically for other sources of risk attitude and where a premium is placed on construct validity. Although there is no guarantee that risk propensities are invariant across time and issues, an analysis of a political decision-maker's orientation toward risk in previous situations might be a useful indicator of present risk attitudes, and for this reason political biographies can be a useful source of data on risk propensities. The George and George (1956) study of Woodrow Wilson is a good example here.

CONCLUSION

Recent attempts to apply prospect theory or some of its key hypotheses to international relations make a significant contribution to the field in a number of respects. First of all, by emphasizing the potential importance of risk propensities, they direct additional attention to an important variable which only recently has begun to attract rigorous and systematic research by international relations scholars (Bueno de Mesquita, 1981, 1985; Morrow, 1987). The fact that the scholars applying prospect theory in international relations come from a different research tradition than the more formally oriented scholars noted above makes this renewed emphasis on risk propensity all the more significant.

The assumption that actors in international relations define value in terms of deviations from a reference point rather than in terms of net asset or power position, and the proposition that gains are treated differently than losses, are also significant contributions to the literature. These ideas have enormous potential in helping to explain the repeated tendency for actors to expend extensive resources and effort to resist even small changes in the status quo contrary to their interests, to make limited changes in order to preserve the overall structure of the status quo, and to persist in losing ventures longer than a rational calculus might predict. Moreover, the framing of a decision problem can affect not only the definition of the reference point but also the evaluation of the utilities of various outcomes. Thus the focus on framing gives renewed emphasis to the old question of the definition of the situation in foreign policy decision-making (Snyder, Bruck, & Sapin, 1962).

In spite of their enormous potential contribution to international relations, applications of prospect theory face a number of potentially difficult conceptual and methodological problems. These difficulties are effectively overcome under highly structured and controlled experimental conditions, but they are much less tractable in the empirical study of international relations through case study or aggregate data methods.

It is not always clear how a decision-maker identifies the reference point; how she defines her available policy options, the possible outcomes that might result from each, and the values and probabilities she attaches to each of these outcomes; which option she perceives as the more risky one; or how she balances immediate versus future risks. For these reasons, it is often difficult to determine whether the preference for one option over another derives from framing, loss aversion, and the over-weighting of certain outcomes; from the adoption of an alternative decision criterion regarding risk; or from a simple utility-maximization criteria. The possible reversal of risk propensities at low probabilities and the highly indeterminant behavior expected at extremely low probabilities further complicate the analysis under certain conditions.

Of course, excessive concern for all of these problems is as likely to lead to paralysis as to better research. We are at an early stage in the application of some of these hypotheses to international relations, and the attitude of the critic should be one of openness and encouragement. Farnham's (1992) conclusion regarding her own study can be fairly applied to the other case studies in this issue as well: "With respect to the theoretical significance of these findings, at the very least they support the demand of prospect theory to be acknowledged as a legitimate alternative for explaining decision-making behavior."

At the same time, however, it is reasonable to suggest that it is not enough for an analyst to demonstrate that observed behavior is consistent with prospect theory. It is also necessary to make a serious effort to rule out the alternative explanation that the observed behavior is also consistent with a rational choice model which posits that decision-makers select the option that has the higher expected value in terms of a standard probability calculus.

ACKNOWLEDGMENTS

I would like to thank Frank Harvey, Patrick James, Cliff Morgan, Ed Rhodes, Janice Stein, and Tom Walker for their helpful comments on earlier versions of this paper.

REFERENCES

Abelson, R. P., & Levi, A. (1985). Decision making and decision theory. In G. Lindzey & E. Aronson (Eds.), *The handbook of social psychology*, 3rd ed., vol. 1 (pp. 231–309). New York: Random House.
Adomeit, H. (1982). *Soviet risk-taking and crisis behavior*. London: George Allen and Unwin.
Bazerman, M. H. (1983). Negotiator judgment. *American Behavioral Scientist, 27*, 211–228.
Bell, D. E., & Raiffa, H. (1988). Marginal value and intrinsic risk aversion. In D. E. Bell, H. Raiffa, & A. Tversky (Eds.), *Decision making: descriptive, normative, and prescriptive interactions* (pp. 384–397). New York: Cambridge University Press.
Bueno de Mesquita, B. (1981). *The war trap*. New Haven, CT: Yale University Press.
Bueno de Mesquita, B. (1985). The war trap revisited: a revised expected utility model. *American Political Science Review, 79*, 156–177.
Davies, J. C. (1962). Toward a theory of revolution. *American Sociological Review, 27*, 5–19.
Dyer, J. S., & Sarin, R. (1979). Measurable multiattribute value functions. *Operations Research, 27*, 810–822.
Einhorn, H. J., & Hogarth, R. M. (1985). Ambiguity and uncertainty in probabilistic inference. *Psychological Review, 92*, 433–461.
Ellsberg, D. (1961). Risk, ambiguity, and the Savage axioms. *Quarterly Journal of Economics, 75*, 643–669.
Farnham, B. (1992). Roosevelt and the Munich crisis: insights from prospect theory. *Political Psychology, 13*, 205–235.
Fishburn, P. C., & Kochenberger, G. A. (1979). Two-piece Von Neumann-Morgenstern utility functions. *Decision Sciences, 10*, 503–518.
Fischer, G. W., Kamlet, M. S., Fienberg, S. E., & Schkade, D. (1986). Risk preferences for gains and losses in multiple objective decision making. *Management Science, 32*, 1065–1086.
Galtung, J. (1964). A structural theory of aggression. *Journal of Peace Research, 1*, 95–119.
George, A. L., & George, J. L. (1956). *Woodrow Wilson and Colonel House*. New York: Dover.
George, A. L. (1969). The 'operational code': a neglected approach to the study of political leaders and decision-making. *International Studies Quarterly, 13*, 190–222.
George, A. L., & Smoke, R. (1974). *Deterrence in American foreign policy*. New York: Columbia University Press.
Gurr, T. R. (1970). *Why men rebel*. Princeton, NJ: Princeton University Press.
Hartman, R. S., Doane, M. J., & Woo, C. (1991). Consumer rationality and the status quo. *Quarterly Journal of Economics, 106*, 141–162.
Hempel, C. G. (1966). *Philosophy of natural science*. Englewood Cliffs, NJ: Prentice-Hall.
Hershey, J. C., & Schoemaker, P. J. H. (1980). Risk taking and problem context in the domain of losses: an expected utility analysis. *Journal of Risk and Insurance, 47*, 111–132.
Huth, P., Gelpi, C., & Bennett, D. S. (1992). International conflict among the great powers: testing the interactive effect of system uncertainty and risk propensity. *Journal of Conflict Resolution, 36*, forthcoming.
Janis, I. L. (1982). *Groupthink*. 2nd ed. Boston: Houghton Mifflin.
Janis, I. L., & Mann, L. (1977). *Decision making*. New York: Free Press.
Jervis, R. (1970). *The logic of images*. Princeton, NJ: Princeton University Press.
Jervis, R. (1976). *Perception and misperception in international politics*. Princeton, NJ: Princeton University Press.
Jervis, R. (1988). War and misperception. *Journal of Interdisciplinary History, 18*, 675–700.
Jervis, R. (1989). *The meaning of the nuclear revolution*. Ithaca, NY: Cornell University Press.
Jervis, R. (1991). Domino beliefs and strategic behavior. In R. Jervis & J. Snyder (Eds.), *Dominoes and bandwagons: strategic beliefs and great power competition in the Eurasian rimland* (pp. 20–50). New York: Oxford University Press.
Jervis, R. (1992). Political implications of loss aversion. *Political Psychology, 13*, 187–204.
Kahneman, D., Knetsch, J. L., & Thaler, R. H. (1990). Experimental tests of the endowment effect and the Coase theorem. *Journal of Political Economy, 98*, 1325–1348.

Kahneman, D., Knetsch, J. L., & Thaler, R. H. (1991). The endowment effect, loss aversion, and status quo bias. *Journal of Economic Perspectives, 5,* 193–206.
Kahneman, D., & Tversky, Amos. (1979). Prospect theory: an analysis of decision under risk. *Econometrica, 47,* 263–291.
Kahneman, D., & Tversky, A. (1982). Variants of uncertainty. In D. Kahneman, P. Slovic, & A. Tversky (Eds.), *Judgment under uncertainty: heuristics and biases* (pp. 509–520). Cambridge, England: Cambridge University Press.
Kahneman, D., & A. Tversky. (1984). Choices, values, and frames. *American Psychologist, 39,* 341–350.
Keohane, R. O. (1984). *After hegemony.* Princeton, NJ: Princeton University Press.
Kim, W., & Morrow, J. (1991). When do power transitions lead to war? Mimeo.
Kirkpatrick, S. A., Davis, D. F., & Robertson, R. D. (1976). The process of political decision-making in groups: search behavior and choice shifts. *American Behavioral Scientist, 20,* 33–64.
Knetsch, Jack L. (1989). The endowment effect and evidence of nonreversible indifference curves. *American Economic Review, 79,* 1277–1284.
Knetsch, J. L., & Sinden, J. A. (1984). Willingness to pay and compensation demanded: experimental evidence of an unexpected disparity in measures of value. *Quarterly Journal of Economics, 99,* 507–521.
Knetsch, J. L., and Sinden, J. A. (1987). The persistence of evaluation disparities. *Quarterly Journal of Economics, 102,* 691–695.
Lakatos, I. (1970). Falsification and the methodology of scientific research programs. In I. Lakatos & A. Musgrave (Eds.), *Criticism and the growth of knowledge* (pp. 91–196). Cambridge, England: Cambridge University Press.
Lamborn, A. C. (1985). Risk and foreign policy choice. *International Studies Quarterly, 29,* 385–410.
Lebow, R. N., & Stein, J. G. (1987). Beyond deterrence. *Journal of Social Issues, 43,* 5–71.
Levin, I. P.., Johnson, R. D., Russo, C. P., & Deldin, P. (1985). Framing effects in judgment tasks with varying amounts of information. *Organizational Behavior and Human Decision Processes, 36,* 362–377.
Levy, J. S. (1983). Misperception and the causes of war. *World Politics, 36,* 76–99.
Levy, J. S. (1987). Declining power and the preventive motivation for war. *World Politics, 40,* 82–107.
Levy, J. S. (1989a). The diversionary theory of war: a critique. In M. I. Midlarsky (Ed.), *Handbook of war studies* (pp. 259–288). Boston: Unwin Hyman.
Levy, J. S. (1989b). Quantitative studies of deterrence success and failure. In P. C. Stern, R. Axelrod, R. Jervis, & R. Radner (Eds.), *Perspectives on deterrence* (pp. 98–133). New York: Oxford University Press.
Levy, J. S. (1990/91). Preferences, constraints, and choices in July 1914. *International Security, 15,* 151–186.
Levy, J. S. (1992). Introduction to prospect theory. *Political Psychology, 13,* 171–186.
Luce, R. D., & Raiffa, H. (1957). *Games and decisions.* New York: Wiley.
McDermott, R. (1992). The failed rescue mission in Iran: an application of prospect theory. *Political Psychology, 13.*
McInerney, A. (1992). Prospect theory and Soviet policy towards Syria, 1966–1967. *Political Psychology, 13.*
McNeil, B. J., Pauker, S. G., Sox, Jr., H. C., & Tversky, A. (1982). On the elicitation of preferences for alternative therapies. *New England Journal of Medicine, 306,* 1259–1262.
Maoz, Z. (1990). Framing the national interest: the manipulation of foreign policy decisions in group settings. *World Politics, 43,* 77–110.
Mayer, A. J. (1977). Internal crises and war since 1870. In C. L. Bertrand (Ed.), *Revolutionary situations in Europe, 1917–1922* (pp. 201–33). Montreal: Interuniversity Center for European Studies.
Midlarsky, M. I. (1975). *On war: Political violence in the international system.* New York: Free Press.
Morgan, P. M. (1977). *Deterrence: a conceptual analysis.* Beverly Hills, CA: Sage.

Morgan, T. C., & Wilson, R. K. (1989). The spatial model of crisis bargaining: an experimental test. ISA paper.
Morrow, J. D. (1987). On the theoretical basis of a measure of national risk attitudes. *International Studies Quarterly, 31,* 423–438.
Payne, J. W., Laughhunn, D. J., & Crum, R. (1981). Aspiration level effects in risky choice behavior. *Management Science, 27,* 953–959.
Pipes, D. (1973). Some operational principles of Soviet foreign policy. In M. Confino & S. Shamir (Eds.), *The USSR and the Middle East.* Jerusalem: Israel University Press.
Pruitt, D. G. (1971). Choice shifts in group discussion: an introductory review. *Journal of Personality and Social Psychology, 20,* 339–360.
Quattrone, G. A., & Tversky, A. (1988). Contrasting rational and psychological analyses of political choice. *American Political Science Review, 82,* 719–736.
Rhodes, E. (1989). *Power and madness.* New York: Columbia University Press.
Rogers, J. P. (1991). Crisis bargaining codes and crisis management. In A. L. George, ed., *Avoiding war: problems of crisis management* (pp. 413–442.) Boulder, CO: Westview.
Ross, D. (1984). Risk aversion in Soviet decisionmaking. In J. Valenta & W. Potter (Eds.), *Soviet decisionmaking for national security* (pp. 237–251). London: Allen & Unwin.
Samuelson, W., & Zechhauser, R. (1988). Status quo bias in decision making. *Journal of Risk and Uncertainty, 1,* 7–59.
Schelling, T. C. (1960). *The strategy of conflict.* Cambridge, MA: Harvard University Press.
Schelling, T. C. (1966). *Arms and influence.* New Haven, CT: Yale University Press.
Schoemaker, P. J. H. (1980). *Experiments on decisions under risk: the expected utility hypothesis.* Boston: Martinus Nijhoff.
Shefrin, H., & Statman, M. (1985). The disposition to sell winners too early and ride losers too long: theory and evidence. *Journal of Finance, 40,* 777–790.
Slovic, P., Fischhoff, B., & Lichtenstein, S. (1988). Response mode, framing, and information-processing effects in risk assessment. In D. E. Bell, H. Raiffa, & A. Tversky (Eds.), *Decision making: descriptive, normative, and prescriptive interactions* (pp. 152–166). New York: Cambridge University Press.
Slovic, P. & Lichtenstein, S. (1983). Preference reversals: a broader perspective. *American Economic Review, 73,* 596–605.
Snyder, R. C., Bruck, H. W., & Sapin, B. (1962). *Foreign policy decision-making.* New York: Free Press.
Stein, J. G. (1992). International cooperation and loss avoidance: framing the problem. In J. G. Stein & L. Pauly (Eds.), *Choosing to cooperate: How states avoid loss.* Baltimore: Johns Hopkins University Press.
Stein, J. G., & Tanter, R. (1980). *Rational decision-making: Israel's security choices, 1967.* Columbus, OH: Ohio State University Press.
Thaler, R. (1980). Toward a positive theory of consumer choice. *Journal of Economic Behavior and Organization, 1,* 39–60.
Tversky, A. (1972). Elimination by aspects: a theory of choice. *Psychological Review, 76,* 31–48.
Tversky, A., & Kahneman, D. (1982). Availability: a heuristic for judging frequency and probability. In D. Kahneman, P. Slovic, & A. Tversky (Eds.), *Judgment under uncertainty: heuristics and biases* (pp. 163–178). Cambridge, England: Cambridge University Press.
Tversky, A., & Kahneman, D. (1986). Rational choice and the framing of decisions. *Journal of Business, 59* (no. 4, pt. 2), S251–S278.

Prospect Theory and Political Analysis: A Psychological Perspective[1]

Eldar Shafir[2]

INTRODUCTION

An important contributor to the shaping of political reality are the decision-making processes that characterize political elites as well as ordinary citizens. The most popular descriptive theory of decision under risk is prospect theory (Kahneman & Tversky, 1979). It is therefore appropriate for political scientists to try to enlist prospect theory in their attempts to analyze political events of particular interest. The contributors to the present collection have embarked on just this course. Each author applies certain qualitative principles derived from prospect theory, and supported by dozens of studies conducted in laboratory settings, to the analysis and explication of political events that seem puzzling from the perspective of standard political thinking.

Farnham, for example, examines President Roosevelt's change of mind during the 1938 Munich crisis, from believing that American intervention was unwarranted to believing that it was necessary, and argues that the shift can be

---

[1] This work was supported by US Public Health Service Grant No. 1-R29-MH46885 from the National Institute of Mental Health.
[2] Department of Psychology, Princeton University, Princeton, New Jersey, 08544. Electronic mail: eldar@clarity.princeton.edu.

understood as resulting from a change in his framing of the decision at hand. McDermott argues that the Iranian hostage crisis gradually became for President Carter a situation involving a choice between losses and led him—in accord with the risk attitudes predicted by prospect theory—to take a risky action that was contrary to his earlier emphasis on a peaceful resolution of the conflict. McInerney suggests that the Soviet leadership in 1966–1967 reluctantly chose the risky option of contributing to the rhetoric and tension that eventually resulted in an Arab-Israeli war because it perceived its relationship with the Syrian neo-Baath party as part of a status quo which it was not willing to lose. Jervis considers the potential role of loss aversion in numerous other political settings.

The application to political analysis of psychological principles derived from prospect theory is at times quite compelling. But findings from other areas of psychology highlight the need for caution. As various researchers have shown (Chapman & Chapman, 1969; see also Nisbett & Ross, 1980), confirming evidence may often be overestimated by investigators who expect to see a phenomenon. While thorough analyses of political decisions and psychological research into decision-making are likely to effect a fruitful synergy, various issues need further investigation. A number of contributors to the present volume discuss the problematics of certain issues that remain unresolved from the point-of-view of political science. They point out, for example, that political leaders may often do all they can to avoid small losses not necessarily because they are averse to a small loss, but rather because they believe that small losses have a tendency—via a domino effect—to pyramid quickly into much greater losses. In fact, the designation of losses and gains may itself be problematic when applied to the political arena, particularly in cases where these are quite different, say, from the perspective of a country's international standing and from that of the domestic standing of its leaders.

In what follows, I discuss some unresolved issues in the application of prospect theory to the analysis of political events, from the point-of-view of psychological theorizing. The discussion refers, whenever applicable, to the aforementioned political studies. The cataloging of unresolved conceptual and methodological problems from a psychological perspective is intended to encourage further explorations of interest to psychologists, decision theorists, and political scientists.

THE PRINCIPAL COMPONENTS OF DECISION

Prospect theory is based on a few simple and compelling assumptions regarding the principal components that characterize any decision under risk. These components are the decision-maker, his or her current position, the values of potential outcomes, and the probabilities of these outcomes. In what follows, we consider each of these components and the issues it raises when prospect theory is applied to the political realm.

The Decision-Maker

Prospect theory is a theory of *individual* decision-making. It is based on specific assumptions regarding people's anticipated pleasure over gains as compared to their pain over losses. Furthermore, it assumes that the desirability of prospects is weighted not by their likelihoods but rather by the subjective weight of these likelihoods for the decision-maker. All this may be significantly different for groups of individuals. Extensive research has shown, for example, that decisions by groups tend to differ from the average of the individual members' decisions prior to group discussion. (See Clark, 1971, for a survey of groups' differential risk attitudes; Mowen & Gentry, 1980, for groups' greater propensity to exhibit "preference reversals"; Brandstatter et al., 1982, for a collection of other relevant studies). In particular, it is important to keep in mind that group preferences ought not to be confounded with the preferences of particular individuals in the group. An intransitive pattern of preferences, for example, may be exhibited by a group, while the same pattern does not apply to any individual member of that group (for discussion, see Luce, 1959). The relationship between individual and aggregate behavior is an intricate problem that has been addressed by a number of researchers (see, e.g., Akerlof & Yellen, 1985; Russell & Thaler, 1985).

Decisions at the level of international relations are frequently made in some form of group setting. McInerney discusses the policies of "the Soviets." Farnham and McDermott, while focusing on decisions officially made by single leaders, present ample evidence suggesting that these decisions were in fact reached in collaboration with, or were strongly influenced by, personal advisers and friends as well as political allies. It is an interesting question as to what extent a group's attitudes change over time as a function of the weight given to the opinions of particular members. It is easy to imagine, for example, that the opinions of military personnel will weigh more heavily once a military action has begun and may yield a change in the risk attitudes of the group although no change has occurred in the attitude of any individual member. Consider McDermott's description of the days preceding the Iranian hostage rescue mission. As a result of Cyrus Vance's (the most risk-averse participant) losing his debate against Zbigniew Brzezinski and eventually resigning, President Carter's group as a whole became more risk prone, even though no change need have occurred in the risk attitudes of any of the participants.

An analysis of framing incorporates similar complications once decisions are made in group settings. Framing refers to the tendency of normatively inconsequential changes in the formulation of a choice problem to affect the ways people represent the problem and, consequently, their preferences. The assumption is that each frame induces a particular perspective. The reason framing effects are sizable and persistent is that the decision-maker does not construct multiple or canonical perspectives but rather adopts the particular perspective induced by the available formulation of the problem. When the decision is reached by numerous participants, however, it is often possible that a plurality of perspectives will be available at once. According to Farnham, for example, President Franklin Roosevelt was presented with different frames of the Munich crisis by, say, Secretary of State Cordell Hull (who advocated inaction), and his Ambassador to France, William Bullitt (who determinedly advised action). Similarly, according to McDermott, President Carter was presented with widely divergent frames of the Iranian hostage crisis by National Security Advisor Brzezinski and Secretary of State Vance. The situation in these scenarios is no longer one in which only a single frame is induced but rather a situation in which one of several available frames must be chosen. While future research may elucidate decision behavior under multiple frames, it may not be trivial to disentangle the choice of a frame from a choice of the alternative which that particular frame supports. One possibility is that two frames simultaneously available behave like a 'mixed' frame, one which combines both formulations. For example, the concurrent presentation of two separate frames, one in terms of gains and another in terms of losses, may behave like a framing of the problem in terms of both gains and losses. Data from McNeil, Pauker, and Tversky (1988) indicate that such mixed frames produce results that are intermediate, leading to behaviors that lie somewhere in between those generated by two opposing frames. To the extent that group deliberations lead to an intermediate framing of a problem, we would expect to observe fewer frame changes in group than in individual decisions and hence relatively infrequent frame changes in decisions regarding international relations.

The Decision-Maker's Current Position

It is important to keep in mind that practically any individual decision is consistent with many candidate theories of choice. Consider, for example, a person's preference for lottery x over lottery y:

x: 90% chance to win $3000 > y: 45% chance to win $6000

Almost any theory of choice can explain this preference by supposing that, for that person, the value of x is higher than that of y. Consider, however, the following additional preference for z over w:

w: .2% chance to win $3000 < z: .1% chance to win $6000

The above pattern of preferences, x > y and z > w (documented in Kahneman & Tversky, 1979), is enough to differentiate between two competing alternatives: it is consistent with prospect theory but cannot be predicted by expected utility theory. In order to distinguish between theories we normally have to document a series of choices that implies an ordering of preferences that is consistent with one theory but not with another. Such an ordering, however, typically needs to be obtained while the decision-maker maintains her current position (economically, socially, politically, psychologically). Once her current assets have changed, the decision-maker is allowed to change her preferences. If, for example, the person had inherited a million dollars in the interval between making the two decisions above, it would be entirely consistent with expected utility theory that she should forfeit the greater chance for what is now perceived as an exceedingly small amount in favor of the smaller chance at a larger sum. All this is rather obvious and relatively easily controlled in various laboratory situations. In the analysis of political events, however, this factor presents a serious problem. Because a single decision is not enough, we need to observe a series of choices that typically extends over some non-negligible period of time. But then we cannot be certain that the protagonists' positions have remained unchanged. Farnham goes to great lengths to show that Roosevelt's political situation in fact had not changed during the two and a half weeks of the Munich crisis. But continuously facing the possibility of a major war is likely to affect the leader of a superpower throughout a variety of dimensions—psychological, physiological, and others— that form an integral part of his current position. It is precisely this "emotional" effect, according to Farnham, that led to Roosevelt's change of frame. The question which then arises is how we distinguish between a decision-maker's change of frame and a change in the decision-maker's current position.

Jervis mentions a number of decisions made by nations who have suffered political losses. In all these cases, however, the assumption that the leaders continue to perceive a loss entails that they have retained their initial reference point. According to McInerney, on the other hand, it took the Soviet leadership less than a year to incorporate the pro-Soviet Provisional Command in Syria into their readjusted point of reference. Other instances, such as Israel's return of the Sinai, indicate that gains may sometimes not be renormalized for much longer periods. Cyrus Vance, according to McDermott, incorporated the Iranian hostage crisis into his new reference point, while Brzezinski and Carter, who had the same information for the same amount of time, did not. A decision-maker's reference point plays a critical role in any analysis based on prospect theory. It determines not only where the decision-maker perceives himself to be but also the perceived nature of his options. McDermott argues that Carter perceived himself as being in the domain of losses. Her ensuing analysis, however, suggests that it was his current position that was perceived by Carter to be below his original reference point: the potential consequences (the release of hostages, the respect of his allies and adversaries, the votes of his constituency) were clearly perceived as gains. Carter's apparent risk attitudes would be interpreted quite differently depending on whether he had retained the original reference point and regarded the hostage crisis as a potential loss or, instead, had shifted his reference point and regarded the resolution of the crisis as a potential gain. For another example, McInerney explains that when the possibility of an Arab-Israeli war became more real, the Soviets promoted the exercise of caution. It then remains to be determined whether the Soviets' perceived status quo included a Syrian ally, with their initial risk-seeking behavior due to the perception of a potential loss, or conversely, whether their status quo did not include a Syrian ally and their eventual risk-avoiding behavior was due to the willingness to forego a potential gain. How long one retains an original point of reference and the dynamics of its eventual change are issues that need to be better understood. As long as we are free to attribute a change of reference point to one advisor in a team but not to another, to one country after one year but to another not even after 10, we risk making it too easy to impose a prospect theory interpretation on almost any political event.

The Values

An essential feature of prospect theory is that the carriers of value are changes in wealth or welfare, rather than final assets. A central characteristic of prospect theory's value function is loss aversion: the function is steeper in the negative than in the positive domain, hence, losses are predicted to loom larger than corresponding gains. Loss aversion plays an important role in all of the aforementioned political analyses. Yet, a convincing demonstration of loss aversion in naturally occurring political settings may be hard to provide. It is not enough to show that a decision-maker is averse to losses: any theory predicts that. Nor does it conflict with prospect theory if we observe preferences for a sure loss over a small probability of a greater loss. This is perfectly consistent with the theory anytime the greater loss is great enough. What one needs to show is that a loss hurts the decision-maker more than an equally large gain makes him happy. (Tversky and Kahneman, 1990, estimate the typical ratio to be a little over 2:1. In other words, a typical decision-maker is about as happy earning a little over $200 as he is sad losing $100.) But to arrive at a political leader's estimated magnitudes of potential gains and losses, and to evaluate his or her attitudes towards the gains and the losses while assuming a single reference point, is not a simple task when interpreting historical events. While the aforementioned analyses successfully illustrate numerous scenarios that are *consistent* with loss aversion, they tend to lack the information and tools required to establish the hypothesized attitudes towards losses and gains.

An immediate consequence of loss aversion is the endowment effect (Thaler, 1980; Kahneman, Knetsch, & Thaler, 1990). This effect, which implies that the disutility associated with giving up a valued good is greater than the utility associated with receiving it, is appealed to in a number of the preceding papers. Like loss aversion, the endowment effect is stated in terms of a precise comparative notion. It does not merely assert that people will be reluctant to give up things in their possession. Rather, it posits that people will find it more painful to part with something they own than they once found it satisfying to come to possess it. Like loss aversion, this delicate balance will not be easy to document in the political arena. For example, McInerney's appeal to the endowment effect as a factor in the Soviets' reluctance to lose control of the Syrian regime is hampered by the fact that we cannot compare the Soviet's reluctance to lose their Syrian ally with their glee when the neo-Baath regime first declared its support.

It is interesting to note, furthermore, that the endowment effect applies somewhat selectively (Kahneman et al., 1990): consumption goods, such as coffee mugs, pens, and chocolate bars, yield the effect, whereas induced value tokens (worth a specific amount of money) do not. A number of features distinguish between consumption goods and tokens. The values of the tokens prescribed by the experimenter are more clearly defined than the values of the consumption goods, and loss aversion is irrelevant to the tokens because transactions are evaluated simply on the basis of net gain or loss. In addition, personal attachment to an item that has been in the individual's possession for some time is likely to contribute significantly to the endowment effect and this attachment may favor coffee mugs and pens over tokens that are exchangeable for money. Now what about occupied lands, or newly situated missiles, or even recently acquired political allies? Are these more like mugs or like tokens? Do political leaders develop a personal attachment to missiles on a distant island or to foreign and deserted territories? Or do they regard them as political tokens, each with its clear political price? Do their preferences show a substantial and immediate effect for items over which their country has just acquired property rights, or do they—in accord with observations made by Kahneman et al.—show much weaker effects for items of which one does not have actual physical possession? The psychology that underlies the perception of political assets and gains will determine when, and to what extent, the endowment effect may be expected to play a role in the conduct and analysis of international politics.

The Chances

Prospect theory, as formulated by Kahneman and Tversky (1979), is a theory about decision under *risk*. It is limited, in other words, to options whose exact probabilities are known to the decision-maker. Most political decisions, on the other hand, involve outcomes whose precise probabilities are uncertain. A rich body of work concerning human probability judgment foreshadows additional intricacies in situations where decision-makers not only have to choose among risky options but must first assess the likelihoods of uncertain alternatives. The formation of belief must combine the strength, or extremeness, of newly obtained evidence with its weight, or predictive validity (see Griffin & Tversky, 1991, for an extensive treatment). But in most political situations, the decision-maker is likely to know a lot more about the strength of evidence than its weight. Hitler's pronouncements throughout September 1938, and the blessings of the Imam for the taking of hostages in Iran, had a strong impact on Roosevelt and Carter, respectively, whereas these occurrences' predictive validity was hard to determine. In many situations, the overweighing of evidence may operate to increase the perceived impact of rare events. Furthermore, phenomena ranging from reliance on various judgmental heuristics (Kahneman, Slovic, & Tversky, 1982; Dawes, 1988) to motivational biases (Kunda, 1990) to self-deception (Quattrone and Tversky, 1984) and feelings of competence (Heath & Tversky, 1991) may intervene in the assessment of likelihoods differentially over time. Thus, a political leader facing an impasse may be motivated to boost his likelihood estimates for the success of a risky solution, or may come to feel more knowledgeable about the domain, thus gaining a greater sense of confidence. While objectively the available options have not changed and no new information has been obtained, the decision-maker's subjective evaluation of likelihoods may shift so as to yield what in effect is a new set of options. All this may occur without a change either in frame or in the underlying attitudes toward loss or risk.

McDermott's portrayal of Carter's deliberations during the hostage crisis seems consistent with such an account. Having begun with a clear preference for diplomatic negotiation over a mission that involved serious military risks, and despite the low estimates of success offered by the Joint Chiefs of Staff, Carter's confidence in the success of the rescue mission increased, and peaked after the decision to proceed was made. Farnham, in turn, argues convincingly that no information had emerged from Godesberg which entitled Roosevelt to increase his subjective likelihood of success for a U.S. diplomatic intervention. Nonetheless, in light of the influences on human judgment mentioned above, it is conceivable that a creeping realization that war was imminent, combined with the fact that the probabilities of success were uncertain and the enemy unpredictable, led to a change in Roosevelt's estimated likelihood of success, however unjustified. Finally, in McInerney's analysis, the Soviets' willingness to contribute to the tensions that resulted in an unwanted war may have been the result of inappropriate probability estimation rather than a risk-seeking attitude. When facing a choice between losses, even the most risk-avoidant may opt for the risky option when its chances appear to be exceedingly small.

Small probabilities, which often characterize potential outcomes in the political realm, present another complication. The common generalization regarding prospect theory's prediction of risk aversion in the case of gains, and risk seeking in the case of losses, is only true for moderate-to-high probabilities. In the case of low probabilities the pattern reverses, yielding a fourfold pattern of risk attitudes: risk aversion for gains and risk-seeking for losses of high probability; risk-seeking for gains and risk aversion for losses of low probability (see, e.g., Cohen, Jaffray, & Said, 1987, and Tversky & Kahneman, 1990, for relevant data). Since political leaders' probability estimates are usually unavailable and can only be very approximately inferred, it may often be hard to determine whether we should expect to observe risk-averse or risk-seeking attitudes. McInerney argues that the Soviets thought an Arab-Israeli war was less likely than the fall of the provisional Syrian government. How much less likely? If their likelihood estimates were low enough (which would explain their willingness to take their chances), then we may expect to see risk avoiding behavior on the part of the Soviets rather than the risk-seeking attitudes that McInerney argues we should find. In a similar vein, in Farnham's analysis of the Munich crisis, some of Roosevelt's change in attitude may be attributed to a change in his subjective probabilities. Initially, as documented by his discussion with Secretary of the Interior Harold Ickes on September 16–17 (Farnham, p. 210), Roosevelt thought a war was unlikely. Within a week, by September 25, war seemed imminent. To the extent that his initial estimates of war were low and the later ones high, we may expect Roosevelt to have switched from a risk-averse to a risk-seeking posture, even if the outcomes were framed as potential losses all along.

Prospect theory's weighting function, π, which transforms stated probabilities into their subjective value for the decision-maker, has a number of additional properties that may predict interesting effects in the realm of political decisions. Let us consider one such property. The overweighting of small probabilities, that is, $\pi(p) > p$ for small p, entails that, for small p, π is generally subadditive. That is, $\pi(.01) + \pi(.04) > \pi(.05)$. Now consider a political leader who obtains probability estimates for various outcomes either separately, from a number of different advisors, or all together, compiled by a single adviser. Assume, for instance, that the Soviets prepared an exhaustive list of possible Israeli actions during the course of 1967 and that, among these, the Soviet generals specializing in Jordan, Egypt, and Syria estimated the chances that Israel would attack these countries to be .01, .02, and .04, respectively (for simplicity, assume that the Soviets regard these events as mutually exclusive). A nuance in political organization is now predicted to have significant psychological impact. The Soviet leader may obtain these estimates from each general separately (in which case the perceived chances that Israel will attack a neighboring Arab nation are $\pi(.01) + \pi(.02) + \pi(.04)$); alternatively, he may obtain a single estimate from a military representative who has compiled the various reports, to the effect that there is a .07 chance of an Israeli attack. According to prospect theory, the Soviets' perceived likelihood of war will be greater in the former than in the latter scenario.

Concluding Remarks

The making of decisions in the political realm is an intricate process, evaluated according to multiple criteria and motivated by conflicting considerations. Various components are likely to enter into the making of political decisions that are ignored in theorizing about individual decision-making under risk. Political leaders tend to be preoccupied with reputation, coalition formation, reciprocity, and power. They are likely to be influenced by their constituents' sentiments of fairness (Kahneman, Knetsch, & Thaler, 1986), as well as by a perceived need for accountability (Tetlock, 1985). They may base their decision on the relative advantages and disadvantages of the available options (Shafir, Osherson, & Smith, in press) and may attempt to minimize the conflict involved in making difficult decisions by searching for convincing reasons and arguments for choosing one option over another (Montgomery, 1983; Simonson, 1989; Tversky & Shafir, 1992a, 1992b). All these factors, which have been shown to affect the outcome of decisions, lie outside the purview of prospect theory's compelling treatment of value and chance.

In their extensive analyses, Farnham, Jervis, McDermott, and McInerney have attempted to isolate those puzzling features of political events that seem best attributable to the psychological processes described by prospect theory. These researchers are driven by the alluring assumption that the more important characteristics of individual decision-making under risk will manifest themselves in political decisions of international proportions. As such, they provide a significant impetus for the continued exploration of ways in which political analysis and the study of decision-making may interact. As suggested by Jervis, the behavior of countries who have made an almost incidental political gain may provide a glimpse into the nature of the endowment effect at the national level. Alternatively, as Farnham points out, the emotions and upheavals of international politics may provide an interesting route by which to explore the dynamics of frame changes. In this vein, interesting extensions of prospect theory recently developed by Tversky and Kahneman (1990) render the theory applicable to an even richer set of contexts. While the original formulation was limited to risky prospects with at most two nonzero outcomes, the enriched, "cumulative" version extends to uncertain prospects and applies to any number of outcomes. There are, in short, plenty of psychological issues as well as political scenarios to pursue along the lines delineated by the present studies.

As has been suggested above, however, true individual attitudes towards risk and value may prove difficult to ascertain in natural settings that are permeated with ambiguous information, group deliberation, ulterior motives, and social constraints. The systematic and predictable trends that psychologists have been able to identify in simple and relatively contrived settings are often hard to verify in the naturally occurring complexity of the political scientists' world. While both endeavors—experimentation in simplified settings and analysis of complex real events—are likely to contribute to our understanding of decisions, we can simultaneously perhaps increase our efforts along the lines where these two disciplines meet. Psychologists and political scientists could collaborate on research in which certain variables are controlled and data collected in otherwise naturally occurring political settings. More effort could be directed, for example, toward obtaining the actual probability estimates of political decision-makers as they make real decisions. Or toward documenting their evaluation of incidentally acquired, recent political gains. Or toward recording their framing of political scenarios, such as the capture of hostages, or the occupation of foreign lands, as time progresses and the reference point is changed. A joint research program by psychologists and political scientists intended to clarify how individual theories of choice apply to the analysis of political events may contribute to our understanding of the decisions people make and the repercussions these have for their political lives.

REFERENCES

Akerlof, G. A., & Yellen, J. 1985. Can small deviations from rationality make significant differences to economic equilibria? *American Economic Review*, 75, 708–20.

Brandstatter, H., Davis, J. H., & Stocker-Kreichgauer, G. (Eds.). 1982. *Group decision making*. New York: Academic Press.

Chapman, L. J., & Chapman, J. P. 1967. Genesis of popular but erroneous psychodiagnostic observations. *Journal of Abnormal Psychology*, 72, 193–204.

Clark, R. D. 1971. Group-induced shift toward risk: A critical appraisal. *Psychological Bulletin*, 76, 251–270.

Cohen, M., Jaffray, J.-Y., & Said, T. 1987. Experimental comparison of individual behavior under risk and under uncertainty for gains and for losses. *Organizational Behavior and Human Decision Processes*, 39, 1–22.

Dawes, R. M. 1988. *Rational choice in an uncertain world*. New York: Harcourt Brace Jovanovich.

Farnham, B. 1992. Roosevelt and the Munich crisis: Insights from prospect theory. *Political Psychology*, 13, 205–235.

Griffin, D., & Tversky, A. 1991. The weighing of evidence and the determinants of confidence. *Cognitive Psychology*, forthcoming.

Heath, C., & Tversky, A. 1991. Preference and belief: Ambiguity and competence in choice under uncertainty. *Journal of Risk and Uncertainty*, 4, 1, 5–28.

Jervis, R. 1992. Political implications of loss aversion. *Political Psychology*, 13, 187–204.

Kahneman, D., Knetsch, J. L., & Thaler, R. 1986. Fairness as a constraint on profit seeking: Entitlements in the market. *American Economic Review*, 76, 728–41.

Kahneman, D., Knetsch, J. L., & Thaler, R. 1990. Experimental tests of the endowment effect and the Coase theorem. *Journal of Political Economy*, 98, 1325–1348.

Kahneman, D., Slovic, P., & Tversky, A. (Eds.). 1982. *Judgment under uncertainty: Heuristics and biases*. New York: Cambridge University Press.

Kahneman, D., & Tversky, A. 1979. Prospect theory: An analysis of decision under risk. *Econometrica, 47*, 263–291.
Kunda, Z. 1990. The case for motivated reasoning. *Psychological Bulletin, 108,* 480–98.
Luce, R. D. 1959. *Individual choice behavior.* New York: Wiley.
McDermott, R. 1992. The Iranian hostage rescue mission. *Political Psychology, 13,* 237–263.
McInerney, A. 1992. Prospect theory and Soviet policy towards Syria, 1966–67. *Political Psychology, 13,* 265–282.
McNeil, B. J., Pauker, S. G., & Tversky, A. 1988. On the framing of medical decisions. In D. Bell, H. Raiffa, & A. Tversky (Eds.), *Decision making: Descriptive, normative, and prescriptive interactions.* New York: Cambridge University Press.
Montgomery, H. 1983. Decision rules and the search for a dominance structure: Towards a process model of decision making. In P. Humphreys, O. Svenson, & A. Vari (Eds.), *Analyzing and aiding decision processes,* Amsterdam: North-Holland.
Mowen, J. C., & Gentry, J. W. 1980. Investigation of the preference-reversal phenomenon in a new product introduction task. *Journal of Applied Psychology, 65,* 715–22.
Nisbett, R., & Ross, L. 1980. *Human Inference: Strategies and shortcomings of social judgment.* Englewood Cliffs, NJ: Prentice-Hall.
Quattrone, G., & Tversky, A. 1984. Causal versus diagnostic contingencies: On self-deception and on the voter's illusion. *Journal of Personality and Social Psychology, 46,* 237–48.
Russell, T., & Thaler, R. 1985. The relevance of quasi rationality in competitive markets. *American Economic Review, 75,* 1071–82.
Shafir, E., Osherson, D. N., & Smith, E. E. In press. The advantage model: A comparative theory of evaluation and choice under risk. *Organizational Behavior and Human Decision Processes.*
Simonson, I. 1989. Choice based on reasons: The case of attraction and compromise effects. *Journal of Consumer Research, 16,* 158–174.
Tetlock, P. E. 1985. Accountability: The neglected social context of judgment and choice. *Research in Organizational Behavior, 7,* 297–332.
Thaler, R. H. 1980. Toward a positive theory of consumer choice. *Journal of Economic Behavior and Organization, 1,* 39–60.
Tversky, A., & Kahneman, D. 1986. Rational choice and the framing of decisions. *Journal of Business, 59,* 251–278.
Tversky, A., & Kahneman, D. 1992. Advances in prospect theory: Cumulative representation of uncertainty. *Journal of Risk and Uncertainty,* forthcoming.
Tversky, A., & Kahneman, D. 1991. Loss aversion in riskless choice: A reference dependent model. *Quarterly Journal of Economics,* forthcoming.
Tversky, A., & Shafir, E. 1992a. Choice under conflict: The dynamics of deferred decision. *Psychological Science,* forthcoming.
Tversky, A., & Shafir, E. 1992b. The disjunction effect in choice under uncertainty. *Psychological Science,* forthcoming.

Conclusion

Barbara Farnham[1]

INTRODUCTION

While many others have tried to assess the potential of psychological theories for enriching political analysis, this symposium on prospect theory and political psychology is perhaps distinctive in its conscious effort to be as comprehensive as possible, a goal which is reflected not only in the participation of scholars from both political science and psychology but also in their decision to adopt a more systematic mode of analysis than is the norm for such inquiries. Thus, in addition to thoroughly exploring the general ability of prospect theory to illuminate political events, the authors have tried to base their prognoses about its possible future contributions on an evaluation of its success in explaining several concrete cases of foreign policy decision-making.

A preliminary review of their findings suggests that these efforts toward a

[1]Institute of War and Peace Studies, Columbia University, New York, New York 10027.

159

broader understanding of the requirements of such an interdisciplinary investigation have been productive in a number of interesting, and sometimes unforeseen, ways. While it is impossible to do justice here to the full scope of a discussion which touches on so many different aspects of both prospect theory and the international political context, it may nevertheless be useful to summarize the major points of agreement.

POTENTIAL AREAS OF APPLICATION

Collectively, these articles suggest that prospect theory's most important contribution to the theory of international relations lies in the opportunity it affords to develop both a more complex understanding of the way decision-makers are likely to define the situation facing them in a variety of conflictual interactions and greater sophistication about how such assessments may affect behavior. As several of the articles make clear, these insights have implications for theory on at least three different levels of analysis. Not only can they help refine our predictions about the behavior of individual political decision-makers, that is, they may also be able to illuminate a variety of operating interactions between states, as well as contribute to a better understanding of phenomena operating at the level of the international system.

With respect to the decision-making level of analysis, for example, prospect theory's notion of framing, together with its concepts of value measurement and risk propensity, suggest that the way a decision-maker characterizes a decision problem has important policy implications. In particular, as Levy shows in his second essay, because people measure value in terms of deviations from a reference point and tend to be risk-averse in the face of gain but risk-seeking for loss, couching a problem in terms of avoiding a loss rather than making a gain can affect a decision-maker's preferences about the options available for dealing with it. Thus, as McDermott, McInerney, and Farnham show, political decision-makers are sometimes willing to engage in behavior to avoid or reverse a loss which they would have judged unacceptably risky had they been contemplating a gain.

Secondly, by affecting the perceptions and choices of decision-makers, these tendencies relating to the measurement of value and risk propensity may also have a critical impact on the outcome of certain interactions between states, such as those involving bargaining and deterrence, although the precise nature of the influence on the incidence of international conflict is still unclear. On the one hand, as Levy notes, such factors as the role of the status quo in focusing states' expectations may make agreement easier to reach. On the other hand, as both Jervis and Levy point out, tendencies like loss aversion can create serious prob-

Conclusion 161

lems for both crisis stability and bargaining, particularly if each party believes itself to be defending the status quo.

Finally, at the level of the international system, the propensity for risk-seeking to avoid loss and risk aversion for gains may have important implications for stability, although, again, the impact of this tendency on the incidence of international conflict is problematical. For example, while risk aversion in the domain of gains might promote acceptance of the status quo and lead to stability, the disposition to engage in risky behavior in the face of loss could, under some conditions, increase the likelihood of conflict.

CONCEPTUAL AND METHODOLOGICAL PROBLEMS

In addition to closely scrutinizing the areas in which applying insights from prospect theory to the analysis of international relations may ultimately prove fruitful, the participants in this symposium have examined a number of conceptual and methodological obstacles which could impede such an enterprise. The most troubling problem, as well as one of the most difficult to address, hinges on the differences between the context in which prospect theory was originally developed and the environment in which it is being applied.

One part of this problem mentioned by all of the analytical papers lies in the disparity between conditions in the laboratory and those found in natural settings. As Levy points out, a number of the difficulties related to applying prospect theory can be "effectively overcome under highly structured and controlled experimental conditions, but . . . are much less tractable in the empirical study of international relations. . . ."

Another dimension of the same problem arises out of the substantive differences between the contextual assumptions underlying prospect theory and the characteristics of most political settings. Shafir identifies at least two of these. First of all, while prospect theory was designed to explain choice under risk, the environment in which political decision-makers must operate is characterized primarily by uncertainty. Secondly, prospect theory was developed as a theory of individual choice, whereas political decision-making takes place in what is largely, if not exclusively, a group setting. Among other things, this poses potentially serious difficulties in applying the concept of framing to the analysis of political choice.

Another major obstacle to using prospect theory to explain political outcomes is that the decision-maker is far from being the only party plagued by the uncertainty characterizing the political context. The analyst, as well, often lacks the kind of information which would allow her to claim with confidence that the behavior of a particular political decision-maker unambiguously accords with the

162 Avoiding Losses / Taking Risks

expectations of prospect theory, as both Jervis and Shafir note. Not only may there be no very good evidence about the precise nature of a decision-maker's reference point (Shafir), or about his utility calculus (Levy), it may also be difficult to ascertain his assessment of the risks involved in any particular venture (Jervis, Levy). Nor is it a simple matter to determine whether a given policy change is the result of loss aversion or merely a shift in utilities. In fact, as Shafir argues, it is all too easy to confuse changes in utilities with changes in frame or domain, and, to make matters worse, according to Levy, a number of factors, such as risk propensity, may have multiple determinants.

Finally, the fact that obtaining evidence about these effects requires a major investment of time and effort only exacerbates the already demanding task of demonstrating the ability of prospect theory to explain political events. As Levy and Shafir both emphasize, it is not sufficient to demonstrate mere consistency between any given behavior and the predictions of prospect theory; one must also show that such behavior cannot be accounted for as well or better by other theories, in particular rational choice theory.

These difficulties mean that, however attractive the notion of applying prospect theory to political phenomena may be, any attempt to do so entails some risk. On the one hand, the political scientist who uses the perspectives of prospect theory to enrich her understanding of political behavior may be charged with claiming too much for insights based on the unsophisticated application of a theory borrowed from another discipline to behavioral phenomena—like risk aversion—whose very existence in the real world is difficult to demonstrate convincingly. On the other hand, as Shafir points out from the perspective of psychology, the risks of interdisciplinary work run in both directions. That is to say, the attempt to apply prospect theory to political events may pose a danger to the integrity of the theory itself as, for example, when an analyst faced with a paucity of information about decision frames, utility functions, or risk propensity is tempted to bend the theory to fit whatever evidence is available.

Mitigating Factors

Despite these hazards, however, the potential rewards of applying prospect theory to political analysis are sufficiently appealing that the attempt to do so is likely to continue. It is, therefore, reassuring that at least some of the problems which have been identified here are neither unique nor insurmountable. Several of them, such as those arising out of the use of a theory developed in one discipline to illuminate the concerns of another, are inherent in any interdisciplinary effort. Not all political scientists, for example, are persuaded that the conceptual and methodological problems associated with borrowing theories from economics to explain behavior in the political context are significantly fewer than those involved in using theories from psychology for the same purpose (see Jervis, for example).

Moreover, the difficulties associated with trying to apply theories developed in highly structured environments to explain behavior occurring in natural settings are not confined to prospect theory alone. Rather, similar problems must be acknowledged and dealt with whenever psychological theories are used to explain political phenomena (On the need to take account of the impact of context on decision-making behavior, see Tetlock, 1983, and Farnham, 1990).

The fact that differences between the laboratory and the political arena clearly do matter, however, does not necessarily mean that theories about decision-making developed in experimental settings should be avoided when explanations are sought for behavior in the vastly more complex environment characterizing the political context. This, after all, is where many of the most interesting problems are to be found. If prospect theory has correctly identified a number of pervasive human tendencies which confound the expectations of rational choice theory, it is crucial to find out whether, and in what manner, those attributes affect the ability of political decision-makers to cope effectively with such problems.

Happily, the papers presented above offer some assistance in dealing with the obstacles to understanding this dynamic. For one thing, their detailed analysis of the problems associated with applying prospect theory should itself provide considerable help to anyone preparing to embark on such a project. Moreover, the authors also suggest ways to alleviate at least some of the difficulties. Levy, for example, spells out a number of conditions which must be satisfied in order for prospect theory to contribute effectively to an understanding of behavior in political settings. Shafir, on the other hand, advances the idea that prospect theory itself may be able to develop in ways which respond to the concerns which have been raised. For example, he suggests the possibility that future research may improve the ability of prospect theory to deal with group decision-making by clarifying "decision behavior under multiple frames."

Crossfertilization

Acknowledgment of the substantial problems that arise in trying to apply insights from psychology to the concerns of political science should not be allowed to obscure the considerable rewards of doing so. As this symposium demonstrates, interdisciplinary collaboration can have a number of theoretical benefits for both of the disciplines involved. In particular, the attempt to use a theory from one discipline to illuminate the concerns of another may not only add to the analytical capacity of the borrower but also aid the development of the theory being tapped.

For one thing, such an attempt can lead to critical examination of the theory by scholars outside the discipline in which it originated, which may yield ideas for possible elaboration or modification. For another, transferring a theory from the laboratory where it was developed to a natural setting may bring to light problems and opportunities that would have been obscured in a more highly structured environment.

This sort of mutual benefit has clearly been a product of the interdisciplinary collaboration attempted here. The advantages for the analysis of international politics of adopting the perspective of prospect theory have been thoroughly canvassed. As Levy observes, in challenging some "basic assumptions and propositions of expected utility theory," prospect theory has become a competitor to rational choice theory, providing an "important alternative theoretical framework for the analysis of social and political behavior." Moreover, to the degree that the empirical studies have been successful in explaining behavior which was puzzling in terms of the predictions of rational choice theory, they too have demonstrated how prospect theory can be used to refine political analysis (cf. Levy's observation on the success of the McInerney, McDermott, and Farnham studies in demonstrating how foreign policy decision-makers frame a choice problem).

More surprisingly perhaps, the attempt to explore the potential of prospect theory for enriching our explanations of political phenomena has also produced some insight into the theory itself. Here again, the empirical studies played an important role. Not only did they perform well in demonstrating how the theory could be applied to concrete cases, but in taking prospect theory out of the laboratory, they may also have contributed to its development. As a consequence of applying prospect theory to problems in a natural setting, for example, at least two of the empirical studies were able to suggest explanations for how frames may be formed in the first place as well as for how they change. McDermott offers a possible elaboration of the theory by pointing to the role of historical analogies in establishing a frame. Farnham, by showing that the experience of strong emotion may have played a crucial role in Roosevelt's reframing of the Munich crisis, suggests a way that changes in decision frames may come about.

CONCLUSION

Taken as a whole, this volume offers a number of insights into how efforts to use prospect theory to refine political analysis might be advanced. Even after thoroughly airing the analytical and methodological problems involved, moreover, the authors retain considerable optimism about the ultimate prospects of doing so, suggesting an outline for future collaboration between political scientists and psychologists in a joint research program exploring some of the issues which have been aired here.

It is equally clear, however, that the debate on these matters is far from over. In fact, the symposium itself has raised a variety of interesting questions for future discussion, not only about the specific merits of employing prospect theory to explain political phenomena but also about the use of theories from psychology to illuminate the concerns of political science generally.

In addition, this exploration of prospect theory and international relations may also have contributed to the discussion by showing the advantages of defining the interdisciplinary character of such undertakings as broadly as possible. The variety of theoretical insights developed in these papers into the problems and the rewards of this kind of enterprise were a direct result of both the inclusion of empirical case studies and the decision to solicit the views of scholars from psychology as well as political science. On the one hand, the case studies provided concrete evidence of several problems in applying prospect theory to political events that would otherwise have only been suspected. On the other, the participation of scholars from both disciplines ensured that the exploration of the potential of prospect theory for enriching political analysis would amount to more than merely a discussion of the mechanics of transferring a theory from one discipline to another, offering instead an opportunity for enriching theory in both disciplines.

REFERENCES

Farnham, B. (1990). Political cognition and decision-making. *Political Psychology*, *11*, 83–11.
Tetlock, P. E. (1983). Accountability: The neglected social context of judgment and choice. *Res. Organ. Behav.*, *7*, 297–332.